HOW TO HOUSE
THE HOMELESS

HOW TO HOUSE
THE HOMELESS

INGRID GOULD ELLEN AND
BRENDAN O'FLAHERTY

EDITORS

Russell Sage Foundation · New York

The Russell Sage Foundation

The Russell Sage Foundation, one of the oldest of America's general purpose foundations, was established in 1907 by Mrs. Margaret Olivia Sage for "the improvement of social and living conditions in the United States." The Foundation seeks to fulfill this mandate by fostering the development and dissemination of knowledge about the country's political, social, and economic problems. While the Foundation endeavors to assure the accuracy and objectivity of each book it publishes, the conclusions and interpretations in Russell Sage Foundation publications are those of the authors and not of the Foundation, its Trustees, or its staff. Publication by Russell Sage, therefore, does not imply Foundation endorsement.

Library of Congress Cataloging-in-Publication Data

How to house the homeless / Ingrid Gould Ellen and Brendan O'Flaherty, editors.
    p. cm.
  Includes bibliographical references and index.
  ISBN 978-0-87154-454-4 (alk. paper)
  1. Homelessness—United States. 2. Housing policy—United States. 3. Housing—United States. I. Ellen, Ingrid Gould, 1965- II. O'Flaherty, Brendan.
  HV4505.H69 2010
  363.5'80973—dc22

                                                                    2010005912

Contents

About the Authors

Ingrid Gould Ellen is professor of public policy and urban planning at the New York University Robert F. Wagner Graduate School of Public Service.

Brendan O'Flaherty is professor of economics at Columbia University.

Jill Khadduri is principal associate of Social & Economic Policy at Abt Associates.

Edgar O. Olsen is professor of economics at the University of Virginia.

Steven Raphael is professor of public policy at the University of California, Berkeley.

Robert Rosenheck is professor of psychiatry and public health in the Department of Psychiatry at the Yale School of Medicine, director of the Division of Mental Health Services and Outcomes Research at the Yale Child Study Center, associate director of health services research at the VA New England Mental Illness Research, Education and Clinical Center, and associate director of the National Center on Homelessness Among Veterans.

Sam Tsemberis is founder and executive director of Pathways to Housing and clinical assistant professor in the Department of Psychiatry at the Columbia University Medical Center.

Acknowledgments

We are indebted to Carol Caton, who first noticed that housing policy was missing from many discussions of homelessness and asked us to put a conference together to reunite the fields. That conference took place at New York University on November 21, 2008, and led to this book. Carol has helped us every step of the way.

The contributors—Robert Rosenheck, Sam Tsemberis, Jill Khadduri, Edgar O. Olsen, and Steven Raphael—produced the contents of this volume. In addition to being wise and insightful, they are an extraordinarily timely, agreeable, and cooperative group of writers. The comments of two anonymous referees and of the discussants at the conference— Jay Bainbridge, Vicki Been, Sewin Chan, Lance Freeman, Sherry Glied, Rosanne Haggerty, Stephen Malpezzi, and Bernard Salanié—clarified many of the ideas and improved the exposition. Ed Olsen deserves special thanks for playing the many roles we asked him to perform: adviser when we were just beginning to plan the conference, discussant when the conference was held, and contributor when a referee recommended that his comments become a paper. He probably would have designed the cover, too, if we had asked.

This project brought together two New York institutions: the Center for Homelessness Prevention Studies (CHPS) at the Columbia Mailman School of Public Health and the Furman Center for Real Estate and Urban Policy at New York University. We needed to have different perspectives. The administrative support that held everything together came from these two centers. We especially thank Mireille Valbrun and Shoshana Vasheetz from CHPS and Vicki Been and Bethany O'Neill from the Furman Center.

The Russell Sage Foundation funded the project and gave us support and guidance along the way. Eric Wanner and Caroline Carr made sure the design was sensible and that the conference happened on time. Suzanne Nichols offered sage editorial guidance and kept refereeing, revisions, and the entire publishing process on track. It is remarkable that someone so patient could actually get us to complete tasks on time.

Finally, we thank our families for their patience and understanding as well. Mary, Niamh, Nell, David, Audrey, and Jacob put up with a lot of distraction but never diminished their love.

Chapter 1

Introduction

INGRID GOULD ELLEN AND BRENDAN O'FLAHERTY

Eliminating homelessness or reducing its volume substantially will take certain changes in how housing markets operate. Homelessness, after all, is ultimately a housing market condition. People who leave homelessness have to live somewhere they weren't living before. It is less clear which housing policies will do the best job of reducing homelessness.

We organized a conference in the fall of 2008 to help identify those policies. We invited leading researchers, with backgrounds ranging from psychiatry to economics and policy, and challenged them to consider how housing policies influence homelessness. The papers collectively consider homelessness both among single adults and families. They look not just at obvious policies, like cranking up existing housing subsidy programs, but also at nonobvious ones, like changing zoning laws and revamping the standard mortgage contract. We find that some policies will likely help and others will not. We synthesize these lessons here. Drawing on the papers and discussion at the conference, we also produce a research agenda outlining the most important questions about housing markets and homelessness that could be answered but haven't yet been.

This volume explores a middle ground between two opposing views of how housing markets affect homelessness. Both views imply that a book like this has little value: one view implies that the question we are trying to answer is impossible to answer (housing market impotence); the other, that it's trivial (housing market omnipotence).

The housing-market-impotence view suggests that people are homeless because of their individual problems, such as illnesses, addictions, or incarceration histories. Thus the only way to reduce homelessness is to reduce the incidence of such problems. This view has considerable appeal because it often mirrors individual biographies: many (though not all) people become homeless after they encounter difficulties with substance abuse, mental illness, or incarceration, and they often end their homelessness when they resolve these difficulties. We would strongly advise any friend of ours who was homeless and a substance abuser to treat his substance abuse problem.

But biography is not always the same as history, and good advice to friends is not always the same as good policy advice. If we thought a Springsteen concert was going to be sold out, we might advise our friends to call early for tickets, but we would not advise the government to subsidize the first calls to Ticketmaster.

Aggregate volumes of homelessness seem to be poorly correlated with aggregate volumes of the conditions that make individuals in a given population more likely to be homeless—for instance, being poor, being male, being a substance abuser, being mentally ill. This appears true both in a number of detailed empirical studies (for a review, see O'Flaherty 2004) and in trends over time. In 1972, for instance, the United States had staggering numbers of alcohol abusers by today's standards, a raging heroin epidemic, deinstitutionalization that was well on its way to completion for the nonelderly mentally ill, no Supplemental Security Income (SSI), poverty rates comparable to today's rates—and almost no homelessness.

The real policy question, however, is not the size of these historical correlations, but whether policies that address housing market conditions are more effective and efficient than those that treat conditions correlated with homelessness on an individual level. To use an analogy, in the 1980s, New Jersey was struck by a wave of bus robberies. No one knew precisely what caused it, and fare-box design was not on anyone's list of causes. But the policy that eliminated bus robberies effectively and efficiently was to redesign fare boxes so drivers had no access to money. Correlation and causality are not always the best guides to policy. This volume will try to answer at least half of the policy question by trying to find the best housing market policies and estimating how much they could reduce homelessness.

The opposing view, housing market omnipotence, looks at homelessness simply as the difference between the number of available homes and the number of households seeking housing; the only way to resolve this shortage is to build more homes and put homeless people in them. A corollary to housing market omnipotence is treatment impotence. Programs that treat the problems homeless people have accomplish nothing more than musical chairs: if person A's life improves and she leaves the streets, she is really only pushing some person B onto the streets if no new housing is built. Or such is the view of housing market omnipotence.

Just as housing market impotence has an appeal if you read only isolated biographies, so too does housing market omnipotence if all you look at are the brute physical facts of doorknobs and noses. But housing markets are much more complex than simple counts. If housing construction were all that mattered, homelessness would have been wiped out during the construction boom of the early 2000s, but instead the numbers of homeless appear to have barely moved. If subsidized housing were all that mattered, then New York City, which has built a huge amount of subsidized housing in the past two decades, would have only a dwindling shelter census.

Real housing markets are not stagnant glasses of water where all you have to measure is the distance to the brim. Instead, they are oceans with tides, ever-shifting currents both horizontal and vertical, evaporation, rainfalls, and waves. You can't control the height of the ocean with a hand pump and a bucket. Housing market players adjust to changing environments by moving in with relatives or moving out; by building, renovating, or abandoning; by exercising more or less caution in screening potential tenants; by looking more or less assiduously for a smaller or larger place to live and accepting more or fewer inconveniences; by raising and lowering advertising budgets; by putting on a new roof, adding a new bathroom, or letting the boiler deteriorate. Players have to adjust to the adjustments that other players make, too, so that in the end the final outcome of a policy's implementation may look nothing like its initial thrust or intended goals. A reputable body of empirical literature, for instance, shows that construction of subsidized housing is offset, at least in part, by reductions in the unsubsidized housing stock (see, for example, Sinai and Waldfogel 2005). In this sense, it may be those who build housing who are playing musical chairs, rather than those who treat personal problems. A detailed understanding of how housing markets work is of course needed to estimate the extent to which either group is playing musical chairs, however.

Major Findings

This book offers three major policy lessons.

First, *housing matters.* Some policies and interventions that make housing more easily available to homeless people can reduce homelessness; policies that don't do this won't reduce homelessness.

Robert Rosenheck and Sam Tsemberis are the only authors in this volume who seriously examine nonhousing interventions. Rosenheck finds that their impacts on housing outcomes are generally small, though they often improve the nonhousing aspects of participants' lives. Tsemberis shows that programs that concentrate on housing rather than treatment do a generally better job of reducing homelessness, and no worse a job in reducing psychiatric and substance abuse problems. Requiring treatment or sobriety as a condition for housing keeps that housing away from the people who need it most and considerably reduces housing retention rates.

The papers identify several housing policies and housing interventions that do reduce homelessness. On the individual level, Jill Khadduri reports on a controlled experiment that showed that housing choice (section 8) vouchers virtually eliminated homelessness among families leaving welfare; Rosenheck finds that the housing aspect of supportive housing reduces homelessness; and Tsemberis shows the effectiveness of

Housing First. On a population basis, looking at cross sections, Steven Raphael finds that housing market regulation is correlated with more expensive housing, and more expensive housing is correlated with more homelessness. Khadduri reports on several cross-sectional studies that find a correlation between homelessness and housing market variables, like rents and vacancy rates.

Before this volume, few papers identified links between a community's housing assistance policies and its level of homelessness. One exception is a study by Dirk Early and Edgar O. Olsen (2002), who find that cities that target subsidies more to low-income recipients have less homelessness, but that the overall volume of subsidies does not matter. Thus we have only weak evidence on a population level of a connection between housing subsidies and homelessness, and no tests of causality. The empirical literature on rent control, which Brendan O'Flaherty reviews in the final chapter of this volume, is extensive, but the conclusion of that literature is that rent control has little impact on homelessness.

Second, *targeting matters.* The best predictor of who will use a particular service in the future is who is using it now. O'Flaherty gives the theoretical basis for this empirical regularity. Rosenheck's analysis shows that interventions that focus on the most severely disadvantaged populations have the highest ratio of benefits to costs, chiefly because they reduce the amount of very expensive services that their participants were receiving. In particular, by making housing available to people who might not otherwise comply with treatment or sobriety requirements, Housing First targets effectively. Olsen argues that we should focus housing assistance on the poorest households, because these households are more likely to become homeless. However, predicting in advance who will become homeless is extremely difficult (again, O'Flaherty gives a theoretical reason for this empirical regularity), and targeting more precisely is therefore very difficult.

Third, *moral hazard inevitably comes with better targeting.* You can target services precisely if you are willing to accept a great deal of moral hazard; you can reduce moral hazard a great deal if you are willing to have poor targeting. But you cannot have both precise targeting and low moral hazard. If only people who are actually homeless receive great services, too many people will be homeless. If everyone receives services, only a tiny percentage of the benefit will inure to people who would otherwise be homeless.

Policy Questions

There are four broad categories of housing policy explored in the book, which vary according to their level of targeting.

The first are policies that aim to make small reductions in risk for large numbers of people, many of whom had low risk to begin with. Raphael's chapter suggests that reducing regulations and thus reducing the price of housing is a good example of such a program; most people who will benefit are not likely to become homeless and the resulting individual risk reductions will be small. Many will benefit, however, and the intervention will not induce any moral hazard.

The second category includes policies that provide traditional subsidized housing to households whose incomes fall below a specified level. Explored in the Khadduri and Olsen chapters, these programs offer few services and include, for instance, public housing, housing choice vouchers, and proposals for a housing entitlement program.

The Rosenheck and Tsemberis chapters focus on the third type of policies, which aim more directly at the population at highest risk. They hope to generate large reductions in risk, but for fewer people, many of whom are highly likely to become homeless. Programs like Housing First and supported or supportive housing are examples. Moral hazard in these programs is mitigated by making participation contingent on criteria that are expensive for most people to fabricate: long periods of homelessness, for instance, or severe mental illness.

The final set of policies, discussed in many of the papers but most directly in the O'Flaherty chapter, concern shelters (or something like them) that are available for emergencies. We might wish that they be rarely used, like fire alarm boxes and air bags in cars, but because surprises and crises are inevitable, it would be irresponsible not to have them.

There are many controversies and questions surrounding these policies, but the key questions center on cost-effectiveness and moral-hazard. Each dollar spent on subsidized housing could achieve how large of a reduction in homelessness? And how great are the moral-hazard costs? How effective is spending on homelessness prevention? How should we manage shelter admission and shelter exit (given that most emergencies don't last forever)? How large are the moral-hazard costs of the widespread practice of rewarding long shelter stays with subsidized housing?

O'Flaherty's is the only theoretical chapter in the volume. Like the conference itself, he tries to span the gap between public-health researchers, who think about dynamic models of individual lives, and housing researchers, who generally use static models of aggregates (or steady states of dynamic models, as in O'Flaherty 1995). His chapter uses dynamic models of individual lives, as in the public-health literature, but the models resemble those of macroeconomics, where individuals must cope with uncertainty as best they can. In colloquial terms, people become homeless when they are down on their luck, and O'Flaherty uses the tools of macroeconomics to take that claim seriously.

The model has many implications for researchers. We have alluded to two already: that entries into homelessness are unpredictable and that the best predictor of who will be in a shelter in the future is who is in a shelter now. The intuition behind unpredictability is pretty simple. Take, for example, fires, another type of bad luck. If you could predict that you would have a fire in your kitchen tomorrow at 3:18 P.M., you would not have a fire then because you would do everything in your power to prevent it. Episodes of homelessness are like fires—they happen by surprise, and no one can predict surprises.

The tie between current and future homelessness is a corollary to the general result that the level of a person's housing consumption in the immediate future is more likely to be close to her consumption today than far from it. Shelter occupancy is a level—usually very low—of housing consumption.

Two other corollaries to this result are that the neighborhoods where people are most likely to live immediately before becoming homeless are those with the cheapest, lowest-quality housing, and that the housing tenure of people immediately before they become homeless is also likely to be the cheapest tenure available (for example, doubling up). These corollaries correspond to well-known empirical regularities, but these regularities have not been previously interpreted in a consistent fashion.

Policy Lessons

Looking at homelessness as bad luck also has implications for policy—particularly subsidized housing, shelter management, and homelessness prevention. This perspective calls for evaluating policies as parts of the safety net and as a form of social insurance for families that temporarily experience bad luck. Subsidized housing has rarely been looked at in these terms: U.S. subsidized housing provides significant insurance for those who are recipients, but none for those who are not but may need insurance.

In terms of broad policies aimed at making small reductions in risk for large numbers of people, Raphael builds on a body of empirical literature, but one that has not previously been connected to homelessness. Housing economists are now pretty certain that housing is more expensive in metropolitan areas where local housing-market regulation is stricter: housing costs more in places where zoning rules and other regulations make building new houses more difficult. Raphael shows that more onerous local housing-market regulation is also associated with more homelessness.

To do this, he uses two relatively new data sets: the Wharton state-level regulatory index that Joseph Gyourko, Albert Saiz, and Anita Summers (2006) describe, and the homeless counts in the 2007 Annual Homeless Assessment Report (AHAR) to Congress. If regulation affects homelessness, it should do so by raising rents. Thus Raphael estimates a two-equation system, with regulation as an instrument for rent-to-income ratios. Regulation works as hypothesized. The estimates imply that reducing regulatory burden in the states that are now above the median to the median level would cut homelessness by 6 to 13 percent—equivalent to 2 million or so more housing vouchers.

A policy of reducing regulations would invite minimal levels of moral hazard and deadweight loss. No one would have to do anything to qualify for the benefits of lower metropolitan-wide rent levels. Some people might reduce the effort they expend on working or sharing if housing prices were lower, but this would not necessarily create deadweight loss because previous housing prices were not an accurate reflection of the true social costs of housing. Effort by itself is not socially valuable. In social terms, homelessness could be reduced for nothing or even less than nothing (that is, with a gain).

Wholesale reduction of local housing-market regulation does not have much political support now, of course. Neither do some of the other ideas discussed in this book, like a housing entitlement program. But we should not dismiss it solely for that reason.

What practical use does this result have then? First, scientific findings are valuable even if they're not immediately useful. It's good to know that the sun is powered by nuclear fusion or that the first humans lived in Africa even if we can't do anything about it.

Second, some regulations are at the political margin in every state. Knowing that these regulations can affect homelessness is not politically irrelevant. Political decisions on these regulations are by definition close and so might be swayed at the margin by these considerations.

Third, realizing that the housing market is distorted in this way can change our evaluation of other policies. Consider, for instance, a housing entitlement program. When we stated that such a program would create deadweight loss by distorting work and sharing incentives, we were implicitly assuming that housing prices reflected social costs accurately. The literature on housing regulation argues that they do not. If housing prices are too high, then ordinary calculations overstate the deadweight loss from a housing entitlement program, especially in heavily regulated metropolitan areas.[1]

Finally, as Raphael argues, the relationship between regulations, which mainly benefit wealthy people, and homelessness leads to a strong compensation argument for using tax revenues to alleviate homelessness.

Khadduri and Olsen describe the current set of programs that subsidize housing for low-income people and examine some of the reforms that might make them more effective at reducing homelessness. The federal government provides about 5 million households with rental subsidies deep enough that people with incomes well below the poverty level can pay the rent. These subsidies are provided under the housing choice voucher (HCV) program, public housing, and the property-based Section 8 program. A randomized controlled experiment has shown that housing choice vouchers virtually eliminate homelessness among welfare families, and a number of studies have shown that individuals and families who leave shelters with vouchers are quite unlikely to return, at least for a few years.

Public housing and the property-based Section 8 program have been moving away from serving people at considerable risk of becoming homeless. More of their small apartments have been designated elderly-only, and new admissions have limits on the number of poor tenants who can be accepted.

These programs continue to reach mainly poor people because they use the housing-gap rent formula—tenants' rent is set at 30 percent of their income. The lower your income, the more attractive these programs are; and if your income is above a certain level, you are not eligible to receive any assistance. Targeting, of course, comes at a cost in moral hazard. The rent-gap formula likely discourages both work effort and the sharing of homes. As O'Flaherty explains in his chapter, the work disincentive has been studied extensively and is probably small; the sharing disincentive has been studied much less and may be large.

Reforms to the HCV program and its expansion appear to both Khadduri and Olsen to be the most expedient route to reducing homelessness. These reforms would include focusing more intensely on the poorest households, allocating more subsidies to places where the risk of homelessness is greater, and expanding outreach efforts to reach more adults without children. More intense focus might be accomplished with a separate program, possibly with time limits and shallower subsidies. The efforts to improve targeting come at a moral-hazard cost: geographic targeting rewards jurisdictions that engage in activities that increase homelessness—for instance, regulatory policies like those that Raphael describes—and rewards those that exaggerate their estimates of the homeless population, making it impossible to rely on local efforts to count the homeless. Tighter income targeting also exacerbates the work and sharing disincentives.

Khadduri and Olsen both discuss the possibility of a universal entitlement program. This proposal calls for shallower subsidies than current programs, but many more of them. Olsen argues strongly that this program would be both more efficient and fair; Khadduri thinks an expanded and reformed HCV program can accomplish many of the homelessness-reducing goals of Olsen's universal entitlement program, but without the dislocations and some of the cost that the latter would entail. She is concerned that shallower subsidies would undermine some of the other goals of the HCV program, like poverty deconcentration.

These issues are crucial for understanding how to house the homeless, and the discussions by Khadduri and Olsen are insightful and extremely knowledgeable. But the empirical findings that we can bring to bear on this question are woefully limited. Not a single study shows clearly that an expansion of HCV will reduce aggregate levels of homelessness.[2] Much debate revolves around what the housing assistance experiments of the 1970s can tell us about how reformed or universalized housing voucher programs might work or how much they would cost, but these experiments have told us nothing about homelessness, because they recorded nothing about it. It would be interesting to see whether diligent researchers could recover a record about homelessness in the communities where these experiments were conducted.

Even the rough numbers we have raise more questions than they resolve. The studies that say anything about the relationship between the volume of assisted housing and the one-night count of homelessness imply that an increase of one hundred assisted units reduces the one-night homelessness count by around four people. There is remarkable uniformity across diverse studies on this sort of estimate.[3] Khadduri and Olsen say that universalizing HCV will bring in HUD's entire "worst-case housing needs" population—about 6 million households. If every one hundred of these additional subsidized households lead to a reduction in aggregate homelessness by four people, then that would reduce the one-night count of homelessness by about 240,000 households—by nearly half.[4]

Understanding whether this somewhat shocking estimate is plausible should probably be the major research question for any effort to house the homeless. The key may well be in questions of time, uncertainty, and household formation.

Rosenheck surveys a body of literature with a much firmer empirical foundation. Several programs have been shown to help homeless people with mental health problems. Programs designed to help in one outcome domain often help in that domain, but the benefits usually don't spill over into other domains. Programs designed to improve housing do that, but they don't reduce symptoms, and programs designed to reduce symptoms don't improve housing. You get what you pay for. Even with supported and supportive housing, which combine housing subsidies and clinical case management, the active ingredient appears to be the housing.

The programs that Rosenheck describes produce a different set of screening and moral-hazard concerns than the programs that Khadduri describes. Almost everyone likes money and a nice place to live, which is what housing programs offer, but most people who are not mentally ill, and many who are, are averse to clinical case management and other techniques of mental health care. Case management and other services could then be seen as screening devices, even if they do not appear to improve housing outcomes among those who are already in the program.

Rosenheck's cost-effectiveness results show that screening is a particularly important issue. The most cost-effective programs are those, like Housing First, that target high-cost, high-risk clients. The question that the housing literature suggests is how that targeting can be accomplished with minimal distortion of incentives. The answer might be by bundling something everybody wants—housing—with something arguably unappealing to those who are not mentally ill—clinical case management.

Tsemberis surveys the history and research on Housing First and contrasts this model with the previous predominant model of "treatment-first." Housing First places severely mentally ill, formerly homeless people into their own apartments, usually in buildings with many other residents from the general community, before beginning any treatment. Consumers, like other renters, have to abide by their lease terms, but they do not have to participate in treatment in order to stay in their apartments. Treatment is available, and consumers are encouraged to take advantage of it. Housing is housing, and treatment is treatment. Tsemberis reviews some of the extensive research that shows how consumers gain from this dichotomy.

In terms of shelter management, O'Flaherty argues that exploiting the analogy with unemployment insurance is likely to be fruitful. For instance, policies that encourage placement into subsidized housing early in a shelter spell are likely to work better than policies that require families to wait a long time before they are eligible for subsidies. Moral hazard is the issue: if you reward people for staying in shelters for a long time, some of them will do so. The popularity of rapid rehousing policies is in part a response to this logic.

Research Questions

In addition to providing us with a richer understanding of the links between housing and homelessness, the papers in this volume also highlight a number of key questions for which we don't have answers.

- Is it possible to reconstruct the history of homelessness in the communities in which the Experimental Housing Allowance Programs were conducted?

- Can characteristics of people early in a shelter spell be used to predict who will have a long shelter spell?

- What do people early in a shelter spell know about how long they will stay in a shelter? If you add self-predictions to all the other available information early in a shelter spell, does it improve the ability to predict who will have a long shelter spell?

- Do housing choice vouchers reduce aggregate homelessness? Do Low Income Housing Tax Credits reduce aggregate homelessness?

- What would be the effects of changing the Housing Choice Voucher Program to provide shallower subsidies to more recipients? What effect would shallower subsidies have on utilization rates and on the quality of neighborhoods reached by HCV holders?

- What affects the proportion of single, nonelderly adults who partic-ipate in HCV program? Why don't more of these individuals receive vouchers?

- Why is living in a neighborhood of concentrated poverty a risk factor for homelessness? Is the relationship causal? Or does it arise because the cheapest housing is located in neighborhoods of concentrated poverty?

- Can a measure of worst-case housing needs be devised that relies on permanent rather than transitory income?

- What effect has the mortgage crisis had on homelessness?

- Can a national database of housing regulations that concentrates on lower-end regulations (such as window space per room requirements), rather than higher-end (such as minimum lot size), be assembled?

- Do lower-end regulations have the same effects as higher-end reg-ulations?

- Will encouraging saving or encouraging borrowing among people at risk of homelessness be more effective in preventing and reducing homelessness?

- Does subsidized housing reduce the volatility of consumption by poor people? Does it reduce the volatility of housing consumption? How do consumption and housing-consumption volatility differ in metropolitan areas with a lot of subsidized housing from volatility in metropolitan areas with little subsidized housing?

- What are the effects of large arrearages on traffic tickets and child-support obligations on the behavior of poor people? What can we learn from this about the effects of homelessness-prevention loans with recourse?

- Would it be possible to design a rental insurance program that would not involve unsustainable levels of moral hazard?

Summary

The conference on which this volume is based was held in November 2008, as the world was heading into the worst economic downturn since the Great Depression. It was held a few subway stops from Wall Street, where company after company had failed in the previous few months. Bad luck was not an inappropriate theme.

But the conference also occurred only a few days after the election of a new president. Recessions, in Schumpeter's words, are times of creative destruction. When the conference was held, huge pieces of the architec-ture of the housing market had been destroyed, and the Obama adminis-tration was beginning to craft a replacement. As a positive proposition, the conference showed that homelessness could not be analyzed separate from housing policy; and as a normative proposition, that housing policy should not be created separate from homelessness.

Notes

1. One might argue that homeowners' tax preferences more than offset the housing price increase from regulation, and so housing prices are too low, not too high. Regulation, however, seems to have the biggest effect on low-income and low-quality housing, while homeowners' tax preferences seem to affect this market very little (Malpezzi and Green 1996). Thus the regulation distortion seems more relevant for discussing homelessness.
2. The randomized controlled study referenced in Jill Khadduri's chapter showed that providing vouchers to individual families receiving welfare reduced the likelihood that those families would become homeless, but it did not answer the question about aggregate effects on population as a whole.
3. Dirk W. Early (2004) estimates the probability of being homeless in the absence of a subsidy for an average household in subsidized housing. His conclusion is a range of 3.8 percent to 5.0 percent. The experimental study of housing vouchers found a treatment-on-the-treated reduction of 9.2 percent in the probability of being homeless during a year (Abt Associates et al. 2006). For comparability, we need a one-night estimate. The 2007 Annual Housing Assessment Report (AHAR; U.S. Department of Housing and Urban Development 2008) found that among sheltered families the one-night estimate was 38 percent as large as the one-year estimate: 248,500 individuals in families in the one-night estimate, of whom 72 percent were sheltered, as compared with a one-year family count of 473,500 individuals. This ratio would imply a reduction of 3.5 homeless families for every one hundred families assisted. Erin Mansur and his colleagues (2002) simulated the effects of a universal voucher program in California cities. In San Francisco, for example, they projected that giving vouchers to all 202,470 poor households would reduce homelessness by 4,426 households, or 2.2 percent.
4. The AHAR found 423,400 single individuals and 248,500 individuals in families who were homeless on a January night. The average family had 3.615 members; hence there were 68,700 homeless family households and 492,700 homeless households.

References

Abt Associates, Gregory Mills, Daniel Gubits, Larry Orr, David Long, Judie Feins, Bulbul Kaul, Michelle Woods, Amy Jones and Associates, Cloudburst Consulting, and the QED Group. 2006. *Effects of Housing Choice Vouchers on Welfare Families.* Washington: U.S. Department of Housing and Urban Development.

Early, Dirk W. 2004. "The Determinants of Homelessness and the Targeting of Housing Assistance." *Journal of Urban Economics* 55(1): 195–214.

Early, Dirk W., and Edgar O. Olsen. 2002. "Subsidized Housing, Emergency Shelters, and Homelessness: An Empirical Investigation Using Data from the 1990 Census." *Advances in Economic Analysis and Policy* 2(1): pp. n.a.

Gyourko, Joseph, Albert Saiz, and Anita Summers. 2006. "A New Measure of the Local Regulatory Environment for Housing Markets: Wharton Residential Land Use Regulatory Index." Wharton School working paper. Philadelphia: University of Pennsylvania.

Malpezzi, Stephen, and Richard K. Green. 1996. "What Has Happened to the Bottom of the U.S. Housing Market?" *Urban Studies* 33(1): 1807–20.

Mansur, Erin, John Quigley, Steven Raphael, and Eugene Smolensky. 2002. "Examining Policies to Reduce Homelessness Using a General Equilibrium Model of the Housing Market." *Journal of Urban Economics* 52(2): 316–40.

O'Flaherty, Brendan. 1995. "An Economic Theory of Homelessness and Housing." *Journal of Housing Economics* 4(1): 13–49.

———. 2004. "Wrong Person AND Wrong Place: For Homelessness the Conjunction is What Matters." *Journal of Housing Economics* 13(1): 1–15.

Sinai, Todd, and Joel Waldfogel. 2005. "Do Low-Income Housing Subsidies Increase the Occupied Housing Stock?" *Journal of Public Economics* 89(11–12): 2137–64.

U.S. Department of Housing and Urban Development, Office of Community Planning and Development. 2008. *The 2007 Annual Homeless Assessment Report.* Washington: Government Printing Office.

PART I

HELPING PEOPLE
LEAVE HOMELESSNESS

Chapter 2

Service Models and Mental Health Problems: Cost-Effectiveness and Policy Relevance

ROBERT ROSENHECK

A recent analysis of data from the National Comorbidity Study Replication, a representative national epidemiological survey, found that 5 percent of U.S. adults reported a past episode of homelessness lasting a week or more. In comparison to other adults, those who had been homeless were six times more likely to have had an alcohol or drug problem and three times more likely to have had a psychiatric illness (Greenberg and Rosenheck n.d). Although it is thus clear that many homeless people have mental illnesses or problems with alcohol or drug use, the link between housing homeless people with such problems and providing them with mental health or social services is not self-evident. One commonsense response would be that, just like any other group of homeless people, the central need of those with mental health problems is a place to live. Mental health care might be needed to address the problems of some homeless people but housing is the logical solution to their homelessness. A logic that could support a more medical treatment model would argue that effective treatment of psychiatric or addictive disorders would allow recovery and subsequent employment with housing through the private market. Certainly, if someone were found on the street having seizures or infected with pneumococcal pneumonia, they would receive treatment for their acute medical crisis before their housing needs would be considered.

In fact, few service initiatives for homeless people with behavioral problems have focused on employment, and most assume that the mental health and addiction problems of homeless people are long-term conditions not likely to be well enough resolved in the immediate future to enable them to become economically self-sufficient. Rather than a medical model, most specialized service programs for people with mental health or addiction problems follow a tacit social rehabilitation model that assumes that such people suffer from impairments in judgment and in social skills and need active assistance coping with the world around them. Such assistance ranges from offers of moral support, such as encouragement to make their own choices, to advice on where to seek material assistance and to more active assistance negotiating with landlords for apartments, with public bureaucracies for income supports or housing subsidies, with criminal justice officials for release from jail, or with health systems to obtain medical or mental health services.

Even though rehabilitation models emphasize personal choice, they also include a surveillance or social control function. Judges are more likely to release arrestees to the community, and landlords to accept tenants of questionable reliability, if they have a case manager—that is, if a case manager is assigned to them to keep an eye on things and provide assistance if it is needed.

Regardless of the underlying logic, a substantial body of research has attempted to test various service models for homeless people with mental health and addiction problems over the past twenty years, with mixed results. This chapter reviews evidence for the effectiveness of five types of intervention: service system integration, supported housing, clinical case management, benefits outreach, and supported employment. Because the primary intention of this research is to guide public policy and identify programs capable of solving the social problem of homelessness, emphasis will be placed both on the effectiveness of such services in helping homeless people obtain housing, and on the cost of such services to society. Public programs are ultimately judged by the cost-effectiveness standard, whether benefits and savings together exceed costs, and we will try to address how various initiatives fare by this standard. But, first, four limitations to the overall enterprise need to be addressed: the constraints imposed by the equipoise standard in human-subjects research (the need to avoid depriving comparison subjects of services that meet current standards for adequate care), the generalizability of data from research samples to the general population, the generalizability of findings from research sites to real-world service systems, and the need for credible, preferably randomized, control groups.

Human Subjects Constraints.   A major limitation of almost all the research reviewed in this chapter is that ethical constraints on human investigation preclude ever testing whether current service models are better than a model of no services or substandard services. Bare neglect, though regrettably practiced in real-world service systems, violates the demand for equipoise in human research—that no subject should suffer disadvantage for participating in a study. The only evaluation-research option, therefore, is to test one acceptable service model against another. As a result, the apparent magnitude of program benefits is diminished and the question of what minimal set of services should be available to all who need them can never be tested. Serendipitously, the national evaluation of the Collaborative Initiative on Chronic Homelessness, discussed shortly, provides a small window through this barrier.

Client Generalizability.   Second, homeless people with mental health and addiction problems are diverse, among many other things, in how long they have been homeless, how serious and chronic their mental health problems are, how serious their ancillary problems are (such as poverty, employability, or being involved in the criminal justice system), and their preference for various mental health services. As a result, the generalizability of research on one sample to others is usually unknown. One of the major determinants of the cost-effectiveness of policies is the population to which they are targeted (Schuck and Zeckhauser 2006). The potential for cost-effectiveness of health-care interventions depends on the potential for cost offsets, which is largely shaped by the baseline costs of the target population (Rosenheck and Neale 1998; Rosenheck et al. 1999). Programs targeted to high-risk, high-cost subpopulations are more likely to pass the cost-effectiveness tests than others, but their results are also less generalizable to the population as a whole.

Site Generalizability.   Third, most studies have been conducted at a single site under the auspices of the proud progenitor of the program being evaluated. If such programs were implemented through a broad public-policy initiative, there would likely be an attenuation of fidelity to the original program model as its implementation passed into less experienced (and less loving) hands, with concomitant attenuation of program effectiveness as well. At a minimum, the generalizability of single-site programs to other locations is typically unknown.

Credible (Randomized) Comparison Groups.   Finally, most studies of services for homeless people, and the most positive and most often publicized studies, are pre–post, or uncontrolled studies in which the effect of regression to the mean cannot be distinguished from true program impact. Evaluation of program impact requires random assignment to treatment or identification of a well-matched control group. Peter Rossi long ago pointed out that the more rigorous the study design, the less likely human-service interventions are to show positive benefits (Shadish, Cook, and Leviton 1990). Accordingly, this review is limited to studies with reasonably well-designed comparison groups, especially those based on random assignment.

These four caveats in fact compound one another, because once we limit ourselves to controlled studies that include cost data, we increase the chances that the samples are not representative, that the comparison treatments will be of above average intensity and quality, and that generalizability to routine real-world care will be limited. Nevertheless, as Fitzgerald wrote in *The Great Gatsby*, "we beat on, boats against the current."

System Integration

One of the most widely voiced complaints about mental health systems in general and about services for homeless people in particular is that they are fragmented, that communication between providers is poor, and that service system integration is much needed (New Freedom Commission on Mental Health 2003). The Continuum of Care initiative of the U.S. Department of Housing and Urban Development (HUD) (Burt et al. 2002) was designed to reduce fragmentation and increase coordination in such systems. Studies of the impact of service-integration initiatives are difficult to conduct because the unit of intervention is the service system and the locus of presumed benefit are the individuals served by the system.

In 1993 the Center for Mental Health Services initiated the ambitious Access to Community Care and Effective Services and Supports (ACCESS) program. This five-year demonstration evaluated the impact of efforts to enhance service system integration in nine communities that received $250,000 per year and extensive technical assistance to bolster system integration using eleven distinct strategies (Randolph et al. 2002). The study also included a matched sample of nine comparison sites that did not receive funds or technical assistance to implement such strategies. Housing and clinical outcomes of more than 7,000 homeless persons with serious mental illness were tracked over twelve months of program participation in four annual cohorts (Rosenheck et al. 2002). The results of this study showed greater use of system integration strategies at intervention sites, greater improvement on measures of system integration (Morrissey et al. 2002), and that many clients successfully exited from homelessness for thirty days or more (Rosenheck et al. 2002). Nonetheless, clients at integration sites showed no greater improvement in exiting homelessness or in symptom outcomes across the four client cohorts as their systems became more integrated than control sites did (Rosenheck et al. 2002). The virtually identical slopes of improvement across all cohorts at both integration and control sites reflect no impact of changes in service system integration on client outcomes. Although ACCESS is just one study, it seems likely that, to improve housing outcomes, integration needs to occur in the direct provision of both housing resources and clinical services to individual clients.

Cost-Effectiveness of Supported Housing

Programs offering such proximal integration of clinical or case management services and augmented housing resources are often called supported housing programs. Although there are many variations, all combine dedicated housing resources or subsidies with human services that represent a combination of community-based mental health services and practical assistance of the kind often associated with the social work profession. It is widely believed that these services need to be intensive, offering contact one or more times per week; flexible, practical, and community-based rather than office-based; and sustained for many years. Only two studies have sought to tease out the specific contribution of housing subsidies and intensive case management: the HUD–Veterans Affairs Supported Housing Program (VASH) (Rosenheck et al. 2003) and the San Diego McKinney Demonstration (Hough et al. 1997).

The VASH program, perhaps the largest of these, is implemented at thirty-four sites nationwide and serves almost 5,000 veterans with access to almost 2,000 Section 8 housing vouchers from 1992 to the present. The program has recently been expanded to 10,000 vouchers that will be linked to more than two hundred case managers at more than 120 VA facilities.

Four sites in the original 1992 demonstration conducted a cost-effectiveness evaluation in which $N = 460$ homeless veterans who were randomly assigned to VASH, involving both Section 8 vouchers and case management ($N = 182$); intensive case management provided by the VASH case managers, but without special-access housing subsidies ($N = 90$); and standard, time-limited VA case-management service for homeless veterans ($N = 188$).

Over a three-year follow-up, the VASH group was housed 65 percent of nights, versus 57 percent for case management alone and 53 percent for the standard care group ($p < .05$) (Rosenheck et al. 2003). The case management–only condition thus had only 4 percent more days housed than the standard care group. The VASH group also experienced 14 percent total days of homelessness compared with the 22 percent of both control groups ($p > .05$), again with no difference between case management only and standard care. Therapeutic alliance, a measure of treatment satisfaction, was stronger in the VASH group than the other groups, and a special analysis addressing differential data attrition with a technique called multiple imputation showed that substance-use outcomes were superior in the VASH group over the other two (Cheng et al. 2007). These results suggest a modest but statistically significant benefit associated with the integration of case management and vouchers, but no independent benefit from intensive case management by itself.

On the cost side, from a societal perspective, including all VA and non-VA health costs as well as shelter use, incarceration, and administrative costs of transfer payments, annual costs for VASH clients over the three years were $2,067 higher than standard care, and those for case-management control clients were $1,167 higher, reflecting both direct case-management services and greater use of other health services.

Figure 2.1   Cost-Effectiveness Acceptability Curve

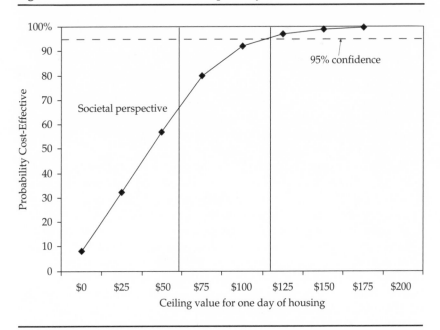

Source: Author's compilation based on Rosenheck et al. (2003).

Cost-effectiveness analysis using incremental ratios showed increased costs of $45 per additional day housed (95 percent confidence interval equals −$19 to +$108) for VASH clients compared with controls. Because societal willingness to pay for a day of housing for a homeless person is unknown, cost-effectiveness acceptability curves can be used to show the likelihood of achieving cost-effectiveness under various shadow prices for such a day from the societal perspective, including VA and non-VA health costs, criminal justice system costs, homeless shelter costs, transfer payments, and productivity through employment (see figure 2.1). Benefits are likely to outweigh costs with a probability of 56 percent if a day of housing is valued at $50, with a probability of 80 percent if valued at $75, and with one of 92 percent if at a $100.

The VASH study was based on random assignment, included a cost component, included a mixture of clients with psychiatric and addiction problems, and was a broad real-world dissemination effort, albeit within the VA system. It showed significant housing benefits, specifically tied to the use of vouchers, but increased costs that would make the intervention less appealing to policymakers. However, with the war in Iraq pushing services for homeless veterans higher on the congressional agenda, the program is now undergoing a major revival and expansion. It is clear that the increased costs of case management could have been reduced by either lowering the intensity of the case management intervention or shortening its duration. In the new iteration, case-load expectations are being increased from twenty-five clients to thirty-five per case manager. What is unknown is whether such cost savings on the delivery of case management services would reduce benefits or, most intriguingly, whether homeless people with mental health or addiction problems could benefit from dedicated vouchers even without any case management.

A second study that tried to differentiate the benefit of intensive case management from that of housing vouchers was the San Diego McKinney Demonstration, which used a two-by-two design crossing access to housing vouchers by two levels, high intensity or low, of case management (Hurlburt, Wood, and Hough 1996; Hough et al. 1997). Clients who received rent subsidies were more likely to be independently housed at the end of the eighteen-month follow-up period, but housing outcomes were no better among clients who received high-intensity case management than among those who received low-intensity, either with or without vouchers. These findings did not represent clear superiority of either intervention because no differences between any of the conditions in the number of days of homelessness were significant, and the high-intensity case management was, in practice, not much more intensive than as the standard intervention had been planned. No cost data were obtained but the lack of robust reductions in homelessness would make the results from San Diego less than attractive from a policy perspective.

Housing First is a third, very well-known supported housing initiative that puts a high emphasis on client choice and emphasizes rapid placement in housing severely mentally ill, often dually diagnosed clients, who otherwise would be unlikely to find housing or would find delayed access through multistage continuum of care programs (Tsemberis, Gulcur, and Nakae 2004). Housing First has among the most robust improvements in housing compared with its randomly assigned control group: over six to twenty-four months, clients spent 60 percent to 80 percent of their time in housing, versus 12 percent to 30 percent for controls ($p < .001$), with similarly robust differences in days of homelessness. Active program maintenance of housing units, unlike referrals to public-housing authorities, may also facilitate more rapid housing and explain the robust findings. Housing First clients saw no benefits in psychiatric or substance-abuse outcomes compared with controls, though they have more choice in programs.

About one-third of clients in the Housing First trial entered the program while they were in a psychiatric hospital bed (Gulcur et al. 2003), creating a substantial opportunity for cost savings. Clear evidence has been published showing that Housing First clients incurred significantly lower costs from institutional care (for example, through a hospital) than controls did during the first twenty-four months of treatment (Gulcur et al.

2003), though by the end of that twenty-four months, significant group differences had disappeared. A full cost-effectiveness analysis that includes the costs of the Housing First intervention itself has yet to be published, but targeting a high-cost sample to begin with increased the chance that Housing First would generate enough savings in institutional care to pay for its own expenses, at least during the first two years. By targeting severely ill clients with dual disorders, which included many psychiatric inpatients, Housing First maximized the opportunity for substantial housing improvements as cost savings. These findings, however, may not be applicable to less severely impaired populations.

Supported Housing Summary

These studies clearly show the potential benefit of housing subsidies but do not provide distinct evidence for the effectiveness of intensive case management, though they certainly do not rule out a critical role for such services. It is notable that even in the VASH study, and to a lesser extent in Housing First, clients who did not receive targeted housing services showed decided improvements in their housing statuses over the follow-up period both in access to independent housing and in reciprocal declines in days of homelessness. Thus, in some studies in which interventions improved housing outcomes, differences were not stark, though they were most robust in Housing First.

Cost-Effectiveness of Case Management

A review of intensive case-management services for homeless people with mental illness identified ten experimental studies, only three of which included cost analyses (Morse 1999). Seven of the ten showed fewer days of homelessness for case management clients, many of whom received poorly defined housing assistance compared with controls, but only two showed reduced symptoms. Four studies have been designed to support cost-effectiveness analysis.

A study conducted in St. Louis compared two models of intensive case management for homeless people with mental illness, one that included community workers on the team and one that used only professionals, against a control. The intensive case-management models cost about $9,000 per client over eighteen months of treatment and were compared with a more standard, brokered case-management model. Although the intensive conditions showed greater symptom reduction and consumer satisfaction than standard care, there were no differences between the two intensive groups in days of homelessness, most likely because no specific housing resources were dedicated to clients in either model. Costs were lowest for the intensive case-management program that used community workers ($39,913), highest for intensive case management that relied on professionals ($49,510), and in the middle for standard, brokered case management ($45,076). The high cost of this program and lack of any greater exit from homelessness does not argue for its policy appeal. It more directly raises doubts about the value of even effective mental health interventions in addressing the problem of homelessness without specific housing resources.

More promising intervention studies, from Baltimore (Lehman et al. 1997, 1999) and from New York (Susser et al. 1997; Herman et al. 2000; Jones et al. 2003), illustrate program elements that can improve cost-effectiveness profiles. The Baltimore Assertive Community Treatment study linked a costly case management intervention ($8,000 per year) with Section 8 vouchers and found significantly greater improvements in symptoms, life satisfaction, and health status and a greater proportion of days in stable housing over a one-year follow-up (59 percent versus 43 percent).

Total health costs for the Baltimore study were $50,748 for the experimental condition and $66,480 for the control, representing a net savings of $15,732 per year. This difference largely reflects thirty fewer inpatient days for the experimental condition during the year, generating a savings of $24,519 in inpatient costs. A key to the favorable cost results was that almost one-third of the sample (29 percent) were recruited from an inpatient unit, thus guaranteeing a high-cost sample, with considerable opportunity for savings. Presumably the availability of housing resources prevented unnecessary extensions of hospital stays. As noted in our summary of study caveats, targeting current inpatients can have an important impact on cost-effectiveness results. Although it limits study generalizability, it also illustrates that thoughtful targeting of policy initiatives can improve their cost-effectiveness, at least during the early phase of treatment.

The New York–based Critical Time Intervention (CTI) program is another modification of the supported-housing case-management model that improved cost-effectiveness. Unlike intensive case-management interventions discussed earlier, CTI is a time-limited, nine-month intervention, designed to facilitate the transition from shelter living to community residence, but does not direct services over the long term. In an experimental study of CTI and standard care, both groups had access to community housing and thus housing rates were very high for both over an eighteen-month follow-up. CTI clients spent 94 percent of their nights in housing and controls spent 79 percent, a difference of fifty-eight days over eighteen months. CTI clients also had lower scores on one measure of psychiatric symptoms.

Total costs from the societal perspective were $725 greater for each CTI client than for each control during the follow-up period. However, because CTI is a time-limited intervention, although costs were $2,263 greater during the first nine months, similar to VASH, they were $1,613 lower during the second nine, after the intervention was over. Thus, though the incremental cost-effectiveness ratio was $94 per night housed during the first nine months, it was only $13 per night over the entire period. Cost-effectiveness acceptability curves showed that CTI was 95 percent likely to be cost-effective if a day of housing is valued at $457 during the first nine months, $120 during the second nine, and $152 over the entire period. CTI cost-effectiveness results are thus similar to those of VASH, except that costs dropped sharply after the supported housing intervention ended, and overall housing rates are higher for both experimental and control groups.

In this review, three points deserve further emphasis. First, it appears both that the availability of dedicated housing resources is a critical ingredient for housing homeless people with mental illness and that intensive case management by itself does not seem to improve housing outcomes. Second, the differences between experimental and control conditions in the studies reviewed are not large: 66 percent versus 53 percent of days in housing through VASH, no difference through the San Diego or St. Louis projects, 59 percent versus 43 percent through Baltimore, and 94 percent versus 79 percent through CTI, but with larger differences in Housing First. Third, though some models were associated with increased costs, others showed cost savings, largely reflecting variability in the baseline costs of the target population and the duration of the intervention. Finally, although these interventions all generate some benefits, from the policy perspective they are not robustly cost-effective and do not provide an exceptionally appealing case for comprehensive implementation.

As noted in our preliminary caveats, differences between experimental and control conditions may be minimized in random assignment studies because of the ethical equipoise requirement that no treatment group be deprived of effective services. To bracket this possibility, we present preliminary data on housing outcomes from the Collaborative Initiative to Help End Chronic Homelessness (CICH), a demonstration program jointly funded by HUD, the Health and Human Services Department (HHS), and VA (Mares and Rosenheck 2007). The CICH evaluation is a nonexperimental study primarily focusing on consumers who received CICH services, a rich array of housing and health-care services using a diversity of case management models. Five of the eleven participating sites voluntarily recruited samples of chronically homeless people from a different part of the city where the enriched services were not available. Baseline data suggest that the CICH sample had more serious health problems than controls and that adjustment was made for these using regression models. These data show more robust differences in housing outcomes, 68 to 90 percent of days housed versus 31 to 55 percent over the first twelve months of service (see figure 2.2), and modest differences in health costs (figure 2.3). They suggest that the impact of supported housing may, in fact, be greater than observed in experimental studies, though the risk of selection biases in the absence of random assignment is of course greater.

Case management programs alone are capable of improving mental health symptoms but seem less likely to improve housing in the absence

Figure 2.2   Outcomes in CICH Supported Housing Program

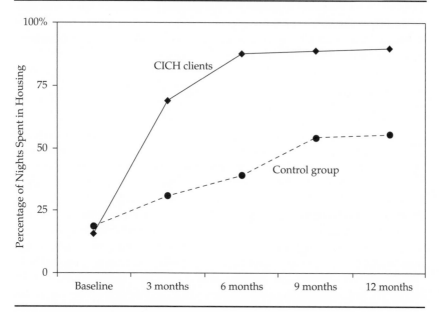

Source: Author's compilation based on Mares and Rosenheck (2007).

Figure 2.3   Health Costs in CICH Supported Housing Program

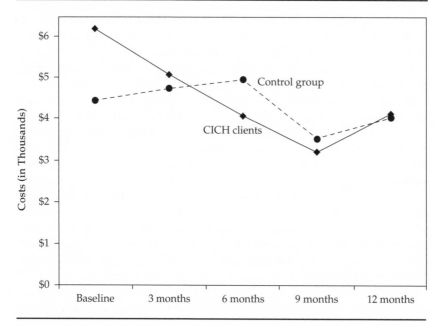

Source: Author's compilation based on Mares and Rosenheck (2007).

of specific housing resources. These programs remain costly, at up to $7,000 to $9,000 per client per year, but, when targeted at high-cost hospitalized patients, can realize enough short-term savings to offset their cost. When delivered on a time-limited basis, costs can be contained enough to allow cost savings after discharge.

Benefits Outreach, Payeeship, and Behavioral Money Management

It is well established that diminished access to public-support payments increases the risk of homelessness among people with mental health and addictions problems and is a more important risk factor than lack of access to mental health treatment (Sosin and Grossman 1991). Although facilitating access to income supports is regarded as one of the services routinely provided by case management teams, several initiatives have been developed improve access to VA income benefits. They show that from 15 to 22 percent of veterans contacted through outreach programs received new benefits over twelve months (Chen et al. 2007; Greenberg et al. 2007). In the absence of comparison groups, however, it is difficult to know how much to attribute these gains to the outreach efforts. Many clients would have received their benefits on their own initiative.

A joint benefits outreach project conducted by VA clinical staff in collaboration with colocated Social Security field-office staff obtained data that allowed for such a comparison. The adjudication of benefits claims can be time-consuming and complex, requiring assertiveness at multiple levels of appeal and deft knowledge of how to develop medical evidence of disability. Project staff included both outreach workers to organize claims and doctoral-level professionals to develop the necessary medical evidence (Rosenheck, Frisman, and Kasprow 1999). The evaluation design compared receipt of Social Security benefits at VA homeless-program sites that were involved in the joint project and comparison sites that were not. Comparing applications for SSA benefits at the demonstration sites in the years before and after the project was initiated shows a sharp increase in applications from 8 to 10 percent of homeless veterans in the years before the project was initiated to 23 percent in the years after, with a small secular upward drift to only 10 to 12 percent at the control sites. Because the rate of award remained the same over these years at both types of sites, the net award rate increased modestly from 5 to 13 percent of veterans (figure 2.4), and that among homeless veterans entering programs at control sites drifted upward from 6 to 7 percent. This improvement in outcomes came at an estimated cost of $1,700 to $3,200 per award (Rosenheck, Frisman, and Kasprow 1999).

A further study of outcomes in the same initiative compared a subgroup of veteran applicants for SSI or Social Security Disability (SSD) payments

Figure 2.4   SSA-VA Joint Outreach

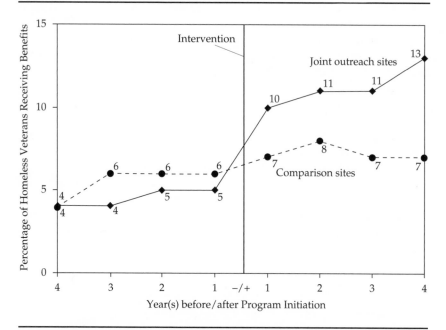

Source: Author's compilation based on Rosenheck, Frisman, and Kasprow (1999).
Note: Rates of award among all outreach veterans (N = 34,431).

who received benefits (N = 50) and those who did not (N = 123). In the three months after the awards, beneficiaries reported not only significantly higher total incomes ($735 versus $458, $p < .001$), higher quality of life (2.96 versus 2.67 on a scale of 1, terrible, to 7, delighted, $p < .004$), and marginally fewer days of homelessness (9.37 versus 31.8, $p = .11$) but also lower employment earnings ($19 versus $108, $p = .013$).

Because receipt of benefits can be a trigger for substance use (Shaner et al. 1995; Phillips, Christenfeld, and Ryan 1999), it is notable that new beneficiaries reported no expenditures on alcohol or drugs, whereas non-recipients reported only $5 expenditures ($p =$ ns), although beneficiaries did spend significantly more money on tobacco products ($31.77 versus $20.28, $p < .007$) (Rosenheck et al. 2000).

Whether the benefits in quality of life and housing are worth the not insubstantial investment in benefits outreach is unclear from these data and would require follow-up information well beyond the first three months after the award.

Concerns about misuse of income benefits for substance abuse have also been widespread. Studies have clearly demonstrated a substantial check effect with increased use of illegal drugs after receipt of benefit checks

(Shaner et al. 1995; Phillips, Christenfeld, and Ryan 1999). However, several studies of participants in VA homeless programs (Rosenheck and Frisman 1996; Frisman and Rosenheck 1997) and in ACCESS (Rosen et al. 2005) have failed to find such effects. A common intervention to curtail such risks, assignment of a representative payee, does not seem to have a significant beneficial effect (Rosenheck, Lam, and Randolph 1997; Rosen, McMahon, and Rosenheck 2008). However, a recently developed behavioral intervention called Advisor-Teller Money Manager (ATM), which is designed specifically to enhance abstinence among drug users by teaching the participants to better manage their funds, shows some promise in reducing substance use (Rosen, Bailey, and Rosenheck 2003; Rosen et al., forthcoming a, forthcoming b).

In summary, benefits outreach to facilitate access to entitlements has been subject to only one controlled study, which revealed some evidence of at least short-term benefits but at substantial cost. Additional research is needed in this intuitively appealing area, but the evidence is still too thin to support policy action.

Supported Employment

We turn, finally, to supported employment, an approach that seeks to return homeless people, many with addiction problems, directly to the labor market. The model of supported employment that has been most carefully evaluated is the individual placement and support (IPS) model (Becker and Drake 2003). IPS emphasizes rapid job placement, a focus on competitive jobs, ongoing support without a time limit, client choice of jobs, integration of vocational support and clinical care, and openness to all who want to work, regardless of clinical status or work experience.

In 2000 a demonstration was implemented at nine VA programs serving homeless veterans. The programs were provided with educational support and funds to hire and train an employment specialist who would provide IPS services (Rosenheck and Mares 2007). Individual client outcomes were assessed with a pre–post nonequivalent–control group design. From six to twelve months before IPS became available, a cohort of thirty homeless veterans who had newly entered the program and expressed an interest in employment was recruited at each site and followed through quarterly interviews for two years (phase 1 cohort, N = 308). Once the employment specialist was hired and trained, a second cohort of thirty-five veterans was recruited and also followed for two years (phase 2 cohort, N = 322). As noted, this kind of comparison, involving real-world, large-scale dissemination without randomization, more closely follows the situation of actual policy implementation, albeit with human-subjects committee approval and written informed consent.[1]

Controlling for significant baseline differences, veterans in phase 2 had on average 13.7 percent more days per month of competitive employment

Figure 2.5   Days Housed in Past Ninety

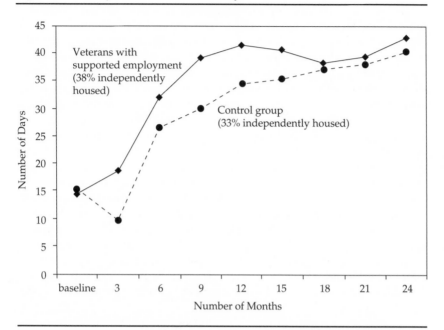

Source: Author's compilation based on Rosenheck and Mares (2007).
Note: Points are means estimated by least squares.

(least square means = 8.4 versus 7.4 days; $F = 16.5$, $p < .0001$). Among workers in either group, no significant differences appeared in hourly wage ($8.51 versus $8.08; $f = 3.2$, $p = .07$) or monthly earnings ($1,238 versus $1,142; $F = 3.1$, $p = .08$). Average annualized employment income among all participants was $1,299 greater for those in the phase 2 group ($8,889 compared with $7,590; $F = 4.5$, $df = 1$ and 596, $p = .01$). There was only one significant difference in any nonemployment outcome. Veterans in phase 2 had a significant, if modestly, greater average numbers of days in housing during the previous ninety days (least square means = 34.0 versus 29.6; $F = 4.5$; $p = .03$) for an annualized difference of sixteen days housed, only 4 percent more per year (see figure 2.5).

This intensive, highly individualized intervention was not inexpensive. Annualized costs for employment specialist services averaged $2,063 per client month (site range = $1,400 to $2,700), though this was partially offset by greater annual earnings (social productivity) of $1,299.

This study suggests that IPS can be implemented in an organization with no previous experience with this model if it undertakes modestly intensive, but sustained, training guided by a single outside expert (Rosenheck and Mares 2007). Increases in days of competitive employment were observed at eight of nine sites and were statistically significant overall. However, these gains are substantially smaller than those reported in other studies. In Gary Bond's (2004) review of research on IPS, almost 2.9 times as many clients in the IPS groups were employed, compared with those in the control groups (56 percent versus 19 percent), whereas in the Employment Intervention Demonstration Program (Cook et al. 2005), another large study, 1.6 times as many clients in the supported-employment group (the experimental model) were employed as in the control group (55 percent versus 34 percent). These effects are much larger than the 15 percent gain in days spent competitively employed that was found in this study. It is possible that group differences were small in this study because training was not intense enough, because the focus was on a homeless sample that included many clients with substance abuse problems rather than on domiciled people predominantly with severe mental illness, or because effectiveness was attenuated in this fairly large-scale, real-world dissemination.

As in our consideration of other interventions for homeless people with special needs, we find evidence not only of modest effectiveness for supported employment but also for increased costs. Rough calculation of incremental cost-effectiveness ratios suggests $129 per night housed for the supported-employment intervention, but only $48 if we consider productivity gains as offsetting intervention costs. These incremental cost-effectiveness ratios are similar to those observed in VASH ($45 per night) and during the active treatment phase of CTI ($94 per night) but are not likely be especially attractive to policymakers with tight budgets.

Conclusion

Controlled research has evaluated the effectiveness and cost of several types of programs intended to meet the needs of homeless people with psychiatric and addictive disorders. Although significantly superior to control treatments, their effects are most often modest in magnitude and primarily center on a single outcome domain, such as housing, symptoms, benefits, or employment. No single intervention seems to spread substantial benefit across multiple life domains. Program costs can be substantial but may be offset by more refined specification of high-cost target populations or in limiting the duration of active treatment, albeit with some risk of loss of effectiveness and applicability to the broader population of homeless people with mental health problems.

These programs provide meaningful, if incremental, benefits, but they do not yet offer a service armamentarium that can be deployed on a large scale in expectation of efficiently eliminating the problem of homelessness among people with mental illness. Incremental progress is clearly in evidence in these studies. Progress nonetheless remains to be made to improve their effectiveness, their efficiency, and their potential for widespread dissemination.

Notes

1. Because the phase 2 comparison group was not identified through random assignment, participants in the two phases were compared on baseline measures revealing that participants in the IPS phase had fewer lifetime years of homelessness, were more likely to have worked in the previous three years (but not in the previous thirty days), had fewer psychiatric symptoms and better physical health, but did not differ on major psychiatric diagnoses or in substance abuse problems. Adjustment for these characteristics was made in subsequent analyses.

References

Becker, Deborah R., and Robert E. Drake. 2003. *A Working Life for People with Severe Mental Illness.* New York: Oxford University Press.

Bond, Gary R. 2004. "Supported Employment: Evidence for an Evidence-Based Practice." *Psychiatric Rehabilitation Journal* 27(4): 345–59.

Burt, Martha, Dave Pollack, Abby Sosland, Kelly Mikelson, Elizabeth Drapa, Kristy Greenwalt, and Patrick Sharkey. 2002. *Evaluations of Continuums of Care for Homeless People.* Washington: U.S. Department of Housing and Urban Development.

Chen, Joyce H., Robert A. Rosenheck, Greg A. Greenberg, and Catherine Seibyl. 2007. "Factors Associated with Receipt of Pension and Compensation Benefits for Homeless Veterans in the VBA/VHA Homeless Outreach Initiative." *Psychiatric Quarterly* 78:63–72.

Cheng, An-Lin, Lin Haiqun, Wesley Kasprow, and Robert A. Rosenheck. 2007. "Impact of Supported Housing on Clinical Outcomes: Analysis of a Randomized Trial Using Multiple Imputation Technique." *Journal of Nervous and Mental Disease* 195(1): 83–88.

Cook, Judith A., H. Stephen Leff, Crystal R. Blyler, Paul B. Gold, Richard W. Goldberg, Kim T. Mueser, Marcia G. Toprac, William R. McFarlane, Michael S. Shafer, Laura E. Blankertz, Ken Dudek, Lisa A. Razzano, Dennis D. Grey, and Jane Burke-Miller. 2005. "Results of a Multisite Randomized Trial of Supported Employment Interventions for Individuals with Severe Mental Illness." *Archives of General Psychiatry* 62(5): 505–12.

Frisman, Linda K., and Robert A. Rosenheck. 1997. "The Relationship of Public Support Payments to Substance Abuse Among Homeless Veterans with Mental Illness." *Psychiatric Services* 48(6): 792–95.

Greenberg, Greg, Joyce H. Chen, Robert A. Rosenheck, and Wesley Kasprow. 2007. "Receipt of Disability Through an Outreach Program for Homeless Veterans." *Military Medicine* 172(5): 461–65.

Greenberg, Greg, and Robert A. Rosenheck. n.d. "Mental Health Correlates of Past Homelessness in the National Comorbidity Study Replication." Unpublished paper.

Gulcur, Leyla, Ana Stefancic, Marybeth Shinn, Sam Tsemberis, and Sean N. Fischer. 2003. "Housing, Hospitalization, and Cost Outcomes for Homeless Individuals with Psychiatric Disabilities Participating in Continuum of Care and Housing First Programmes." *Journal of Community & Applied Social Psychology* 13:171–86.

Herman, Daniel, Lewis Opler, Alan Felix, Elie Valencia, Richard J. Wyatt, and Ezra Susser. 2000. "Critical Time Intervention with Mentally Ill Homeless Men: Impact on Psychiatric Symptoms." *Journal of Nervous and Mental Disease* 188: 135–40.

Hough, Richard L., Patricia A. Wood, Michael S. Hurlburt, H. R. Tarke, R. Quinlivan, S. Yamashiro, A. Crowell, and E. Morris. 1997. *Housing, Quality of Life and Mental Health Outcomes in an Evaluation of Supported Housing for Homeless Mentally Ill Individuals.* San Diego, Calif.: San Diego State University.

Hurlburt, Michael S., Patricia A. Wood, and Richard L. Hough. 1996. "Effects of Substance Abuse on Housing Stability of Homeless Mentally Ill Persons in Supported Housing." *Psychiatric Services* 47: 731–36.

Jones, Kristine, Paul W. Colson, Mark C. Holter, Shang Lin, Elie Valencia, Ezra Susser, and Richard J. Wyatt. 2003. "Cost-Effectiveness of Critical Time Intervention to Reduce Homelessness Among Persons with Mental Illness." *Psychiatric Services* 54(6): 884–90.

Lehman, Anthony F., Lisa B. Dixon, Jeffrey S. Hoch, Bruce DeForge, Eimer Kernan, and Richard Frank. 1999. "Cost-Effectiveness of Assertive Community Treatment for Homeless Persons with Severe Mental Illness." *British Journal of Psychiatry* 174: 346–52.

Lehman, Anthony F., Lisa B. Dixon, Eimer Kernan, Bruce R. DeForge, and Leticia A. Postrado. 1997. "Randomized Trial of Assertive Community Treatment for Homeless Persons with Severe Mental Illness." *Archive of General Psychiatry* 54: 1038–43.

Mares, Alvin S, and Robert A. Rosenheck. 2007. *HUD/HHS/VA Collaborative Initiative to Help End Chronic Homelessness National Performance Outcomes Assessment Preliminary Client Outcomes Report.* West Haven, Conn.: Northeast Program Evaluation Center.

Morrissey, Joseph P., Michael O. Calloway, Neil Thakur, Joseph Cocozza, Henry J. Steadman, and Deborah Dennis. 2002. "Integration of Service Systems for Homeless Persons with Serious Mental Illness Through the ACCESS Program. Access to Community Care and Effective Services and Supports." *Psychiatric Services* 53(8): 949–57.

Morse, Gary A. 1999. "Review of Case Management for People Who are Homeless: Implications for Practice, Policy and Research." In *Practical Lessons: The 1998 National Symposium on Homelessness Research,* edited by Linda B. Forsberg and Deborah Dennis. Washington: U.S. Department of Housing and Urban Development and U.S. Department of Health and Human Services.

New Freedom Commission on Mental Health. 2003. *Achieving the Promise: Transforming Mental Health Care in America; Final Report.* DHHS Pub. No. SMA 033–832. Rockville, Md.: U.S. Department of Health and Human Services.

Phillips, David P., Nicholas Christenfeld, and Natalie M. Ryan. 1999. "An Increase in the Number of Deaths in the United States in the First Week of the Month— An Association with Substance Abuse and Other Causes of Death." *New England Journal of Medicine* 341: 93–98.

Randolph, Frances, Margaret Blasinsky, Joseph Morrissey, Robert A. Rosenheck, Joseph Cocozza, Howard H. Goldman, and the ACCESS National Evaluation Team. 2002. "Overview of the ACCESS Program." *Psychiatric Services* 53(8): 945–48.

Rosen, Marc I., Margaret Bailey, and Robert A. Rosenheck. 2003. "Principles of Money Management as a Therapy for Addiction." *Psychiatric Services* 54(2): 171–73.

Rosen, Marc I., M. K. Carroll, A. E. Stefanovics, Robert A. Rosenheck, and the VA New England VISN 1 MIRECC Study Group. Forthcoming a. "A Randomized Controlled Trial of a Money-Management Based Intervention Targeting Substance Use." *Psychiatric Services.*

Rosen, Marc I., Thomas J. McMahon, HaiQui Lin, and Robert A. Rosenheck. 2005. "Effect of Social Security Payments on Substance Abuse in a Homeless Mentally Ill Cohort." *Health Services Research* 41(1): 173–91.

Rosen, Marc I., Thomas J. McMahon, and Robert A. Rosenheck. 2008. "Does Assigning a Representative Payee Reduce Substance Abuse?" *Drug and Alcohol Dependence* 86(2–3): 115–22.

Rosen, Marc I., Robert A. Rosenheck, K. Ablondi, and B. Rounsaville. Forthcoming b. "Advisor-Teller Money Manager (ATM) Therapy for Substance Abuse." *Psychiatric Services.*

Rosenheck, Robert A., Joyce Cramer, Allan Edward, Joseph Erdos, Linda K. Frisman, Weichun Xu, Jonathan Thomas, William Henderson, and Dennis Charney. 1999. "Cost-Effectiveness of Clozapine in Patients with High and Low Levels of Hospital Use." *Archives of General Psychiatry* 56(6): 565–72.

Rosenheck, Robert A., David J. Dausey, Linda K. Frisman, and Wesley Kasprow. 2000. "Impact of Receipt of Social Security Benefits on Homeless Veterans with Mental Illness." *Psychiatric Services* 51(12): 1549–54.

Rosenheck, Robert A., and Linda K. Frisman. 1996. "Do Public Support Payments Encourage Substance Abuse?" *Health Affairs* 15(3): 192–200.

Rosenheck, Robert A., Linda K. Frisman, and Wesley Kasprow. 1999. "Improving Access to Disability Benefits Among Homeless Persons with Mental Illness: An Agency-Specific Approach to Services Integration." *American Journal of Public Health* 89(4): 524–28.

Rosenheck, Robert A., Wesley Kasprow, Linda K. Frisman, and Wen Liu-Mares. 2003. "Cost-Effectiveness of Supported Housing for Homeless Persons with Mental Illness." *Archives of General Psychiatry* 60: 940–51.

Rosenheck, Robert A., Julie Lam, Joseph P. Morrissey, Michael O. Calloway, Marilyn Stolar, Frances Randolph, and the Access National Evaluation Team. 2002. "Service Systems Integration and Outcomes for Mentally Ill Homeless Persons in the ACCESS program." *Psychiatric Services* 53(8): 958–66.

Rosenheck, Robert A., Julie Lam, and Frances Randolph. 1997. "Impact of Representative Payees on Substance Use Among Homeless Persons Diagnosed with Serious Mental Illness and Substance Abuse." *Psychiatric Services* 48: 800–806.

Rosenheck, Robert A., and Alvin S. Mares. 2007. "Implementation of Supported Employment for Homeless Veterans with Psychiatric or Addiction Disorders: Two-Year Outcomes." *Psychiatric Services* 58: 315–24.

Rosenheck, Robert A., and Michael S. Neale. 1998. "Cost-Effectiveness of Intensive Psychiatric Community Care for High Users of Inpatient Services." *Archives of General Psychiatry* 55(5): 459–66.

Schuck, Peter H., and Richard J. Zeckhauser. 2006. *Targeting in Social Programs: Avoiding Bad Bets and Removing Bad Apples.* Washington, D.C.: Brookings Institution.

Shadish, William R., Thomas D. Cook, and Laura Leviton. 1991. *Foundations of Program Evaluation: Theories of Practice.* Newbury Park, Calif.: Sage Publications.

Shaner, Andrew., Thad A. Eckman, Lisa J. Roberts, Jeffrey N. Wilkins, Douglas E. Tucker, John W. Tsuang, and Jim Mintz. 1995. "Disability Income, Cocaine Use, and Repeated Hospitalization Among Schizophrenic Cocaine Abusers: A Government-Sponsored Revolving Door?" *New England Journal of Medicine* 333: 777–83.

Sosin, Michael R., and Susan Grossman. 1991. "The Mental Health System and the Etiology of Homelessness: A Comparison Study." *Journal of Community Psychology* 19: 337–50.

Susser, Ezra, Elie Valencia, Sarah Conover, Alan Felix, Wei-Yann Tsai, and Richard J. Wyatt. 1997. "Preventing Recurrent Homelessness Among Mentally Ill Men: A 'Critical Time' Intervention After Discharge from a Shelter." *American Journal of Public Health* 87(2): 256–62.

Tsemberis, Sam, Leyla Gulcur, and Maria Nakae. 2004. "Housing First, Consumer Choice, and Harm Reduction for Homeless Individuals with a Dual Diagnosis." *American Journal of Public Health* 94(4): 651–56.

Chapter 3

Housing First: Ending Homelessness, Promoting Recovery, and Reducing Costs

SAM TSEMBERIS

Case Vignette: Candice

Candice, a fifty-three-year-old native New Yorker, was homeless for more than fifteen years when she was referred to Pathways. She stayed on the streets but slept in a tent that she frequently pitched in an Upper West Side park. Other campsites included the meridian that separates the northbound and southbound lanes of Broadway above 72nd Street. Her highly visible blue tent drew immediate attention from concerned citizens, outreach teams, and the police and typically resulted in a hasty involuntary transport and admission to one of the local psychiatric hospitals. A few weeks later, after discharge, this cycle would repeat.

Because of her prominent symptoms of psychosis, which featured paranoia and fear about government control, most outreach and other aid workers encouraged her to seek treatment. The workers knew that without treatment they would be unable to admit her to a supportive housing program. She repeatedly and adamantly refused all psychiatric and medical treatments.

In their first meeting with Candice, Pathways staff offered to help her with anything she needed, including an apartment of her own—no strings attached. It took several visits to convince her that the housing offer was genuine, unconditional, and free of government controls. She accepted the apartment on the condition that her signature would not be required and that she would be permitted to pitch her tent inside her new home.

After she moved in, staff continued to work with her and better understand her circumstances. They learned that she had been employed as a nurse at the time of her first psychotic episode, more than twenty years ago. As she grew more comfortable and felt safer in the apartment, she stopped using the tent and began sleeping first on the couch in the living room and eventually in her own bed. After years of eating canned and uncooked foods, she began to enjoy her own home-cooked meals. The relationship between her and her family was transformed from arguments about her treatment refusals to enjoyable visits at holidays. Her condition has continued to improve, and she has had only one hospitalization in the four years since receiving Pathway's services.

The Housing First Program

The Pathways' Housing First (HF) program, an evidence-based practice (Pathways to Housing 2007), was originally developed for people like Candice, the chronically homeless and severely mentally ill. Most consumers also suffer from serious health problems and addiction disorders. A key feature of the program is that it does not require participation in psychiatric treatment or sobriety as a condition for obtaining housing. Eliminating psychiatric and sobriety prerequisites to housing removes what often prove to be insurmountable barriers for the most vulnerable sector of the homeless. Another feature that accounts for the program's effectiveness is the enormous value of what HF offers—an apartment of one's own in a normal community setting. An invitation is an offer that many chronically homeless find irresistible. Consumers move from living in the streets directly into apartments of their own and are provided with significant support services. The program requires that consumers agree to two conditions: that they accept a weekly staff visit to their apartment as well as the terms and conditions of a standard lease with full tenant rights and payment of 30 percent of their income toward the rent. Most consumers readily agree, but staff have the flexibility of deferring enforcement of the agreement if, as in Candice's case, they feel such enforcement would interfere with the larger goal of engagement with a consumer.

In the past five years, the number of HF programs has grown from a few dozen to a few hundred. The National Alliance to End Homelessness (NAEH) reports that more than four hundred cities and counties have completed ten-year plans to *end* homelessness and 67 percent of all plans include a Housing First program (www.endhomelessness.org). In California, an estimated one hundred HF programs were recently implemented using funds generated by California Assembly Bill 2034, Integrated Services for Homeless Adults with Serious Mental Illness (Gilmer, Manning, and Ettner 2009). The programs are growing in Canada as well. The Mental Health Commission of Canada recently funded a $110 million national initiative to implement HF programs in five cities and to conduct a cross-site randomized control trial to evaluate its effectiveness (www.mentalhealthcommission.ca).

Rarely does a social service, housing, or mental health intervention see such rapid growth and dissemination. Various questions are addressed in this chapter: Why was HF developed? Who does it serve? How does the program operate? Is it effective? A series of questions on cost are also posed: How much does it cost? How is it funded? Is it cost-effective? Describing the context in which HF was developed helps answer some of these questions.

The Linear Continuum:
Treatment Compliance First

Mental health systems were among the first responders to the current epidemic of homelessness, which began around 1980 and has grown ever since. Having observed that the homeless on the streets included a disproportionately high number of people with mental illness, mental health programs mobilized to create a range of programs that begin with outreach, then move to service provision and transitional housing and end with permanent housing. This linear residential treatment (LRT) continuum remains the dominant program model today. It is well developed in communities throughout the United States and is a model that has been supported and funded by the U.S. Department of Housing and Urban Development (HUD) through its annual Continuum of Care process.

A fully developed LRT system is comprised of outreach teams, drop-in centers, safe havens, shelters, several types of transitional housing with limits on stay ranging from six months to two years, and an array of permanent supportive housing (PSH) programs. PSH can include community residences, small and large single-room occupancy (SRO) buildings with social services on site, and some mixed-use housing where people with psychiatric disabilities share the building with people with a variety of special needs or low-income residents from the community. Independent and shared apartments, clustered or scattered-site, are also a component of the LRT but almost all permanent housing options, especially apartments, are available to consumers on the condition that they demonstrate continued participation in psychiatric treatment and achieve a period of sobriety.

Most permanent supportive housing provided through LRT programs comprises studio-like units in buildings that also offer treatment and social services on-site. The construction of these projects has met with some not-in-my-back-yard opposition from the community, but they have generally proven popular with supportive housing providers, funders, and developers, especially in communities with vacant or deteriorated properties. The buildings create jobs and a permanent asset for the community. The development and construction of these projects is labor intensive, expensive, and time-consuming (projects require anywhere from three to five years to complete). Consider the average PSH construction project of twenty-five to forty units. A group of partners must work together for three years or more and obtain financing for predevelopment work and capital costs, which can range from $75,000 to $175,000 per housing unit. Financing includes obtaining bank loans, tax-credit incentives, and low-interest loans, as well as funding for ongoing rental subsidies, approximately $10,000 per person per year, and ongoing service costs, between $6,000 and $10,000 per person each year. Even if the high costs of construction and operation could be justified, the success of this model would have to be documented, and the rate at which these units are being developed would have to be accelerated substantially for this approach to meet the increasing demand for supportive housing.

In addition to high costs and inadequate supply, research shows that single-site facilities that bundle housing and treatment services also face several programmatic and ethical challenges. After evaluating a number of supportive housing programs in New York City, Frank R. Lipton and his colleagues (2000) found that bundling housing and social services can jeopardize housing stability. A consumer living in a single-site building who suffers a relapse is often evicted from housing and discharged by the social-service provider only because the site-based service provider does not have the capacity to provide follow-up treatment in either another building or within the community. A HUD-funded study of twenty-eight permanent supportive-housing programs in Philadelphia showed that about 50 percent of residents stayed three or more years, and that among those who left, one-third went to independent and other living situations (positive outcomes) and two-thirds returned to homelessness, institutions, and unspecified locations (negative outcomes) and had more severe mental illness, greater incidence of substance abuse, and higher supportive service needs than those who remained housed (O'Hara, 2007).

John Monahan and his colleagues (2001) as well as others argue that housing offered only as a reward for participation in treatment includes, by definition, an element of coercion. Can such coercion be justified on therapeutic, legal, or ethical grounds? Does it lead to greater compliance with treatment? Most mental health experts argue that it does not. In an article summarizing the literature on this subject, Michael Allen concludes that coercion violates the therapeutic alliance, violates ethical principles of mental health practitioners, and "does not work as well as programs that take a 'housing first' approach" (2003, 5).

The annual HUD homeless count provides some indirect evidence that the housing-first approach may be succeeding where the old treatment-first approach has failed. In 2006, after the widespread dissemination of HF programs, the data showed new annual reductions: from 175,914 in 2005 to 155,623 in 2006, an 11.5 percent decrease, and then in 2007 to 123,833, an additional 20.4 percent decrease (Sermons and Henry 2009).

One journalistic report of the results of the count quotes experts attributing the reduction to the Housing First approach (Swarns 2008).

Moreover, a large number of consumers are unable either to gain admission or to retain housing in LRT programs. Others, who have been homeless for years and, like Candice, have severe mental illness that interferes with their thinking and perceptions, would never apply. This subgroup has recently been dubbed the chronically homeless. Some LRT housing providers argue that these consumers remain homeless because of some personal failing or personality characteristic that makes them treatment-resistant or hard to house.

It may be, however, that the continued presence of the chronically homeless is evidence not of their individual failures, but of failings inherent in the LRT model of care. From the hard-to-house consumers' perspective, the treatment-first programs are simply not compatible with their priorities—survival, safety, and security. Much of their time is consumed with being concerned and afraid about where, when, or whether they will be able to get food; wondering where they will find a safe place to sleep; fending off illness, pain, exhaustion; and avoiding the attention of authorities. Most consumers who have been homeless for years have likely tried and failed, whether voluntarily or involuntarily, on many occasions to enter treatment simply to obtain housing. Housing is fundamental to survival and meets a basic human need of refuge and safety.

Regardless of their level of awareness of mental health symptoms, basic survival needs are of paramount concern for the homeless mentally ill with addiction disorders. For this group, treatment-first housing programs are often puzzling. Indeed, the priorities of the LRT system and the priorities of the homeless consumer are almost antithetical. Can people with severe mental illness know and articulate their priorities? The following vignette illustrates how a person who is homeless, diagnosed with schizophrenia, and experiencing an urgent medical problem makes choices and articulates his preferences in very difficult circumstances.

Case Vignette: Stan

The day Pathways staff met Stan, aged fifty-five, he was sitting in front of a coffee shop in his favorite downtown neighborhood occasionally waving or saying hello to passersby. He was charming and articulate, and the benefit of the Ivy League college he had attended at the time of his first psychotic break could still be seen. The staff introduced the idea of enrolling him in the HF program. Having lived in the streets for decades, he was tentative about accepting offers of any kind because he had been in and out of many programs before.

His shoes were too small for his swollen feet, which were infected and oozing puss in several places. When the staff expressed their concern for his condition, he agreed to be taken to the emergency room on the provision that the staff would accompany him though the admission process.

The emergency admissions nurse interviewed Stan about his complaints: "My feet," he told her, pointing to them. "I am in pain, considerable pain." She looked at his feet, wrote some notes, and continued, "Any other problems or conditions?" "Yes," he replied, "I also have schizophrenia, but that isn't bothering me so much right now."

When considering the LRT model from the consumer's perspective. it is evident that the treatment-first model was developed from the clinician's perspective rather than the homeless person's. In fact, the LRT model seems to be loosely based on several erroneous assumptions about consumers' disabilities that are still prevalent in many psychiatric inpatient units. These assumptions include the belief that consumers must work to earn privileges (in the LRT model, the privilege of housing) by demonstrating compliance with treatment and ward rules; that clinicians must set goals for consumers because they are incapable of making choices or settings goals for themselves; that consumers with severe mental illness need to live in residences with on-site staff because they require around-the-clock supervision; that consumers must first demonstrate they can live successfully in transitional congregate housing before they can manage independent housing; and that consumers with co-occurring addiction disorders must be clean and sober before they can be housed.

These assumptions persist even in light of a growing body of research indicating that consumers are capable of setting their own goals and, with support, live independently without first living in transitional settings. Indeed, the evidence suggests that not only are consumers able to make choices but they are also far more likely to remain in housing programs that allow them greater choice. Studies in psychiatric rehabilitation indicate that the most effective way to learn the skills necessary for living independently in the community is not in a group or transitional setting, but in the community where the skills will be used.

If the treatment-then-housing approach is riddled with erroneous clinical assumptions and contributes to creating chronic homelessness, why does it persist? Part of the answer concerns the enormous discrepancy between the supply and the demand of affordable supportive housing. For every available supportive housing slot, literally hundreds apply. Thus providers can easily meet their targets selecting only those applicants who have successfully met their treatment-based program requirements.

Unfortunately, not every consumer can or will meet these criteria. Those who do not can remain homeless for years, often cycling in and out shelters, emergency rooms, detox, and jail (Hopper et al. 1997). Such continued exposure to stressors of homelessness has profoundly adverse effects on a person's physical, psychological, social, economic, legal, and spiritual well-being. The ordinary day-to-day tasks of survival, such as getting a meal or sleep, become a challenging and exhausting ordeal. Being homeless exposes individuals to extremes of weather, vulnerability to violence and other life-threatening situations, drug and alcohol dependence, harassment and arrest, exposure to acute and chronic health problems, and premature mortality (Barrow et al. 1999).

The Housing First Model

The Housing First (HF) model, developed by Pathways to Housing in 1992, has created a paradigm shift in the field of housing and treatment options. Equally important, the program has expanded the range of what is considered possible for people who are homeless and suffer from mental illness and addiction disorders. The program provides immediate access to permanent affordable housing (one's own apartment) along with support and treatment services. The program effectively ends chronic homelessness by using a consumer-directed service approach and immediately provides consumers with what they want most: an apartment of their own, free of treatment and sobriety conditions. HF is based on a belief that housing is a basic human right rather than something the person with mental illness has to earn or prove that they deserve by being in treatment. It is also based on the belief that people who are homeless and who have psychiatric disabilities are capable of defining their own goals. A fundamental principle of the program is that consumers should have a choice in the housing and services they receive and that services should be geared toward supporting their recovery.

The Housing First model includes four essential elements: consumer choice, separation of housing and treatment, recovery orientation, and community integration.

Consumer Choice

Making choices about important aspects of one's life and learning from the consequences of those choices are fundamental to the process of recovery. Most traditional supportive-housing programs are highly structured and permit only a narrow range of consumer choices. In sharp contrast, HF programs are driven by consumer choice. The starting point is to ask consumers what they want; the program begins by honoring and fulfilling the request that most homeless people say they want, first, a place to live. Support staff are available for help, but consumers actively participate to select the neighborhood they wish to live in, choose their apartment, select furniture and household items, and live with someone if they wish.

Once housed, with safety and security no longer a daily struggle, consumers begin to focus on other areas of their lives, some long neglected and others representing new beginnings. The range and variety of goals that consumers set after they are housed are as diverse as the people themselves: family reconnection, employment, treatment of chronic health problems, shopping for food, or simply recovery from the extreme stress of street life. Consumer choice means encouraging and supporting consumers to select from among many priorities to begin building a life they wish to live. Consumers determine the type, intensity, and frequency of treatment and support services they receive.

Instead of requiring psychiatric treatment or sobriety as a condition of housing, the HF approach focuses on a harm-reduction approach when addressing mental health and substance abuse issues. When drug or alcohol use interferes with the consumer's functioning, staff will attempt to engage the consumer in an open and honest discussion about the pros and cons of using or drinking and try to help the consumer make the kinds of choices that will reduce harm to themselves and lead to a healthier life. The program incorporates a stages-of-change model and attempts to develop plans with consumers that are consistent with their stage of treatment readiness. Staff members also encourage participation in mental health treatment and support and celebrate reductions in drug and alcohol use. However, consumers are not required to accept any formal clinical services, such as taking psychiatric medication, seeing a psychiatrist, or working with a substance-use specialist.

All consumers are required to meet with the program staff at least once each week. A typical home visit consists of a conversation about such issues as how things are going, next steps to take, current unmet needs, as well as an informal assessment of the consumer's living environment and general well-being. It is essential to keep the channels of communication between the consumer and program staff open. Staff members offer assistance with any domain the consumer wishes to address, from fixing a leaky faucet to mending broken ties with family members.

Honoring consumer choice is especially important in times of difficulty or crisis, such as when consumers deplete their financial resources, are under threat of eviction, or have relapsed into addiction. Unless there is a danger to the consumer or to others, staff must support one another to resist desire to control or resolve a chaotic situation and make every effort to remain in communication with the consumer exploring options while allowing the consumer to make the decisions. For example, if a consumer is facing eviction by the landlord because she has invited too many of her homeless friends to stay in her apartment, staff should work with the consumer to determine the best course of action: What options do we have here? Try to negotiate with the landlord? Leave this apartment and start over in another apartment? They discuss the lease violations that led the landlord to file for eviction and how this may be prevented from happening again, and they explore what steps can be taken. By making their own decisions under difficult circumstances, consumers can learn to make better decisions in the future. Experiential learning, in which consumers are supported in making and observing the consequences of their decisions, is one of the cornerstones of recovery.

Separation of Housing and Services

The Pathways HF program uses a scattered-site, independent housing model and rents affordable, decent apartments from landlords in the community. This model is consistent with research that honors consumers' preferences for neighborhoods and apartments of their own choosing. Naturally, housing and neighborhood choices are restricted by affordability and suitability of available units. To ensure that people with psychiatric disabilities are integrated into the community, the program limits leases to no more than 20 percent of the units in any one building. Apartments are rented at fair market value and meet HUD's housing-quality standards. In sum, consumers are not moving into a housing program; they are moving into a safe and affordable apartment of their choice.

Consumers have the same rights and responsibilities as all other tenants holding a standard lease, and they are required to pay 30 percent of their income, typically Supplemental Security Income (SSI), in rent; the program pays the remainder. The program may offer to become a consumer's representative payee or offer other budgeting services to help ensure that bills are paid. In HF programs, housing loss occurs only for lease violations, not for treatment noncompliance or hospitalization. Some consumers lose their apartments after they relapse and stop paying bills. However, because the housing component is separate from the clinical component, eviction from an apartment does not mean being discharged from the program. Program staff continues to work with the consumer through a housing loss, preventing a return to homelessness and ensuring continuity of care through crises.

Because the inventory of apartments consists of rental units available on the open market, no lengthy project planning and construction are needed. HF programs can be operational within three months of funding being secured. The average annual cost for housing is approximately $10,000 per apartment per year for a studio or a one-bedroom unit in major U.S. cities.

HF consumers have access to treatment and comprehensive support services. These are usually provided through a multidisciplinary approach, such as Assertive Community Treatment (ACT) or an intensive case-management team. The teams are located off-site but are available on-call twenty-four hours a day, seven days a week, and provide most services in a consumer's natural environment, such as an apartment, workplace, or neighborhood. The service is time-unlimited in that it is offered as long as a consumer needs the given level of support.

A slightly modified version of the traditional ACT team, one that includes peers and a primary-care nurse as staff, has been incorporated into the Housing First model. Since its inception more thirty years ago, and the initial research demonstration study of ACT (Stein and Test 1980), this intervention has proven to be a robust model of community-based treatment for people with severe psychiatric disabilities. Numerous controlled studies document the effectiveness of ACT in the treatment of consumers with extensive histories of psychiatric hospitalizations, although some recent studies with strong comparison conditions (for example, Essock et al. 2006) have found that intensive case-management programs can be as effective as ACT. ACT is remarkable for the articulation of its structural and functional features and for having a widely used fidelity scale to assess a team's adherence to an ideal ACT model for staffing and services (Teague, Bond, and Drake 1998). ACT is also an efficient program model from which to provide other interventions, including supported employment, integrated dual-disorder treatment, and illness management and recovery (Salyers and Tsemberis 2007). Consistent with these research findings, the HF program uses intensive case management instead of ACT when on admission it is determined that the consumer does not require the intensity of ACT services or a consumer has received ACT services for a time and shows significant improvement.

Consumers' participation in treatment is aimed at addressing their mental health problems, and this effort is separate and distinct from their homelessness or housing issues. For example, a consumer who needs inpatient treatment goes into the hospital and, on discharge, returns home to the apartment. By separating the criteria for getting and keeping housing from a consumer's treatment status and yet maintaining a close ongoing relationship between these two components, HF programs help prevent recurrence of homelessness when consumers relapse into substance abuse or a psychiatric crisis. When necessary, team members can provide intensive treatment or facilitate admission to a detox center or a hospital to address the clinical crisis. The need for eviction is bypassed; after treatment, the person simply returns home.

Similarly, in the event of an eviction for a lease violation, support services can facilitate a move into another apartment and provide continuity of care with the same team members.

As consumers continue to recover, they may need fewer services. This can be accomplished by using an ACT step-down team or an enhanced case-management team. Such a flexible adjustment process provides a better match between consumer and service needs, increases program capacity, and reduces cost. When the person is fully recovered, housing and services remain separate. The consumer continues to live in and pay for the apartment but no longer needs program services. The services may be simply discontinued, avoiding the need for a potentially disruptive transition.

Recovery Orientation

HF embodies a recovery orientation that is now the cornerstone of mental health service reform (New Freedom Commission 2003). This philosophy and practice places consumer choice and shared decisionmaking at the foundation of the program model. Service plans are not based on clinician assessments of consumers' needs but driven by consumers' own treatment goals. This approach helps ensure that consumers remain engaged with the team, particularly during crisis. The harm-reduction approach creates the conditions under which consumers are free to have an honest exchange about symptoms or substance use because treatment compliance is not linked to housing retention.

One of the main goals of recovery-oriented services is to help staff and the consumer develop a recovery-oriented working relationship. Staff must constantly be offering choices, encouraging self-directed care, and conveying a message of belief that recovery is possible and inevitable. In practice, they must be cognizant that though *doing things for* the consumer may be acceptable during the engagement or the initial phase of the program, they want to be moving toward *doing things with* consumers and finally to teaching and supporting consumers *to do things for themselves.*

Community Integration

Housing First promotes community integration by using the scattered-site apartment model, under which consumers live in normal apartments rented from community landlords. This arrangement enables people with psychiatric disabilities to be immediately integrated into the community and eliminates the potential for community resistance. Community norms and social pressures in their environments sustain normative behaviors among consumers. Program staff encourage and facilitate social connection by encouraging consumers to reconnect with families, meet their neighbors, and make friends by participating in groups, classes, or social events sponsored by the program or their community. This scattered-site housing design renders consumers virtually indistinguishable from other neighborhood residents with similar socioeconomic and ethnic-racial characteristics. The model is also consistent with the Olmstead Supreme Court decision that integration is fundamental to provisions of the Americans with Disabilities Act and that states may be required to provide community-based rather than institutional care to people with disabilities (Allen 2003).

Research Evidence for Housing First: Residential Stability and Improved Mental Health

Research studies have provided compelling evidence that HF is effective for achieving residential stability for people who have remained homeless for years. Initial evaluations of HF in urban areas with primarily street-dwelling samples yielded convincing results. Using archival data over a five-year period, 88 percent of HF consumers remained housed as compared to 47 percent of consumers in traditional LRT programs (Tsemberis and Eisenberg 2000). In a randomized clinical trial of housing alternatives, individuals assigned to HF spent approximately 80 percent of their time stably housed compared with only 30 percent for participants assigned to traditional LRT or treatment-first services after two years (Tsemberis, Gulcur, and Nakae 2004).

In 2004, the U.S. Interagency Council on Homelessness launched its national Collaborative Initiative to Help End Chronic Homelessness, which was funded by HUD, the Department of Health and Human Services (HHS), the Substance Abuse and Mental Health Services Administration (SAMHSA), and the Department of Veterans Affairs (VA). Seven of the eleven cities funded used the Pathways HF model and achieved 85 percent housing retention rates after twelve months (Mares and Rosenheck 2007). Two years later, HUD sponsored a study of three programs using the HF approach, which reported an 84 percent housing retention rate (Pearson, Montgomery, and Locke 2009). A study of consumers who were long-term shelter dwellers in a suburban county found similar outcomes; approximately 78 percent of HF participants remained stably housed over a four-year period (Stefancic and Tsemberis 2007). This provides evidence for the model's utility for street dwelling, as well as shelter-using segments of the homeless population, and its effectiveness in both urban and suburban environments.

Although the hallmark of HF's effectiveness has been its success in providing residential stability for people whom other agencies would not house, both quantitative and qualitative research has also documented that HF delivers advantages that go beyond residential stability. For instance, greater choice in housing and services and living in scattered-site as opposed to single-site housing programs, both essential components of the HF model, are significant predictors of consumers' psychological well-being and social integration, respectively (Greenwood et al. 2005; Gulcur et al. 2007). Consumers report significantly higher housing satisfaction when living in more independent, scattered-site supported-housing settings as compared to congregate supportive housing or community residences (Siegel et al. 2006). Consumers living in their own scattered-site apartments describe the importance of having a home in terms of privacy, normalized daily activities, and a secure base for self-discovery, all of which foster a greater sense of belonging in the world (Padgett 2007). Although some consumers reported feeling lonely in their apartments, they preferred independent living to congregate housing options (Yanos, Barrow, and Tsemberis 2004). Additionally, although consumers in traditional programs receive more extensive substance-use treatment, HF consumers appear to have no greater rates of alcohol or substance use (Padgett, Gulcur, and Tsemberis 2006).

The Cost of Homelessness

Funding is needed to support rental costs in HF programs, but these costs are offset to some degree through reduction and eventually elimination of outreach, drop-in, shelter, and transitional housing programs because these programs are unnecessary when using the HF model. Moreover, the group targeted by HF, homeless adults with a serious psychiatric disability illness, also has very high use rates of emergency rooms and inpatient services. Placement directly into HF programs can reduce institutional-services use, and the related cost reductions can be diverted to provide the support-services component of HF programs.

Thus, achieving residential stability for a subset of the homeless population considered hard to house may ultimately be cost-effective. Dennis P. Culhane notes that homeless advocates have long argued that providing HF or other permanent supportive housing is significantly less costly than having a person remain homeless (2008). In a HUD-funded review of cost studies dating back to 1998, Culhane and his colleagues find that the national average cost for shelter beds is $13,000 per year and the price goes up from there depending on the region and the services available (2008). In New York City, service-enriched shelter beds can range from $23,000 to $33,000 per year and institutional settings, such as hospitals or jails, can quickly bring those costs to more than $100,000 per year. Put simply, choosing to leave people on the streets has a price. One study found that the combined average annual cost associated with services such as drop-in centers, shelters, emergency services, police interventions, and incarcerations for individuals who are chronically homeless with severe mental illness is $40,500. When this same group is provided HF, the combined rent-and-service costs range from $17,000 to $24,000, depending on the services used (Culhane et al. 2008).

Malcolm Gladwell put a face on this counterintuitive discussion of cost, homelessness, mental illness, and service utilization. His memorable *New Yorker* profile "Million-Dollar Murray" (2006) is about a man he met in Reno.

Million-Dollar Murray

Murray was a middle-aged, homeless man who lived for ten years in Reno, Nevada. He was well-known downtown, a veteran who suffered from schizophrenia. Everyone, it seemed, knew Murray. The police, the local merchants, homeless outreach teams, the emergency room staff, the detox center staff, and ambulance drivers, all knew him well.

Why does Gladwell give Murray this million-dollar handle? Because Gladwell, with the assistance of a local police officer, tallied all the services Murray had received from the city of Reno over the course of the previous ten years. These included EMS transports, police interventions, jail days, detox days, hospital days. In those ten years, the City of Reno had spent more than $1 million on Murray, yet Murray remained homeless until the day he passed away.

The service providers in Murray's life repeatedly offered the same services, presumably expecting a different result. Trying to entice some homeless people into treatment over and over again as an incentive for housing has proven incredibly costly. More important, it simply has not worked and will not work for the chronically homeless.

Several studies examine patterns of service use and cost-effectiveness of HF programs for homeless persons with severe mental illness or other high service needs. The first study was conducted in San Diego and focused on 177 participants in a HF program who were compared to 161 clients receiving standard treatment (Gilmer, Manning, and Ettner 2009). The control group was matched using propensity scoring. Demographic and clinical characteristics were similar across the two groups. Mental health service use and costs, including case management, outpatient services, inpatient and emergency services, criminal justice services, and total services, were tracked for treatment and control groups over a two-year period. Cost of housing and services provided over this period was essentially offset by the savings from a reduction in inpatient care, emergency services, and mental health services that had been provided by the criminal justice system.

The second study was conducted in Seattle and compared use and cost of services for ninety-five chronically homeless individuals who received housing in a single-site HF program with use and costs for thirty-nine wait-list controls over a two-year period. This study also used propensity scoring to match its samples and tallied the cost of jail bookings, incarceration, shelters, sobering centers, hospital-based medical services, medical emergency services, and other Medicaid-funded services. Study participants had a primary diagnosis of severe alcoholism and were identified as high users of medical service systems. Mary E. Larimer and her colleagues (2009) reported that in the year before entering HF, HF participants had median costs of $4,066 per month. In the six months after enrollment, this was reduced to $1,492 per month and after twelve months to $958 per month. In addition to these significant cost savings, a reduction in alcohol use was found for individuals in the HF program relative to control-group members.

Third, Robert Rosenheck and his colleagues (2003) conducted an experimental study that randomly assigned homeless veterans with severe mental illness to one of three conditions: supported housing that included a

Section 8 voucher and intensive case management, case management only, and standard care provided by the VA. The study made use of administrative data to track VA health-services use and relied on self-reported interviews to record non-VA service use, such as shelters, jail, and non-VA health and mental health services. Those placed in supported housing recorded significantly more days in stable housing than either of the other two groups. Moreover, the study found that due to a cost offset resulting from a reduction in acute services use, the supported housing had an annual net cost of only about $2,000 per unit.

Fourth, in a longitudinal, randomized control trial study conducted in New York City, Leyla Gulcur and her colleagues (2003) examined hospital days and use and costs of other services by homeless persons with serious mental illness randomly assigned to either an HF program or to programs using the LRT Continuum of Care model. Results indicate that those in the HF group used fewer services and spent less time hospitalized than their counterparts in the control group. In addition, estimated costs based on study participants' self-reported service use suggest a significant cost difference, with those in the control group costing more overall.

Finally, a recently published study compared the costs of providing discharge planning that included case management services that started in the hospital and followed patients through discharge to supportive housing (N = 204) to a group that received "usual care" consisting of the hospital-based social worker providing discharge planning (N = 201). The study sample was a group of chronically homeless individuals with serious medical conditions. Laura Sadowski and her colleagues (2009) explored whether the costs of the intervention were offset by reduced service use. Although not focused exclusively on persons with severe mental illness, this randomized control trial conducted in Chicago found that the group receiving case management support outside the hospital to reach supportive housing ultimately cost less than the usual care group because of greater residential stability and reduced post-discharge service needs.

In addition to studies using rigorous research designs, more than forty municipalities throughout the United States have conducted cost analysis studies since 2003 to generate strategic-planning information as part of their ten-year plans to end chronic homelessness. Culhane and his colleagues summarize a number of these studies and their results (2008). Conducted by a variety of consultants, academics, advocates, and planners, these studies do not involve random assignment and seldom include comparison or control groups. Moreover, the study populations are selected through convenience sampling and frequently are chosen based on their presumed heavy use of services. These studies thus likely overestimate cost reductions and should be interpreted with caution. Still, the findings are striking in their consistency. The intervention studies all demonstrate reduced service use subsequent to housing placement, finding cost reductions ranging from $5,266 to $43,045 (Culhane et al. 2008). Many find that the reduced costs of services use fully offset the intervention cost.

Despite this consistency, Culhane (2008) points out that even when reduced services costs associated with the interventions partially or wholly offset their cost, cost savings do not necessarily transfer between public agencies. Savings accrued from the reduced services are not easily reinvested in housing solutions. Clearly, even when cost savings associated with housing interventions are apparent, complicated issues that must be addressed remain.

Rosenheck (2000) and others argue that the cost-effectiveness of particular interventions should not be the sole arbiter of a program's merit. Homelessness imposes many unmeasured costs, such as dehumanization, social isolation, and susceptibility to violence (Culhane 2008). Although establishing a monetary value is difficult, from a moral standpoint, these costs alone may justify the expense of more effective housing programs. Overall, estimates of benefits of housing programs should consider both monetary and humanitarian costs in adopting change in housing policy.

Indeed, it seems unlikely that the larger goal of ending homelessness can be accomplished without incurring cost somewhere. HF and other supportive housing interventions may end homelessness but do not cure psychiatric disability, addiction, or poverty. These programs, it might be said, help individuals graduate from the trauma of homelessness into the normal everyday misery of extreme poverty, stigma, and unemployment. Economic recovery should be part and parcel of the plan to end homelessness. It includes increases in minimum wage, health benefits, entitlements, and, most of all, the availability of decent affordable housing. These larger structural changes would not only help to end homelessness but are also the best way to prevent it.

Implementation Issues

Even if a consensus is reached that HF approaches are more effective than traditional LRT supportive housing, the transition needs to be handled with care. Agencies currently operating LRT supportive-housing programs that require treatment and sobriety before housing should develop a transition plan to help them move to an HF approach. Their plan will need three elements. First, it will define new roles for staff currently employed by outreach, shelter, or transitional programs (such as changing case-management job descriptions from shelter-based work to providing support as part of a home visit). Second, it will inform every stakeholder in the agency from consumers to boards of directors of the principles about HF and, especially, of its consumer-driven philosophy and harm-reduction practice. Third, it will require training for clinicians in recognizing consumers' stages of change, motivational interviewing techniques, harm-reduction approaches, and other recovery-focused interventions to help clinicians learn to allow clients to make their own decisions and lead the treatment process.

Clinicians also need to be trained in how to transition from working as solo practitioners to working in a team approach. This is extremely useful when applying a harm-reduction approach in which the team allows consumers to learn by reducing but not fully eliminating potentially harmful behaviors until ready to do so. Team members can support each other when confronted with difficult situations and continue to allow consumers to direct their own treatment even after an initial failure. When challenging situations are confronted this way, successful outcomes build consumers' confidence in managing their crises and reinforce the continued use of consumer-directed interventions by the team.

Conclusion

The weight of the evidence, then, clearly shows that HF is an effective program for helping consumers with multiple problems and little or no likelihood of access to traditional LRT housing. As HF becomes more widely available, assessment of residential stability, cost-effectiveness, levels of psychiatric symptoms, substance use, and community integration will continue to be important outcome measures. However, new HF programs should expand their repertoire of services so that they can improve outcomes in a number of other domains (including health, wellness self-management, employment, and social integration) and help consumers identify and realize individual capabilities that are important to them.

References

Allen, Michael. 2003. "Waking Rip van Winkle: Why Developments in the Last 20 Years Should Teach the Mental Health System Not to Use Housing as a Tool of Coercion." *Behavioral Sciences and the Law* 21(4): 503–21.

Barrow, Susan M., Daniel B. Herman, Pilar Cordova, and Elmer L. Struening. 1999. "Mortality Among Homeless Shelter Residents in New York City." *American Journal of Public Health* 89(4): 529–34.

Culhane, Dennis P. 2008. "The Costs of Homelessness: A Perspective from the United States." *European Journal of Homelessness* 2(1): 97–114.

Culhane, Dennis P., Kenneth S. Gross, Wayne D. Parker, Barbara Poppe, and Ezra Sykes. 2008. "Accountability, Cost-Effectiveness, and Program Performance: Progress Since 1998." Paper presented at the National Symposium on Homelessness Research. Phoenix. (June 11–14, 2008). Available at: http://works.bepress.com/dennis_culhane/22.

Essock, Susan M., Kim T. Mueser, Robert E. Drake, Nancy H. Covell, Gregory J. McHugo, Linda K. Frisman, Nina J. Kontos, Carlos T. Jackson, Flora Townsend, and Karin Swain. 2006. "Comparison of ACT and Standard Case Management for Delivering Integrated Treatment for Co-occurring Disorders." *Psychiatric Services* 57(2): 185–96.

Gilmer, Todd P., Willard G. Manning, and Susan L. Ettner. 2009. "A Cost Analysis of San Diego County's REACH Program for Homeless Persons." *Psychiatric Services* 60(4): 445–50.

Gladwell, Malcolm. 2006. "Million Dollar Murray." *The New Yorker,* February 13, p. 96.

Greenwood, Ronni M., Nicole J. Schaefer-McDaniel, Gary Winkel, and Sam Tsemberis. 2005. "Decreasing Psychiatric Symptoms by Increasing Choice in Services for Adults with Histories of Homelessness." *American Journal of Community Psychology* 36(3/4): 223–38.

Gulcur, Leyla, Ann Stefancic, Marybeth Shinn, Sam Tsemberis, and Sean N. Fischer. 2003. "Housing, Hospitalization, and Cost Outcomes for Homeless Individuals with Psychiatric Disabilities Participating in Continuum of Care and Housing First Programs." *Journal of Community and Applied Social Psychology* 13(2): 171–86.

Gulcur, Leyla, Sam Tsemberis, Ann Stefancic, and R. M. Greenwood. 2007. "Community Integration of Adults with Psychiatric Disabilities and Histories of Homelessness." *Community Mental Health Journal* 43(3): 211–29.

Hopper, Kim, John Jost, Terri Hay, Susan Welber, and Gary Haugland. 1997. "Homelessness, Severe Mental Illness, and the Institutional Circuit." *Psychiatric Services* 48(5): 659–65.

Larimer, Mary E., Daniel K. Malone, Michelle E. Garner, David C. Atkins, Bonnie Burlingham, Heather S. Lonczak, Kenneth Tanzer, Joshua Ginzler, Seema L. Clifasefi, William G. Hobson, and G. Alan Marlatt. 2009. "Health Care and Public Service Use and Costs Before and After Provision of Housing for Chronically Homeless Persons with Severe Alcohol Problems." *Journal of American Medical Association* 301(13): 1349–57.

Lipton, Frank R., Carole Siegel, Anthony Hannigan, Judy B. Samuels, and Sherryl Baker. 2000. "Tenure in Supportive Housing for Homeless Persons with Severe Mental Illness." *Psychiatric Services* 51(4): 479–86.

Mares, Alvin S., and Robert A. Rosenheck. 2007. "National Performance Outcomes Assessment: Preliminary Client Outcomes Report." Collaborative Initiative to Help End Chronic Homelessness. Washington: U.S. Department of Health and Human Services, Assistant Secretary for Planning and Evaluation. Available at: http://aspe.hhs.gov/hsp/homelessness/CICH07/outcomes07/index.htm (accessed April 30, 2010).

Monahan, John, Richard J. Bonnie, Paul S. Appelbaum, Pamela S. Hyde, Henry J. Steadman, and Marvin S. Swartz. 2001. "Mandated Community Treatment: Beyond Outpatient Commitment." *Psychiatric Services* 52(9): 1198–1205.

New Freedom Commission on Mental Health. 2003. *Achieving the Promise: Transforming Mental Health Care in America: Final Report.* DHHS Pub. No. SMA-03 3832. Rockville, Md.: U.S. Department of Health and Human Services.

O'Hara, Ann. 2007. "Housing for People with Mental Illness: Update of a Report to the President's New Freedom Commission." *Psychiatric Services* 58:907–13.

Padgett, Deborah K. 2007. "There's No Place Like (a) Home: Ontological Security Among Persons with Serious Mental Illness in the United States." *Social Science and Medicine* 64(9): 1925–36.

Padgett, Deborah K., Leyla Gulcur, and Sam Tsemberis. 2006. "Housing First Services for People Who Are Homeless with Co-occurring Serious Mental Illness and Substance Abuse." *Research on Social Work Practice* 16(1): 74–83.

Pathways to Housing. 2007. "Pathways' Housing First Program." SAMHSA's National Registry of Evidence-Based Programs and Practices. Washington: U.S. Department of Health and Human Services, Substance Abuse and Mental Health Services Administration. Available at: http://www.nrepp. samhsa.gov/programfulldetails.asp?PROGRAM_ID=195 (accessed November 1, 2007).

Pearson, Carol, Ann Elizabeth Montgomery, and Gretchen Locke. 2009. "Housing Stability Among Homeless Individuals with Serious Mental Illness Participating in Housing First Programs." *Journal of Community Psychology* 37(3): 407–17.

Rosenheck, Robert. 2000. "Cost-Effectiveness of Services for Mentally Ill Homeless People: The Application of Research to Policy and Practice." *American Journal of Psychiatry* 157(10): 1563–70.

Rosenheck, Robert, Wesley Kasprow, Linda Frisman, and Wen Liu-Mares. 2003. "Cost-Effectiveness of Supported Housing for Homeless Persons with Mental Illness." *Archives of General Psychiatry* 60(9): 940–51.

Sadowski, Laura S., Romina A. Kee, Tyler J. VanderWeele, and David Buchanan. 2009. "Effect of a Housing and Case Management Program on Emergency Department Visits and Hospitalizations Among Chronically Ill Homeless Adults." *Journal of American Medical Association* 301(17): 1771–78.

Salyers, Michelle P., and Sam Tsemberis. 2007. "ACT and Recovery: Integrating Evidence-Based Practice and Recovery Orientation on Assertive Community Treatment Teams." *Community Mental Health Journal* 43(6): 619–41.

Sermons, M. William, and Meghan Henry. 2009. "Homelessness Counts: Changes in Homelessness from 2005 to 2007." Washington, D.C.: National Alliance to End Homelessness. Available at: http://www.endhomelessness.org/content/article/detail/2158 (accessed January 12, 2010).

Siegel, Carole E., Judith Samuels, Dei-In Tang, Ilyssa Berg, Kristine Jones, and Kim Hopper. 2006. "Tenant Outcomes in Supported Housing and Community Residences in New York City." *Psychiatric Services* 57:982–91.

Stefancic, Ana, and Sam Tsemberis. 2007. "Housing First for Long-Term Shelter Dwellers with Psychiatric Disabilities in a Suburban County: A Four-Year Outcome Study of Housing Access and Retention." *Journal of Primary Prevention* 28: 265–79.

Stein, Leonard I., and Maryann Test. 1980. "An Alternative to Mental Health Treatment I: Conceptual Model, Treatment Program and Clinical Evaluation." *Archives of General Psychiatry* 37(4): 392–97.

Swarns, Rachel L. 2008. "U.S. Reports Drop in Homeless Population." *New York Times,* July 30, p. 1.

Teague, Gregory B., Gary R. Bond, and Robert E. Drake. 1988. "Program Fidelity in Assertive Community Treatment: Development and Use of a Measure." *American Journal of Orthopsychiatry* 68(2): 216–32.

Tsemberis, Sam, and Rhonda F. Eisenberg. 2000. "Pathways to Housing: Supported Housing for Street-Dwelling Homeless Individuals with Psychiatric Disabilities." *Psychiatric Services* 51(4): 487–93.

Tsemberis, Sam, Leyla Gulcur, and Marie Nakae. 2004. "Housing First, Consumer Choice, and Harm Reduction for Homeless Individuals with a Dual Diagnosis." *American Journal of Public Health* 94(4): 651–56.

Yanos, Philip T., Susan M. Barrow, and Sam Tsemberis. 2004. "Community Integration in the Early Phase of Housing Among Homeless Individuals Diagnosed with Severe Mental Illness: Success and Challenges." *Community Mental Health Journal* 40(2): 133–50.

PART II

USING HOUSING POLICY
TO PREVENT HOMELESSNESS

Chapter 4

Rental Subsidies: Reducing Homelessness

JILL KHADDURI

A growing literature on the relationship between housing markets and homelessness suggests that subsidies to make housing more affordable for poor individuals and families can play an important role in reducing homelessness in the United States. Several recent papers show that rates of homelessness are higher in high-cost housing markets. For example, John Quigley, Steven Raphael, and Eugene Smolensky (2001) demonstrate that homelessness is more extensive in areas with low vacancy rates and high rents, based on counts of people homeless in various U.S. cities and metropolitan areas and in California counties. They conclude that "homelessness may be combated by modest supply policies combined with housing assistance directed to those for whom housing costs consume a large share of their low incomes" (50). An earlier study by Marjorie Honig and Randall K. Filer (1993) found that rent levels at the 10th percentile of the rent distribution had a large impact on the relative level of homelessness across cities and concluded that "public policies to reduce the cost of providing minimally adequate housing could have a powerful impact in reducing homelessness" (250).

Dirk Early and Edgar Olsen (2002) demonstrate that higher housing prices are related to increased rates of homelessness among the poverty population across 224 of the metropolitan areas in which homeless people were counted in the 1990 census. They show that the rate of homelessness is lower in areas in which a larger proportion of subsidized rental housing is targeted to very poor households. Brendan O'Flaherty (2004) argues that, though these and other studies of the determinants of aggregate rates of homelessness may seem inconsistent with studies that predict homelessness based on the characteristics of particular individuals and families, in fact there is no inconsistency. He uses a theoretical model to demonstrate that the interaction of personal characteristics, such as mental illness and poverty, and housing market characteristics, such as inelastic housing supply, is what drives homelessness.

Most recently, an experimental design study of the effects of housing vouchers on welfare families found that this form of subsidy leads to dramatic reductions in both unstable housing situations and homelessness. Almost 45 percent of families who did not use vouchers reported that they did not have a place of their own to stay at some point during the year before they were interviewed. About one-third of the families in the control group (31.4 percent) had stayed with friends or relatives, and 12.5 percent spent time on the street or in a shelter. Families with vouchers experienced much lower levels of housing insecurity, and literal homelessness was reduced to 3.3 percent by the use of a housing subsidy (Wood, Turnham, and Mills 2008).

The results of the voucher study imply that for every one hundred additional housing vouchers put into use, nine fewer families would be homeless. Dirk Early (2004) estimates that between 3.8 and 5 percent of households in subsidized households would be homeless in the absence of a subsidy. Estimates based on the results of other studies are in the same ballpark.[1]

A Separate Residential System for Homeless People

For most homeless people, homelessness is a temporary state, not a way of life. Appropriate attention has focused on chronic homeless individuals—those who are homeless for long periods or who have repeated episodes of homelessness—because they are the most likely among the homeless to spend part of the time sleeping on the streets or in abandoned buildings (Metreaux et al. 2001; Burt et al. 2001). A consensus has emerged across the American political spectrum that unsheltered homelessness is inhumane and unacceptable. An equally powerful reason for focusing on individuals with chronic patterns of homelessness is that they drain the budgets of public systems, such as emergency rooms, inpatient medical facilities, police forces, jails, and emergency transport (Caton, Wilkins, and Anderson 2007).

However, the chronically homeless, whether for long periods or with repeated episodes, are a small minority of all those who become homeless in the United States. The best national estimate available, as of 2009, is that 19 percent of those who are homeless on a given night fit the profile of chronic homelessness (U.S. Department of Housing and Urban Development 2009a). The percentage of chronically homeless people among all those who are homeless at some time during a year is lower, because by definition a one-night snapshot will capture a larger proportion of those who remain homeless for long periods (Burt et al. 2001). Most people who become homeless will remain homeless for a few days or weeks but not become homeless again (Kuhn and Culhane 1998; Culhane et al. 2007a, 2007b; U.S. Department of Housing and Urban Development 2008, 2009a; Spellman et al. 2010).

Who Becomes Homeless?

Administrative data now make it possible to describe the demographic characteristics of sheltered homeless people. Local Homeless Management Information Systems (HMIS) collect data from individuals and families when they enter shelter and during their shelter stays.[2] Each year the U.S. Department of Housing and Urban Development (HUD) analyzes HMIS data provided by a nationally representative sample of communities and produces a report to Congress called the Annual Homeless Assessment Report (AHAR). The most recent data show that 48 percent of those who use a homeless shelter at some time during the course of a year are individual men; 18 percent are individual women; and 32 percent are members of families, as in, groups of people who are homeless together and that include at least one adult and one child (HUD 2009a, Appendix D).[3] Comparisons with the poverty population show that both African American individuals and families are at particularly high risk of becoming homeless (HUD 2008, 2009a).

With some exceptions, administrative data do not describe people who are homeless on the street. However, most people who live on the street come into shelters periodically (Maguire, Culhane, and Poulin 2005) and therefore are among the chronically homeless individuals described in data on sheltered homeless people. The extent to which families with children are found in places unfit for human habitation is debatable, but estimates are getting better as HUD insists on street counts that follow rigorous methodologies (HUD 2008, 2009a).

Distinguishing between individuals and families has proved useful for understanding vulnerability to homelessness and patterns of homelessness. However, many people who become homeless as individuals are parents who are without their minor children (Burt et al. 2001). HMIS data that tracked homeless families over at least eighteen months in four communities (Houston; the District of Columbia; Kalamazoo, Michigan; and upstate South Carolina) show that people who become homeless with their children have unstable family composition. If their period of homelessness has any gaps—that is, if they appear in the shelter system, disappear, and then return—they are very likely to come back into the residential system for homeless people with a different household configuration: fewer people, more people, or different people (Spellman et al. 2010).

Studies that use a variety of data sources to predict which types of households are most likely to become homeless confirm that, in addition to poverty, gender (men), age (middle age), and race (African American) are risk factors. For individuals, chronic patterns of homelessness are also associated with mental illness, substance abuse, unemployment, and a history of arrests (Caton, Wilkins, and Anderson 2007). For families, risk factors for becoming homeless include mental health problems, substance abuse, domestic violence, and having newborns or young children. Families that often become homeless are involved with the child-welfare system (Rog and Buckner 2007). Nonetheless, only a small percentage of individuals or families with any particular profile become homeless, even among those who would seem to have notably high risks.

Both families and individuals are very likely to have been in someone else's housing unit (a friend's or a relative's) immediately before becoming homeless. Of individuals not already homeless at the time that they entered an emergency shelter or a transitional housing program, the 2008 Annual Homeless Assessment Report shows that 43 percent had been staying with family or friends and that 18 percent had been in their own housing unit. Among families, 57 percent had been staying with family or friends and 26 percent had been in their own housing unit (HUD 2009a).

Where Do People Become Homeless?

More than three-quarters of sheltered homeless people are in principal cities of metropolitan regions. Because virtually all homeless people are poor, it is instructive to compare this rate with the percentage of poor people living in principal cities: only 36 percent, in contrast to the 68 percent of homeless people. In many states, a very large proportion of all homeless people are in the state's largest city. For example, according to local one-night counts, 44 percent of California's homeless population is in the city and county of Los Angeles, 41 percent of all homeless people in Illinois are in Chicago, and 82 percent of all homeless people in New York are in New York City (HUD 2009a). Furthermore, census tracts with sheltered homeless populations of one hundred or more are most likely to be in the largest cities (Lee and Farrell 2004). Something we know for certain about homelessness is that it is an urban phenomenon.

Dennis Culhane, Chang-Moo Lee, and Susan Wachter (1996) show that in two large cities with high rates of homelessness, New York and Philadelphia, families entering the public system of shelters had previous addresses more highly concentrated in only a few census tracts than the city's general poverty population had. These tracts had concentrations of poor, African American, and female-headed households with young children. These findings suggest that highly concentrated urban poverty, a phenomenon found mainly in the largest U.S. cities (Jargowsky 2003), is a separate risk factor beyond the individual characteristics that make people vulnerable to homelessness. The lower cost and greater availability of housing (higher vacancy rates) in these distressed neighborhoods do not

protect families against homelessness. Culhane and his coauthors conclude that "policies designed to counteract racial segregation, concentrated poverty, and poor housing and neighborhood conditions, as well as more narrowly defined homelessness-prevention programs, could target the neighborhoods found to be at greatest risk for generating shelter admissions" (355–56).

Residential Homeless-Services System

A system of residential programs for homeless people has evolved over the past thirty years and includes three broad types of programs targeted explicitly to homeless people: emergency shelters, transitional housing programs, and permanent supportive housing (sometimes called supported housing). Nationally, as of 2008, more than 600,000 beds were available within the residential homeless system, somewhat more than 200,000 each within emergency shelters and transitional housing and somewhat fewer than 200,000 within permanent supportive housing (HUD 2009a). People are still considered homeless during their stays in emergency shelters and transitional housing. Rules on permitted lengths of stay for these types of programs vary from community to community and from program to program, but residents do not have long-term tenure rights or expectations, as they do in permanent housing.

Permanent supportive housing (PSH) is part of the homeless services system, not because it is temporary, but because it is available only to people leaving homelessness. To be eligible for the PSH funded by HUD under the McKinney-Vento Shelter Plus Care program, individuals or family heads must also have a disability. Providers of HUD-funded PSH must demonstrate that the rent subsidy is matched by case management and other services of equal or greater value (Fosburg et al. 1997). The services are often provided by mainstream systems such as the state or city mental-health department.

Housing programs linked to services for people with disabilities also are funded through the HUD Section 811 program for people with disabilities, the Low Income Housing Tax Credit, and state and local funding sources. Whether this housing is part of the homeless services system or mainstream subsidized housing is ambiguous, but Martha Burt (2005) found that about a third of all supported housing units are occupied by people who formerly had chronic patterns of homelessness.

Most homeless people use both emergency shelters and transitional housing for short periods. A recent study based on unduplicated records of people in emergency shelters and transitional housing programs during a one-year period showed that 43 percent of individual men who used emergency shelters had stays of a week or less, as did 41 percent of individual women and 23 percent of members of families with children (HUD

2008). A study that tracked homeless people in six communities found that, over the eighteen months following their entry into the homeless residential system, the median number of nights that people spent in homeless programs (including emergency shelters, transitional housing, and, sometimes, permanent supportive housing) ranged from eleven to twenty-four nights across the three communities where individual homeless people were studied and from thirty-one to 129 nights over the four communities where families were studied. In each of the communities studied, a substantial proportion of the study population had single short stays in emergency shelters (Spellman et al. 2010).

Lengths of stay in permanent supportive housing typically are longer, although many individuals and families leave PSH after a few months or a few years rather than making it their long-term home (Morris Davis and Company, 2006). However, the study that tracked homeless people over an eighteen-month period found that few of these first-time homeless individuals and families used PSH; most Shelter Plus Care and other PSH units were already occupied by people who had been homeless before the start of the study period. Although the study did not collect direct information on disabilities, rates of involvement with mental health systems were high (Spellman et al. 2010). Thus, although HUD has encouraged communities to add units of PSH as part of its focus on ending chronic homelessness (Caton, Wilkins, and Anderson 2007; HUD 2008), the supply of PSH remains insufficient.

Mainstream Rental-Housing Assistance to Prevent Homelessness

The federal government provides about 5 million households with rental housing subsidies that require a rent payment that is roughly 30 percent of the actual income of the assisted household. Because of this benefit formula, the subsidies can be used by people with incomes far below the poverty standard—that is, those most vulnerable to becoming homeless. The programs that provide these subsidies—the housing choice voucher (HCV) program, public housing, and the property-based Section 8 program—are collectively known as assisted housing.

A few other programs help provide subsidies for building affordable housing. However, these programs have shallower subsidies that do not reach poor people. The rent of an affordable housing unit is flat—that is, not tied to actual income—so an individual or a family with little income cannot afford to pay it (McClure 2010). The federal Low Income Housing Tax Credit (LIHTC) is the largest affordable-housing program. Given its focus on people with relatively higher incomes among those with modest incomes, the LIHTC probably does little to prevent homelessness. However, the program can be used together with other funding to provide supported housing for people who otherwise would experience chronic patterns of homelessness, as will be discussed later.

Housing vouchers account for about 2 million of the 5 million housing assistance slots. In general, vouchers are superior to public housing and Section 8 projects because of the greater choice that they provide to their users and because they avoid the inefficiencies inherent in property-based programs (Khadduri and Wilkins 2008). Furthermore, because vouchers are not attached to buildings with particular unit sizes or other features, they can be easily used for special purposes and population groups, even if those were not the original intended uses.

While the housing choice voucher program is the most important housing-subsidy program for preventing homelessness, public housing and Section 8 developments account for a major portion of all units of assisted housing. Simply replacing these types of assisted housing with vouchers would do nothing to lower the numbers of people who become homeless in the United States. What is needed is a larger total number of assisted housing units beyond the current 5 million units or subsidy slots.[4]

Expanding the Housing Voucher Program

An obvious proposal for preventing homelessness is to make housing assistance an open enrollment program or entitlement, like the Supplemental Nutrition Assistance Program (formerly food stamps) and like programs in other countries that provide, as part of their social safety nets, housing allowances to all households that meet certain eligibility criteria. Discussion of an open enrollment program has focused on vouchers, because the voucher program relies on already built private-market housing and can be expanded more easily than property-based assisted housing programs. Proposals to move toward an open enrollment program have been put forward since the beginning of the tenant-based housing assistance program in the 1970s (Khadduri and Struyk 1982). The problem has always been cost.

An open enrollment program would add several million households to the 5 million currently using vouchers, public housing, and privately owned assisted housing. The size of an open enrollment program would depend on the generosity of the subsidy, as a lower subsidy produces a benefit larger than zero for fewer households, as well as on the fraction of those qualifying for a subsidy who would apply for and accept it. The rate of participation in an open-enrollment voucher program is hard to estimate, because the only experience with such a program is thirty years old and based on a program that differs somewhat from the current housing choice voucher program and was implemented in two midwestern cities.[5]

Both program size and the cost of serving each household could be reduced by lowering the voucher program's benefit standard. Edgar Olsen has recommended such an approach (Olsen 2008; Olsen, this volume). But a voucher program with a sharply reduced benefit level has not been tested and probably is not politically feasible, given the multiple purposes and constituencies that the program has come to serve.[6]

For preventing homelessness, housing assistance does not need to become an open enrollment program. A larger program with shorter waiting lists would alleviate housing crises for many high-risk households and would also make the public housing agencies (PHAs) that administer the housing choice voucher program more willing to focus resources on groups with particularly high risks of becoming homeless.

The voucher program grew between the late 1990s and 2009 only because vouchers were used to replace public housing and Section 8 projects that had been downsized or had left the assisted housing stock. Expansion of the program through a return to the 1970s to 1990s pattern of appropriating funds to support incremental vouchers would be easy. At one point, such slots were added to the program at the rate of 100,000 units a year.

The system for administering vouchers could absorb this or an even higher rate of growth. The voucher program is currently administered by some 2,400 separate PHAs, many of which have small programs and staffs. However, in the event of an expansion of the program, the current capacity of larger programs—which are typical of major metropolitan areas—could be used. It would be a long overdue occasion to favor administration of vouchers on a regional or even a statewide basis. Because the administration of the voucher program is currently on the local rather than the state level, it can be difficult to coordinate vouchers with state programs that serve vulnerable clients, such as those administered by state mental health agencies (Khadduri 2003).

Just as it is not necessary to assume that a larger housing-assistance program must have open enrollment, so also is there no need to assume that the budget for housing assistance is fixed. The willingness of taxpayers and their elected federal officials to spend more on housing subsidies has been demonstrated by the recent increase in per capita funding for the Low Income Housing Tax Credit and by on-budget appropriations for housing and related activities in the wake of both natural disasters (Hurricanes Katrina and Rita) and the foreclosure crisis (the Neighborhood Stabilization Program that subsidizes the purchase of foreclosed properties). An effective articulation of the link between homelessness and assisted housing could persuade Congress to return to providing funding for substantial increments of housing vouchers each year.

Structuring Subsidies to Reach People at Greatest Risk of Homelessness

The clear answer for how to reduce homelessness is to create a system of assisted housing that reaches a larger number of households. However, the number of households that can be served by the assisted housing program is not the only dimension of a system best suited to prevent homelessness. In addition:

- Subsidies should be structured to reach the families and individuals most likely to become homeless.

- Subsidies should be large enough to prevent homelessness *and* to reduce the spatial concentrations of poverty that appear to breed homelessness.

- Subsidies should be allocated to locations with the highest rates of homelessness.

Focusing Housing Assistance on the Poorest Households.   Targeting assisted housing to the poorest households could be increased as part of a policy that emphasizes the program's objective of reducing homelessness. HUD estimates of rental housing needs (sometimes called the worst-case-needs estimates) demonstrate that most households with severe rent burdens have extremely low incomes, or incomes below 30 percent of the area median (HUD 2007). Individuals and families that become homeless have even lower incomes, typically at half the poverty level or below (Burt et al. 2001).

Currently federal law requires that at least 75 percent of vouchers be used by households that have extremely low incomes at the time of their first use. The cutoff, 30 percent of area median income and adjusted for household size, varies by geography but approximates the poverty level. Most PHAs, especially those with large voucher programs and central city or statewide jurisdictions, exceed this requirement (Dawkins 2007), often because they put families and individuals in that income group ahead of others on the waiting list, given that this is an administratively simple way of ensuring that they meet the statutory requirement.

Public housing and Section 8 projects have lighter income targeting. Only 40 percent of households entering those programs must have incomes below 30 percent of area median income (AMI). However, like the voucher program, the project-based programs mainly serve the poverty population, probably because of two factors: the location of a large percentage of public housing and Section 8 projects in low-income neighborhoods and the income-based rent formula, which makes this housing particularly attractive to the poorest households who pay the lowest rents.

Targeting of housing assistance exclusively to poor families and individuals, in the interest of preventing homelessness, might be opposed by those who want to help families make a transition to full-time work and increase their wages. Many currently assisted households work, but often less than full time, at low wages, and with intermittent job histories. A demonstration program enacted in 1996 permits some PHAs to alter the rules for the size and shape of the housing subsidy—for example, to charge flat rents rather than rents based on income or to phase out subsidies in order to encourage income growth.[7] As of 2009, such Moving to Work (MTW) PHAs administer approximately 10 percent of the housing choice voucher program units and manage roughly 10 percent of all public housing units.[8] However, few of the PHAs with MTW authority have made substantial changes to the assisted housing subsidy formula based on actual household income. Most PHA staff are reluctant to do so because they view their core mission as serving poor households at affordable rents.[9]

A housing subsidy program with the explicit goal of encouraging increased work should be separate from the voucher and other assisted housing programs, with a separate source of revenue. In effect, such a program already exists: the Low Income Housing Tax Credit, which charges flat rents and requires them to be affordable for households with incomes at 60 percent of the area median. An assisted housing program with a central goal of ending homelessness should continue to be based on the housing gap formula (benefit standard minus a percentage of actual income) that enables the program to help the poorest families.

Serving More Single-Person, Nonelderly Households

Dirk Early (1998, 2004) points out that vouchers are used mainly by families and elderly people, and not much by nonelderly, single men, who comprise a large percentage of people who become homeless. He finds that housing assistance could better reach those at risk of becoming homeless if PHAs more often targeted assistance to poor single persons who had not reached their sixty-second birthday.

Ingrid Ellen and Brendan O'Flaherty (2007) make the opposite point. Vouchers—like some other social safety net programs—provide a greater benefit per capita to smaller households because these programs take economies of scale in household budgets into account when determining the maximum benefit. Thus housing assistance creates an incentive for fewer adults to live in a household. Experimental design research confirms that the use of vouchers results in fewer adults in families with children. The program does not discourage marriage or cohabitation but does result in fewer households consisting of a parent and his or her children living together with grandparents or other relatives (Mills et al. 2007). However,

Table 4.1   Household Sizes Below Poverty Threshold

Household	Homeless People	Poor People
One person	70.3%	37.4%
Two people	8.0	4.8
Three people	8.2	13.1
Four people	6.5	16.7
Five or more people	6.9	28.0

Source: Author's calculations based on data collected for the 2007 Annual Homeless Assessment Report (HUD 2008).

this program incentive for smaller households has not resulted in widespread use of the program by single adults without children present.

Homeless people are overwhelmingly people from smaller households. Table 4.1, based on data collected for the 2007 Annual Homeless Assessment Report (HUD 2008), shows the household size distribution of the sheltered homeless population compared to the U.S. poverty population. Almost none of the single homeless adults are sixty-two years of age or older. The implication is that for preventing homelessness, the voucher program should be more rather than less focused on single, nonelderly individuals.

Single, nonelderly people have been fully eligible for housing assistance since about 1980, and studies of the rate of success that households issued vouchers have in using them find that success rates generally do not vary by household size (Finkel and Buron 2001).[10] The de facto targeting of the voucher program to families and elderly people by housing authorities is largely a function of the information flows through which people find their way to housing assistance programs, such as referrals from welfare and social service agencies. Families and elderly people are much more likely than younger individuals with incomes below poverty to be connected with these agencies and, therefore, to be encouraged to get on the PHA voucher waiting list. Single, nonelderly individuals also are less likely to be in social networks that include people already using vouchers who can advise them on the processes for applying and using housing assistance.

The voucher program does not need to be redesigned to better reach the poor single men at particularly high risk of becoming homeless. Instead, part of a policy that makes preventing homelessness a major goal of the voucher program should be an outreach campaign to single-person households, perhaps those in their middle or late middle age (forty to sixty-one years), because people in that age group are particularly vulnerable to chronic patterns of homelessness. The campaign could, for example, use soup kitchens and other programs that serve poor individuals to overcome their hesitations in applying to the voucher program. The information campaign should include PHAs, their staffs, and their boards of directors, so that single individuals are not discouraged by PHAs when they come through the door of the housing assistance program.

The justification for the information campaign need not be limited to preventing homelessness. HUD's worst-case-needs estimates have consistently found that single, nonelderly people make up a large proportion of all unassisted, very low income renters with severe rent burdens. For example, as of 2005, 34 percent of households with worst-case needs, some 2.1 million, were single, nonelderly people. Based on receipt of Supplemental Security Income (SSI), at least 540,000 of those individuals had a disability (HUD 2007).

The sizes and types of households served by public housing and Section 8 projects are also relevant to preventing homelessness. These programs have almost 3 million units combined as of 2009, which is more units than the voucher program has. Furthermore, the developments that have left the public housing program since the mid-1990s mainly housed families and offered multiple bedrooms. A large and increasing fraction of the public housing program consists of one- or zero-bedroom units suitable for occupancy by individuals or elderly couples.

Since the early 1990s, some PHAs that own and manage developments with small units have taken advantage of statutory provisions that permit them to be designated as elderly-only properties. HUD estimates that since 1994, 70,000 public housing units may be occupied only by elders as a result of such designations.[11] However, there remain many public housing units that are suitable for occupancy by nonelderly individuals and potentially available for formerly homeless people with special needs.

Many Section 8 projects have been replaced by vouchers as owners have taken their developments out of the assisted housing stock. Sometimes these developments have been preserved as assisted housing, with their Section 8 subsidies, or affordable housing, without their Section 8 subsidies, by transferring ownership and redeveloping the property using the LIHTC or other sources of development funds under state and local control (Finkel et al. 2006). Section 8 owners have been more likely than PHAs to take advantage of authority to reserve properties for exclusive use by the elderly. As many as 400,000 of the 500,000 studio and one-bedroom units in these privately owned housing developments have been reserved for the elderly. Some of these Section 8 units are no longer part of the assisted housing inventory in any case, because their owners have exercised their option to leave the program.[12]

Preventing Homelessness and Reducing Concentrations of Poverty

Voucher subsidies are scaled to the local cost of housing. Payment standards are set at the discretion of the local administrator, but may deviate only to a limited extent from annually adjusted estimates of local housing costs published by the HUD Fair Market Rents (FMRs). FMRs are set at about the midpoint of local rents.[13] The basic concept is that households assisted by vouchers should have access to about the same fraction of the housing market in each part of the country.[14]

Analysis by Edgar Olsen and Amy Crews Cutts (2002) has demonstrated that the FMRs used for the program are higher than the minimum needed for units that pass the program's housing quality standard. However, the purpose of the voucher program is not just to induce households to occupy housing of standard physical quality. As the physical quality of the U.S. housing stock has risen, the purposes of the voucher program have expanded to include reducing severe rent burdens and increasing opportunities for low-income and minority households to live in economically and racially integrated neighborhoods (President's Commission on Housing 1982; Millennial Housing Commission 2002; Turnham and Khadduri 2001; Mills et al., 2007; Khadduri 2001; Newman 2008). Both purposes are highly relevant to the use of housing assistance to prevent homelessness. Housing costs so high that they replace other needed consumption are not sustainable over time and contribute to housing instability patterns that can end in homelessness. Concentrations of poverty in particular neighborhoods in large U.S. cities may even constitute an independent risk factor for homelessness and help explain why homelessness is both a big-city phenomenon and most prevalent among African American individuals and families.

Notably, a growing number of voucher holders use the program to move to new units. The most recent study of the process of program participation found that only 21 percent of voucher holders leased in place (Finkel and Buron 2001). The program is used mainly by households seeking new units, including a substantial number using the program to leave doubled-up housing conditions and form independent households. The utility of the program for households leaving crowded conditions is particularly relevant to preventing homelessness, and the program should continue to have FMRs set at levels that permit most of the program's participants to live somewhere other than where they live now and to move to neighborhoods with low rates of poverty.

An experimental design evaluation of vouchers used by welfare families showed that, even without special efforts to encourage mobility, voucher users on average move to neighborhoods with somewhat lower poverty rates (Mills et. al. 2007). Further analysis of the data from that study shows that families starting in neighborhoods with the highest poverty rates are particularly likely to use their vouchers to move to locations with lower rates (Gubits, Khadduri, and Turnham 2009).

The voucher program's benefit level has from time to time been adjusted downward, by altering the percentile of rents of recently occupied units of standard quality at which the FMRs are set, from the 50th to the 45th and then the 40th percentile. In addition, FMRs are "re-benchmarked" as new census data on rents become available.[15] These downward adjustments have occurred without damaging the program's outcomes, as measured by success rates or by the range of neighborhoods in which voucher users live (Leger and Kennedy 1990; Finkel and Buron 2001; Newman and Schnare 1997; Devine et al. 2003).

We do not know how much lower FMRs could be without eviscerating the program's purposes: the Cutts and Olsen estimates of rents (2002) at which program users could find standard units are intended to be illustrative rather than determinative. Any proposal to reduce the level of FMRs should be based on two analyses: the effect of the proposed subsidy level on the nonhousing consumption budgets of assisted households, and the spatial and socioeconomic distribution of neighborhoods in which voucher users would be able to rent.

Allocating Subsidies

If one of the main purposes of the voucher program is to prevent homelessness, then additional allocations of vouchers should go to places where the risk of homelessness is particularly high. The allocation formula that distributes incremental voucher "slots" should favor cities and metropolitan areas where vacancy rates are low, housing costs have grown relative to incomes, and severe rent burdens are common among low-income renters. HUD's worst-case-needs estimates are based mainly on severe rent burden and should be the starting point for a formula.[16] To be most relevant to reducing homeless, the allocation formula should include a measure of overcrowded housing as well, since doubling up is a common path to homelessness.

The other parts of the system of assisted housing—public housing and Section 8 projects—already are heavily concentrated in some of the places that also have high rates of homelessness: large cities in large metropolitan areas. Allocation of incremental vouchers based on rent burden and crowding would help offset the relatively lower amounts of project-based housing in the West and, especially, in urban California.

In addition to focusing the allocation of new vouchers on places where the risk of homelessness is high, policies related to the transformation of public housing and Section 8 should be handled in a way that does not reduce the overall amount of housing assistance in the largest U.S. metropolitan areas and cities. At times HUD has reallocated voucher funding that a particular PHA has failed to use to a different geographic area, including the vouchers that are intended to replace public housing and Section 8 projects. Reallocation policies should keep the funding in the same jurisdiction and find an alternative administrator when a PHA's administrative practices result in underuse of voucher funds.

Noting that race is an important predictor of homelessness, Dirk Early (2004) observes that "it is doubtful such a factor could legally or ethically be used to select recipients." However, objective factors such as rates of housing distress by geographical area can be used to a similar effect.

At the same time, the use of voucher allocations should not be locked into central cities with high concentrations of poverty. The program's incentives for the use of vouchers across jurisdictional lines in areas with low poverty rates and racial diversity should be increased, through bonus administrative funding for PHAs that make progress toward achieving this goal, metropolitan-wide program administration, or administration of the voucher program by states (Katz and Turner 2008; Khadduri 2003). State administration of new voucher funding or reallocated voucher funding would have another beneficial result, in that states would be more able than most cities to allocate vouchers for use with mental health and substance abuse funding in areas with high rates of homelessness.

Forestalling Episodes of Homelessness

A larger voucher program that is well targeted geographically, by income, and by household type and that continues to use a housing-gap benefit formula will go far toward preventing homelessness. Reducing overall levels of homelessness through a larger assisted housing system will reduce flows into the emergency shelter and transitional housing programs and permit those systems to shrink. At the same time, it has been amply demonstrated that homeless people can use vouchers successfully to leave homelessness, shortening time spent homeless and leading to sustained, stable housing.

A larger voucher program will encourage PHAs to create linkages to the homeless services system, helping to shorten stays in emergency shelters and transitional housing and to provide the long-term housing assistance that many homeless individuals and families need. The voucher program formerly had a federal preference system that gave homelessness equal weight with severe rent burden and substandard housing. PHA administrators sometimes gave people on the street, in shelters, or about to become homeless an absolute priority.

The federal preference was repealed in 1998 and replaced by additional focus on households with incomes below 30 percent of the area median and flexibility for PHAs to adopt their own preferences. PHAs now often make first-come, first-served among households with extremely low incomes their preference system, though some retain homelessness as one of several preferences given equal weight. Interviews with organizations responsible for planning and coordinating local responses to homelessness, as well as with individual providers of emergency shelters and transitional housing, suggest that outplacement with vouchers has become much more difficult over time.

Explicit and absolute preferences for homeless people can be problematic because they can encourage people to enter the emergency shelter system to obtain housing assistance and to lengthen their shelter stays while waiting for their placement into permanent housing (O'Flaherty and Wu 2006). However, this would be a much smaller problem if the voucher program were large enough to have short waiting lists.

People with Immediate Housing Crises

A larger voucher program, even an open enrollment program, would not solve housing crises that arise suddenly and do not provide enough time for an individual or a family to go through the processes created to ensure that voucher assistance is used for eligible households in eligible housing units. These processes include verifying income, finding housing that meets the program standards (the housing quality standard and a reasonable rent compared with other private-market units), and signing a lease with a willing landlord. To avert homelessness by helping households with immediate crises, communities also need homelessness prevention programs that provide assistance quickly. Prevention assistance can pay rent and utilities arrears for a currently occupied housing unit or deposits and move-in expenses for another housing unit. The assistance can include help with a few months' rent. Because this assistance is shallow and temporary, it need not be subject to the same controls on inappropriate use needed for a substantial long-term benefit such as a housing voucher.

Shallow and temporary subsidies also can be used for people whose housing crisis has led to a shelter admission. An advantage is that the modest nature of the subsidy makes it less likely that the effect of the subsidy will be to drive up the use of shelters. People are less likely to enter a shelter with the specific purpose of obtaining a subsidy of modest size and duration than is the case when permanent rental assistance is set aside to help families or individuals leave a shelter.

Short-term assistance may help some families and individuals get well enough established in a job that enables them to pay for housing on their own or to move into someone else's housing unit in which they will be able to stay long term. Shallow and temporary rent subsidies for homeless people have not been evaluated, but researchers studying the use of such subsidies for people with HIV/AIDs have found them to be effective (Dasinger and Speiglman 2007).

A few communities have been experimenting for several years with short-term rental subsidies for shelter diversion and rapid exit (Burt, Pearson, and Montgomery 2005; Burt and Spellman 2007). A larger number will adopt such programs now that Congress, as part of the American Recovery and Reinvestment Act (the stimulus package), enacted a Homelessness Prevention and Rapid Re-Housing Program (HPRP). In early 2009 HUD allocated $1.5 billion to states and cities and published program rules and guidance.

Federal HPRP rules set broad standards for state and local administrators to follow in implementing the program, including an income limit (50 percent of area median income), a maximum rent subsidy (full rent up to the market value of the housing unit), maximum duration of the rent subsidy (eighteen months), and a requirement that any housing unit to which a household moves with a rent subsidy must be physically safe (HUD 2009b).[17]

HUD guidance encourages program administrators to establish lower income limits to better target assistance to those at greatest risk of becoming homeless. While the maximum permitted subsidy is full rent for eighteen months, cities and states are encouraged to serve more households by providing subsidies smaller than the maximum. For example, the assistance could cover less than the full rent, or the subsidy could be stepped down over time to avoid creating a new housing crisis when the household suddenly goes from paying no rent to full rent. Grantees also are required to document that but for the assistance, the family or the individual would have become homeless or would not have been able to leave the shelter (HUD 2009b). Training materials have stressed the importance of using caseworker assessments of individual situations made as close as possible to the decision on shelter admission, when HPRP funds are used for prevention.[18]

Despite the temporary nature of stimulus funds, prevention and rapid re-housing are likely to become increasingly important components of the residential homeless services system that is administered separately from mainstream housing assistance—both because of communities' experience using HPRP and because the 2009 reauthorization of HUD Mc-Kinney-Vento programs[19] made prevention an eligible use of funds and created incentives for rapid re-housing approaches.

The current HPRP model might be characterized as a "voucher lite" program, which can serve households in crisis more quickly and flexibly than the housing choice voucher program. However, while implementation is likely to vary greatly from place to place, a major concern is that many communities may not target prevention assistance to people at highest risk of becoming homeless.[20]

Another concern is that, given the pressures on the federal government to avoid program abuse, HPRP rules will become even more like the rules of the voucher program than they are now—with full-blown income verification, housing quality inspections, and controls over rents. If that happens, the program will lose its ability to respond to housing crises quickly.

An alternative approach that should be considered for prevention of homelessness would be to allocate funds to states and the largest U.S.

cities for use by agencies that serve highly vulnerable people, such as mental health, substance abuse, and child welfare agencies.

More Than a Short-Term Rental Subsidy

Not all people who become homeless can be kept from becoming homeless again by a short-term rental subsidy. Some individuals and families are likely to need permanent-housing assistance. Some may need services packaged together with the housing or concentrated case management to link them to services provided by mainstream agencies.

When permanent-housing assistance is set aside for people who have become homeless, it should be used to the maximum extent possible for individuals and families whose profiles suggest that they are at high risk of becoming long-stayers in the residential system for homeless people or experiencing sustained periods of unstable housing. Using set-asides only for high-risk people will help avoid making shelters a queuing system for subsidized housing.

Individuals with Chronic Patterns of Homelessness.   For individuals, a definition of chronic homelessness has been created that includes a diagnosed disability and is based roughly on a body of research (Caton, Wilkins, and Anderson 2007; Kuhn and Culhane 1998). The policy goal of ending patterns of chronic homelessness among individuals with disabilities by providing permanent housing together with supportive services should continue.

A debate continues about the way in which housing and services should be combined: for example, whether services should be packaged directly with the housing or delivered separately, the appropriate degree of encouragement to accept services, and whether a housing program should accept active substance abusers or mentally ill people not complying with treatment (Pearson et al. 2007; Caton, Wilkins, and Anderson 2007; see also chapters 2 and 3, of this volume). This issue concerns the design and delivery of services and treatment, not housing subsidy programs. It does not need to be resolved to determine how affordable housing policies can be used to reduce homelessness. Whatever the treatment model, long-term housing subsidies are essential for a population for whom a successful exit from homelessness means access to income support (SSI for people with disabilities) and opportunities to work, but usually not to earn income sufficient to pay a private-market rent (Long, Rio, and Rosen 2007).

Supported housing based on various approaches to housing subsidy has been shown to be effective for people with chronically homeless profiles. For example, Robert Rosenheck and his colleagues (2003) find that HUD-VA Supportive Housing (VASH) program was successfully used by homeless veterans with psychiatric or substance abuse disorders or both.

Case managers helped the VASH participants apply for and use their vouchers—for example, by meeting with prospective landlords. Those with vouchers had superior outcomes for housing stability, with 35 percent and 36 percent fewer days homeless during a three-year follow-up, compared with one control group that had intensive case management alone and another that had usual care from the Veterans Administration.

Sandra Newman (1994) uses a pre–post research design to analyze data from a demonstration program sponsored by the Robert Wood Johnson Foundation and HUD that provided vouchers to people with severe mental illness. She shows that a program of scattered-site housing with services works for people at high risk of chronic homelessness: it reduces their hospitalizations and increases their housing stability. Michael Hulbert, Patricia Wood, and Richard Hough (1996) show that a majority of homeless individuals who were selected for a demonstration program because they had severe and persistent mental illness were able to use housing vouchers successfully and to achieve stable, independent living. Participants received help getting through the voucher application process and finding a suitable housing unit.

Homeless Families with High Needs.   The definition of high-needs households, consisting of parents who become homeless together with their children, is less well formed than the definition of chronic homelessness for individuals. High-needs families should include those that have long stays in the residential system for homeless people and families that have trouble maintaining stable housing, leaving emergency shelters or transitional housing relatively quickly but reappearing after gaps during which they apparently were in their own or someone else's housing unit.

Transitional housing has been a widely used approach for serving homeless families with high needs. Families are placed in temporary housing and receive intensive case management and services to prepare them for success in finding and maintaining permanent housing and achieving other goals related to the well-being of parents and children. However, some research suggests that families actually using transitional housing are less needy than other groups of families that become homeless, based on comparing their rates of use of psychiatric, inpatient mental-health and substance-abuse services and the placement of their children in foster care (Culhane et al. 2007a).[21] A recent study of the costs of first-time homelessness (Spellman et al. 2010) shows that long transitional-housing stays are costly to the system but does not measure the outcomes of those stays. In a study of those who successfully leave transitional housing programs, Martha Burt (2010) finds that spending more time in transitional housing is associated with higher educational attainment and employment at the time of moving out and with sustained employment over the following year. In addition, those with longer stays are less likely to be without a place of their own over the following year. However, because the study has no control group it is not possible to determine the degree of bias—that is, whether women who stayed longer in the programs and took advantage of educational and employment opportunities would have been more likely to do better than women with shorter stays in any case.

Burt also finds that having a housing subsidy (a voucher) at move-out is the most important factor in predicting whether the transitional-housing leaver would have his or her own place over the next year. Given the high cost of transitional housing compared with the cost of a voucher in most housing markets (Spellman et al. 2010), the weight of evidence is that policy should be based on providing an early subsidized transition out of programs explicitly targeted to homeless families, whether those programs are defined as emergency shelter or as transitional housing.

Families that leave shelters or transitional housing fairly quickly but then come back into the homeless services system after several months have high rates of involvement with the criminal justice and child welfare systems. During their long total period of homelessness, including any gaps between stays in shelters, households that follow this pattern are very likely to change household composition, whether gaining or losing adults or children. Although most families that become homeless have only female adults, families that follow this pattern often include men during some of their stays in shelters (Spellman et al. 2010). In short, this is a group of highly unstable families, with chaotic lives that likely have high societal costs stretching across generations. Their appearance in the homeless services system may provide an opportunity for intervention, based on assessments made when they first appear in shelters and placements into programs that involve intensive and targeted services.

Too little is known about this group of highly unstable families to say definitively how they can be helped by subsidized housing. However, receipt of such housing has been found to be the best predictor of whether families will avoid returning to shelters (Shinn et al. 1998). In addition, the Family Reunification Program, a special allocation of housing vouchers targeted to families referred by child welfare agencies, was shown by a descriptive evaluation to be a promising approach for alleviating combinations of housing and family instability (Rog, Gilbert-Mongelli, and Lundy 1997).

Increasing the Supply of Permanent Housing

Set-Asides of Vouchers.   For individuals with chronic patterns of homelessness and for homeless families with high needs, the source of a larger supply of permanent housing depends on how large the housing voucher program becomes. With a large enough voucher program, providers of services to people with disabilities and other indicators of high needs would have access to vouchers both for tenant-based, scattered-site program models and for models in which the voucher provides a rent subsidy while a development program such as the Low Income Housing Tax Credit provides the housing.[22] Supportive housing need not be targeted explicitly to formerly homeless people, if the supply of such housing—tenant-based or property-based—is ample.

Set-asides of new voucher funding sometimes have focused on homeless people. The HUD-VA Supportive Housing Program (VASH) used tenant-based housing vouchers together with intensive case management. The HUD 2009 Omnibus Appropriations Act had the first new funding of VASH since the early 1990s, enough to support about 10,000 units.

Allocations of Family Reunification vouchers totaled about 37,000 units between 1992 and 2001. The 2009 Appropriations Act funded the program for the first time in eight years and at a level that will support between 2,500 and 3,000 families. This renewed funding could be focused on families with a history of housing instability and supported by a rigorous evaluation based on random assignment.

Although these set-aside programs can help particular families and individuals leave homelessness, the number of people served is too small to have any discernable effect on numbers of homeless people or patterns of homelessness. What the programs have done is demonstrate the feasibility of using vouchers for people with intense needs (Rosenheck et al. 2003; Rog, Gilbert-Mongelli, and Lundy 1997), as well as the important role of vouchers in preventing homelessness (Mills et al. 2007).

Such special set-asides need not continue indefinitely. If evaluations suggest they are successful, incentives short of set-asides can be created to encourage administrators of the voucher program to continue them.

In the absence of a substantially larger voucher program, another policy option is a substantial increase in funding for the McKinney-Vento Shelter Plus Care Program, which would ensure a source of supported housing for formerly homeless people with disabilities. In addition to its explicit targeting, Shelter Plus Care has a matching requirement that has been successful in attracting funding for case management and services from mainstream funding sources. Its housing subsidy is essentially the same as a voucher subsidy and costs the same as a voucher.

Use of LIHTC for Supportive Housing.   Despite its shallower subsidy (a flat rent affordable only for households substantially above the poverty level), the LIHTC program can help to reduce homelessness for individuals and families because it can be used to develop supported housing for formerly homeless people and people with disabilities. Other subsidies can be used to create very low flat rents in an LIHTC development, or LIHTC housing can be used together with an income-based voucher.

LIHTC produces more than 100,000 units every year (Climaco et al. 2009). A key feature of LIHTC is that decisions about the geographic location of housing and whether it is intended for use by families, elderly people, or people with special needs are made by state governments. This state locus of decision making can facilitate linking rental housing projects to services provided through state programs for people with mental illness or substance abuse disorders. Many states provide preferences for supported housing in systems for allocating tax credits to particular developments through threshold requirements, set-asides, or scoring incentives, and some states' Qualified Allocation Plans require substantial detail about the services to be provided in connection with the housing (Tassos 2007, 2008).

Data collected from state housing finance agencies show that 4.5 percent of the 5,756 LIHTC developments placed in service between 2003 and 2006 had some or all units targeted to homeless people, and 12.5 percent had some units reserved for people with disabilities. Most properties were relatively large, with between twenty-one and ninety-nine units, and these properties likely have a portion rather than all their units targeted to people with special needs (Climaco et al. 2009). Federal rules for the LIHTC could provide a larger tax credit for individual properties when used for supportive housing and linked to mental health agencies (Spellman et al. 2006).[23]

Public Housing and Section 8 Projects.   The redevelopment or refinancing of public housing and Section 8 projects can provide an opportunity for setting aside units for people with special needs for supportive services. As of 2009, replacement of public-housing units with vouchers has come about mainly through redevelopment of distressed public housing into smaller and often mixed-income communities that include units subsidized by the LIHTC Program and occupied by the somewhat higher-income families reached by the LIHTC.[24]

To the extent that public housing and Section 8 projects are preserved and redeveloped rather than dropped out of the assisted housing stock, those undertaking the redevelopment should be encouraged to make set-asides of units available for formerly homeless people. PHAs and private owners of subsidized rental housing are most likely to agree to designate units for younger disabled and formerly homeless people, rather than excluding them from the context of redevelopment that brings in additional resources to support housing and includes linkages to agencies providing services to people with disabilities.

A Continued Role for the Residential Homeless-Services System

A goal of ending homelessness rather than managing it, as espoused by the National Alliance to End Homelessness starting in 2000, has been an effective counterpoint to the emergence of a system that may be institutionalizing a parallel system of care for a certain group of needy people (Leginski 2007; Culhane et al. 2007b; Burt and Spellman 2007). However, maintaining a residual system of emergency shelters may be more cost-effective than completely shutting down the shelter system and attempting to forestall all short-term episodes of homelessness through emergency cash or casework. Completely closing down the emergency-shelter system for individuals might not be feasible in any case, given its heavily nongovernmental sponsorship and, in some cases, the combination of religion and therapy that impels these programs.

The case may be different for families. The system of shelters for families has evolved away from congregate-style shelters—perceived to be dangerous for children—to self-contained dwelling units that are, in many ways, indistinguishable from transitional or even permanent housing but cost more to maintain because of intensive staffing and administration (Spellman et al. 2010). Apartment-based emergency shelters also run the risk of making the homeless services system too attractive, discouraging families from finding other solutions to their housing crises and serving as a de facto queuing system for subsidized housing (Culhane et al. 2007a). It may be both realistic and cost-effective for communities to redefine the shelter system for families using a combination of prevention programs and programs that place families who become homeless immediately into permanent housing, with supportive services when needed. However, some residual system for immediate housing emergencies that aims for very short-term stays and uses low-cost approaches to staffing may be needed.

Notes

1. Calculations based on other studies are available from Brendan O'Flaherty.
2. These new data amplify and confirm what we already knew from the mid-1990s National Survey of Homeless Providers and Clients (NSHPC), conducted by the U.S. Census Bureau in 1996. NSHPC survey results were analyzed by Martha Burt and her colleagues at the Urban Institute (Burt, Aaron, and Lee, 2001).
3. The remaining 2 percent consists of unaccompanied people under eighteen years of age and two or more adults who are homeless together.
4. For convenience, vouchers are often discussed as units, even though the program does not produce housing units but instead provides subsidies to be used for housing units. Although there was no new funding of incremental vouchers during the first decade of the 21st century, the voucher program grew as vouchers were used to replace public housing and Section 8 projects that left the assisted housing stock. The process of replacing public housing and Section 8 program units with equivalent numbers of vouchers has been imperfect, and there has been some reduction in total assisted units in many locations, even though this was not the explicit policy.
5. The Housing Allowance Supply Experiment conducted in the 1970s in Green Bay, Wisconsin, and South Bend, Indiana. Among other differences from the

voucher program that could affect participation, subsidies were paid directly to households rather than to landlords.

6. Edgar Olsen (this volume) proposes eliminating all public housing and Section 8 projects and claims that this would provide funding for much more than the equivalent number of vouchers. Whether that is the case is debatable, given the amounts per unit spent now and likely to be spent in the future on those programs. The higher costs of project-based programs include the costs incurred to build the projects, which are sunk costs. Together the 2.9 million units of public housing and project-based Section 8 used appropriations of only $16 billion per year as of 2008, a much smaller amount per unit than the $15 billion appropriated for the 2 million vouchers (Rice, Sard, and Fischer 2008). Current backlogs and future accruals of capital needs might be shown to add enough to the operating costs of property-based programs that the future per-unit costs of these programs could be shown to be higher than the per-unit cost of a voucher. However, shifting to vouchers may not provide enough realizable savings to fund additional vouchers, since deferring capital expenditures is a reality of multifamily housing management for appropriators of housing-subsidy funds, just as it is for unsubsidized property owners.

7. Sandra Newman (2008) reviews the extensive literature on whether housing assistance encourages or impedes work.

8. Abt Associates estimates based on HUD and PHA data.

9. Based on surveys of PHAs conducted for a study of rent policies by Abt Associates (principal investigator Larry Buron) for the U.S. Department of Housing and Urban Development.

10. An exception is families with five or more members, who have lower success rates. Families of that size make up a small fraction of those using vouchers and of those likely to become homeless. Only 7 percent of sheltered homeless people are in households with five or more people.

11. Information from http://www.hud.gov/offices/pih/programs/ph/dhp/designated.xls (accessed April 30, 2010).

12. Information from HUD websites assembled by the Technical Assistance Council.

13. Technically, the 40th percentile rent of standard-quality units that have had new tenants during the past two years. The exclusions, particularly basing the FMR estimates on units that are without the tenure discounts typically enjoyed by sitting tenants, raise the FMRs to roughly the midpoint of the distribution of rents.

14. This is not the same as providing access to the same quality housing unit in different parts of the country, as the distribution of housing quality differs from place to place, depending on such factors as the age of the rental housing stock and the income levels of unassisted renters.

15. Re-benchmarking corrects for the tendency of FMRs to be adjusted upward, but rarely downward, as PHAs appeal the level at which their FMRs have been set, using local housing-market data as evidence.

16. The worst-case-needs estimates also include renters living in severely substandard housing without a severe rent burden, but that condition is not common.

17. In the housing choice voucher program, housing quality standards also apply to a unit that was occupied by a household before it began to receive rental assistance.

18. In addition to HUD's training materials and guidance, the National Alliance to End Homelessness published guidebooks that reflect the 2009 state-of-the-art design of prevention and rapid-re-housing programs (NAEH 2009a, 2009b).

19. The Homeless Emergency Assistance and Rapid Transition to Housing (HEARTH) Act.

20. Burt, Pearson, and Montgomery (2005) review the literature on the difficulty of targeting homeless-prevention programs to the households most at risk of becoming homeless.

21. Culhane and his colleagues do not distinguish between emergency shelter and transitional housing in their analysis of lengths of stay.

22. See Khadduri and Wilkins (2008) for the advantages of a split subsidy approach to providing subsidized rental housing.

23. Some states already provide relief from state-imposed caps on development costs for LIHTC developments serving populations with special needs (Tassos 2007, 2008). The Housing and Economic Recovery Act of 2008 (HERA, PL 110–289) permits states to provide an increase of 30 percent to the "eligible basis" for any LIHTC development. The federal government could provide additional incentives for supported housing by exempting some of the tax-credit amounts allocated for supported housing from the state's per capita ceiling on LIHTC authority.

24. Sometimes properties redeveloped through HOPE VI or similar programs also include market-rate rental units or homeownership units.

References

Burt, Martha R. 2005. *Taking Health Care Home: Baseline Report on PSH Tenant Programs, Policies, and Funding.* Oakland, Calif.: Corporation for Supportive Housing.

———. 2010. *Life After Transitional Housing for Homeless Families.* Washington: U.S. Department of Housing and Urban Development.

Burt, Martha, Laudan Y. Aron, Edgar Lee, and Jesse Valente. 2001. *Helping America's Homeless: Emergency Shelter or Affordable Housing?* Washington, D.C.: Urban Institute Press.

Burt, Martha, Carol Pearson, and Ann Elizabeth Montgomery. 2005. *Strategies for Preventing Homelessness.* Washington: U.S. Department of Housing and Urban Development.

Burt, Martha, and Brooke Spellman. 2007. "Changing Homeless and Mainstream Service Systems: Essential Approaches to Ending Homelessness." In *Towards Understanding Homelessness: The 2007 National Symposium on Homelessness Research,* edited by Deborah Dennis, Gretchen Locke, and Jill Khadduri. Washington: U.S. Department of Health and Human Services: U.S. Department of Housing and Urban Development.

Caton, Carol L. M., Carol Wilkins, and Jacquelyn Anderson. 2007. "People Who Experience Long-Term Homelessness: Characteristics and Intervention." In *Towards Understanding Homelessness: The 2007 National Symposium on Homelessness Research,* edited by Deborah Dennis, Gretchen Locke, and Jill Khadduri. Washington: U.S. Department of Health and Human Services and U.S. Department of Housing and Urban Development.

Climaco, Carissa, Meryl Finkel, Bulbul Kaul, Ken Lam, and Chris Rodger. 2009. *Updating the Low Income Housing Tax Credit (LIHTC) Database: Projects Placed in Service Through 2006.* Cambridge, Mass.: Abt Associates.

Culhane, Dennis P., Chang-Moo Lee, and Susan M. Wachter. 1996. "Where the Homeless Come From: A Study of the Prior Address Distribution of Families Admitted to Public Shelters in New York City and Philadelphia." *Housing Policy Debate* 7(2): 327–65.

Culhane, Dennis P., Stephen Metraux, Jung Min Park, Maryanne Schretzman, and Jesse Valente. 2007a. "Testing a Typology of Family Homelessness Based on Patterns of Public Shelter Utilization in Four U.S. Jurisdictions: Implications for Policy and Program Planning." *Housing Policy Debate* 18(1): 1–28.

Culhane, Dennis, Wayne Parker, Barbara Poppe, Kennen Gross, and Ezra Sykes. 2007b. "Accountability, Cost-Effectiveness, and Program Performance: Progress Since 1998." In *Towards Understanding Homelessness: The 2007 National Symposium on Homelessness Research,* edited by Deborah Dennis, Gretchen Locke, and Jill Khadduri. Washington: U.S. Department of Health and Human Services and U.S. Department of Housing and Urban Development.

Cutts, Amy Crews, and Edgar O. Olsen. 2002. "Are Section 8 Subsidies Too High?" *Journal of Housing Economics* 11(3): 214–43.

Dasinger, Lisa K., and Richard Speiglman. 2007. "Homeless Prevention: The Effect of a Shallow Rent Subsidy on Housing Outcomes Among People with HIV or AIDS." *AIDS and Behavior* 11(2): 128–39.

Dawkins, Casey J. 2007. "Income Targeting of Housing Vouchers: What Happened After the Quality Housing and Work Responsibility Act?" *Cityscape* 9(3): 69–94.

Devine, Deborah J., Robert W. Gray, Lester Rubin, and Lydia B. Taghavi. 2003. *Housing Choice Voucher Location Patterns: Implications for Participants and Neighborhood Welfare.* Washington: U.S. Department of Housing and Urban Development.

Early, Dirk W. 1998. "The Role of Subsidized Housing in Reducing Homelessness: An Empirical Investigation Using Micro-Data." *Journal of Policy Analysis and Management* 17(4): 687–96.

———. 2004. "The Determinants of Homelessness and the Targeting of Housing Assistance." *Journal of Urban Economics* 55: 195–214.

Early, Dirk W., and Edgar Olsen. 2002. "Subsidized Housing, Emergency Shelters, and Homelessness: An Empirical Investigation Using Data from the 1990 Census." *Advances in Economic Analysis and Policy* 2(1): 1–34.

Ellen, Ingrid, and Brendan O'Flaherty. 2007. "Social Programs and Household Size: Evidence from New York City." *Population Research Policy Review* 26(4): 387–409.

Finkel, Meryl, and Larry Buron. 2001. *Study on Section 8 Voucher Success Rates, vol. 1: Quantitative Study of Success Rates in Metropolitan Areas.* Washington: U.S. Department of Housing and Urban Development.

Finkel, Meryl, Charles Hanson, Richard Hilton, Ken Lam, and Melissa Vandawalker. 2006. *Multifamily Properties: Opting In, Opting Out, and Remaining Affordable.* Bethesda, Md., and Cambridge, Mass.: Econometrica and Abt Associates.

Fosburg, Linda B., Gretchen Locke, Laura Peck, and Meryl Finkel. 1997. *National Evaluation of the Shelter Plus Case Program.* Cambridge, Mass.: Abt Associates.

Gubits, Daniel, Jill Khadduri, and Jennifer Turnham. 2009. *Housing Patterns of Low Income Families with Children: Further Analysis of Data from the Study of the Effects of Housing Vouchers on Families with Children.* Cambridge, Mass.: Harvard University Joint Center for Housing Studies.

Honig, Marjorie, and Randall K. Filer. 1993. "Causes of Inter-city Variation in Homelessness." *American Economic Review* 83(1): 248–55.

Hulbert, Michael S., Patricia A. Wood, and Richard L. Hough. 1996. "Providing Independent Housing for the Homeless Mentally Ill: A Novel Approach to Evaluating Long-Term Longitudinal Housing Patterns." *Journal of Community Psychology* 24(3): 291–310.

Jargowsky, Paul A. 2003. *Stunning Progress, Hidden Problems: The Dramatic Decline of Concentrated Poverty in the 1990s.* Washington, D.C.: Brookings Institution.

Katz, Bruce, and Margery Austin Turner. 2008. "Rethinking U.S. Rental Housing Policy: A New Blueprint for Federal, State, and Local Action." In *Revisiting Rental Housing: Policies, Programs, and Priorities,* edited by Nicholas Retsinas and Eric Belsky. Washington, D.C.: Brookings Institution.

Khadduri, Jill. 2001. "Deconcentration: What Do We Mean? What Do We Want?" *Cityscape* 5(2): 69–84.

———. 2003. "Should the Housing Voucher Program Become a Block Grant?" *Housing Policy Debate* 14(3): 235–69.

Khadduri, Jill, and Raymond J. Struyk. 1982. "Housing Vouchers for the Poor." *Journal of Policy Analysis and Management* 1(2): 196–208.

Khadduri, Jill, and Charles Wilkins. 2008. "Designing Sustainable Subsidized Rental Housing Programs: What Have We Learned?" In *Revisiting Rental Housing: Policies, Programs, and Priorities,* edited by in Nicholas Retsinas and Eric Belsky. Washington, D.C.: Brookings Institution.

Kuhn, Randall, and Dennis Culhane. 1998. "Applying Cluster Analysis to Test of a Typology of Homelessness: Results from the Analysis of Administrative Data." *American Journal of Community Psychology* 26(2): 207–32.

Lee, Robert, and Chad R. Farrell. 2004. "Metropolitan Neighborhoods with Sheltered Homeless Populations: Evidence from the 1990 and 2000 Censuses." *Living Cities Census Series.* Washington, D.C.: Brookings Institution.

Leger, Mireille, and Stephen D. Kennedy. 1990. *Final Comprehensive Report of the Freestanding Voucher Demonstration.* Cambridge, Mass.: Abt Associates.

Leginski, Walter. 2007. "Historical and Contextual Influences on the U.S. Response to Contemporary Homelessness." In *Towards Understanding Homelessness: The 2007 National Symposium on Homelessness Research,* edited by Deborah Dennis, Gretchen Locke, and Jill Khadduri. Washington: U.S. Department of Health and Human Services and U.S. Department of Housing and Urban Development.

Long, David, John Rio, and Jeremy Rosen. 2007. "Employment and Income Supports for Homeless People." In *Towards Understanding Homelessness: The 2007 National*

Symposium on Homelessness Research, edited by Deborah Dennis, Gretchen Locke, and Jill Khadduri. Washington: U.S. Department of Health and Human Services and U.S. Department of Housing and Urban Development.

McClure, Kirk. 2010. "Are Low-Income Housing Tax Credits Locating Where There Is a Shortage of Available Units." *Housing Policy Debate* 20(2).

Maguire, Marcella, Dennis Culhane, and Steve Poulin. 2005. "Using the HMIS to Identify Chronic Homelessness, Service Patterns, and Costs." Presentation to the 2005 National HMIS Conference. St. Louis (September 13, 2005).

Metraux, Steven, Dennis Culhane, Stacy Raphael, Matthew White, Carol Pearson, Eric Hirsh, Patricia Ferrel, Steven Rice, Barbara Ritter, and Stephen Cleghorn. 2001. "Assessing Homeless Population Size Through the Use of Emergency and Transitional Shelter Services in 1998: Results from the Analysis of Administrative Data from Nine U.S. Jurisdictions." *Public Health Reports* 116(4): 344–52.

Millennial Housing Commission. 2002. *Meeting Our Nation's Housing Challenges: Report of the Bipartisan Millennial Housing Commission Appointed by the Congress of the United States.* Washington: Millennial Housing Commission.

Mills, Gregory, Daniel Gubits, Larry Orr, David Long, Judie Feins, Bulbul Kaul, Michelle Wood, Abt Associates, Amy Jones & Associates, Cloudburst Consulting, and the QED Group. 2007. *Effects of Housing Choice Vouchers on Welfare Families: Final Report.* Washington: U.S. Department of Housing and Urban Development.

Morris Davis and Company, Inc., and University of Pennsylvania. 2006. *Predicting Staying in or Leaving Permanent Supportive Housing That Serves Homeless People with Serious Mental Illness.* Washington: U.S. Department of Housing and Urban Development.

National Alliance to End Homelessness. 2009a. *Homeless Prevention: Creating Programs That Work.* Washington: NAEH.

———. 2009b. *Rapid Re-Housing: Creating Programs That Work.* Washington: NAEH.

Newman, Sandra. 1994. "The Effects of Independent Living on Persons with Chronic Mental Illness: An Assessment of the Section 8 Certificate Program." *Millbank Quarterly* 72(1): 171–98.

Newman, Sandra. 2008. "Does Housing Matter for Poor Families? A Critical Summary of Research and Issues Still to be Resolved." *Journal of Policy Analysis and Management* 27(4): 895–925.

Newman, Sandra J., and Ann B. Schnare. 1997. "And a Suitable Living Environment: The Failure of Housing Programs to Deliver on Neighborhood Quality." *Housing Policy Debate* 8(4): 703–41.

O'Flaherty, Brendan. 2004. "Wrong Person and Wrong Place: For Homelessness, the Conjunction Is What Matters." *Journal of Housing Economics* 13(1): 1–15.

O'Flaherty, Brendan, and Ting Wu. 2006. "Fewer Subsidized Exits and a Recession: How New York City's Family Homeless Shelter Population Became Immense." *Journal of Housing Economics* 15(2): 99–125.

Olsen, Edgar O. 2008. "Getting More from Low-Income Housing Assistance." Hamilton Project discussion paper. Washington, D.C.: Brookings Institution.

Pearson, Carol L., Gretchen Locke, Ann Elizabeth Montgomery, and Larry Buron. 2007. *The Applicability of Housing First Models to Homeless Persons with*

Serious Mental Illness. Washington: U.S. Department of Housing and Urban Development.

President's Commission on Housing. 1982. *Report of the President's Commission on Housing.* Washington: President's Commission on Housing.

Quigley, John, Steven Raphael, and Eugene Smolensky. 2001. "Homeless in America, Homeless in California." *The Review of Economics and Statistic* 83(2): 37–51.

Rice, Douglas, Barbara Sard, and Will Fischer. 2008. "HUD Budget Contains Major Funding Shortfalls." Paper. Washington, D.C.: Center on Budget and Policy Priorities.

Rog, Debra J., and John C. Buckner. 2007. "Homeless Families and Children." In *Towards Understanding Homelessness: The 2007 National Symposium on Homelessness Research,* edited by Deborah Dennis, Gretchen Locke, and Jill Khadduri. Washington: U.S. Department of Health and Human Services and U.S. Department of Housing and Urban Development.

Rog, Debra J., Ariana M. Gilbert-Mongelli, and Ezell Lundy. 1997. *The Family Reunification Program: Final Evaluation Report.* Washington, D.C.: Vanderbilt Institute for Public Policy Studies.

Rosenheck, Robert, Wesley Kasprow, Linda Frisman, and Wen Liu-Mares. 2003. "Cost-Effectiveness of Supported Housing for Homeless Persons with Mental Illness." *Archives of General Psychiatry* 60(9): 940–51.

Shinn, Marybeth, Beth C. Weitzman, Daniela Stojanovic, James R. Knickman, Lucila Jimenez, Lisa Duchon, Susan James, and David H. Krantz. 1998. "Predictors of Homelessness Among Families in New York City: From Shelter Request to Housing Stability." *American Journal of Public Health* 88(11): 1651–57.

Spellman, Brooke, Jill Khadduri, Melody Fennel, and Chris Lord. 2006. *A Federal Tax Credit Program for Permanent Supportive Housing: Design and Feasibility.* Washington, D.C.: National Alliance to End Homelessness.

Spellman, Brooke, Jill Khadduri, Brian Sokol, and Josh Leopold. 2010. *Costs Associated With First Time Homelessness for Families and Individuals.* Washington: U.S. Department of Housing and Urban Development.

Tassos, James. 2007. *Housing Credit Policies in 2007 That Promote Supportive Housing: A State-by-State Analysis.* Washington, D.C.: Enterprise Community Partners and Corporation for Supportive Housing.

———. 2008. "Summary of Select 2008 Low Income Housing Tax Credit QAP Policies Encouraging Supportive Housing." Washington, D.C.: Enterprise Community Partners and Corporation for Supportive Housing.

Turnham, Jennifer, and Jill Khadduri. 2001. "Issues and Options for HUD's Tenant-based Assistance Program." Prepared for the Millennial Housing Commission. September 2001.

U.S. Department of Housing and Urban Development HUD. 2007. *Affordable Housing Needs 2005: Report to Congress.* Office of Policy Development and Research. Washington: U.S. Government Printing Office.

———. 2008. *The 2007 Annual Homeless Assessment Report.* Washington: U.S. Government Printing Office.

———. 2009a. *The 2008 Annual Homeless Assessment Report.* Washington: Office of Community Planning and Development.

————. 2009b. *Notice of Allocations, Application Procedures, and Requirements for Homeless Prevention and Rapid Re-Housing Program Grantees Under the American Recovery and Reinvestment Act of 2009.* Washington: Office of Community Planning and Development.

Wood, Michelle, Jennifer Turnham, and Gregory Mills. 2008. "Housing Affordability and Family Well-Being: Results from the Housing Voucher Evaluation." *Housing Policy Debate* 19(2): 367–412.

Chapter 5

Fundamental Housing Policy Reforms to End Homelessness

EDGAR O. OLSEN

The failure to offer assistance to all who become homeless is a major defect of the current system of low-income housing assistance. Replacing this system with an equally costly entitlement housing voucher program would ensure that housing assistance is available to all individuals who would otherwise be homeless. Such fundamental reform is justified on other grounds as well. Plausible assumptions about taxpayer preferences argue strongly for replacing the current patchwork of nonentitlement low-income housing programs with an entitlement housing assistance program for the poorest individuals. Evidence on the excessive costs of all forms of project-based housing assistance argues for exclusive reliance on tenant-based assistance.

Replacing the current system of low-income housing programs with an entitlement program of tenant-based assistance has been espoused by housing policy analysts for many years (Khadduri and Struyk 1982; Olsen 1982, 2008; Weicher 1997; Quigley 2008). It has also attracted political support at the highest level. The Clinton administration proposed comprehensive legislation for phasing out project-based assistance (U.S. Department of Housing and Urban Development 1995), and in his campaign against President Clinton, Robert Dole also proposed vouchering out public housing. Although the Clinton proposals were not adopted, the 1998 Housing Act mandated the conversion of public housing projects to recipient-based assistance under certain circumstances and allowed it under others.

A politically feasible reform would involve a transition that does not harm the overwhelming majority of current recipients of low-income housing assistance, or it would involve a transition that even benefits them. However, because more than 600,000 households give up their assistance each year, the transition to an entitlement housing voucher program could be structured to eliminate homelessness within a relatively short time without reducing benefits for current recipients and without spending more money. Targeting recycled and new assistance to the poorest individuals would ensure that housing assistance is available to all who would otherwise be homeless.

Offering housing assistance to all the poorest individuals is a necessary but not a sufficient condition for eliminating homelessness. Some will need encouragement to seek assistance and help in navigating the system. Many will need temporary shelter while applications are processed and during the search for an apartment, and many will need help in finding housing in the private market. With the bulk of the cost of housing assistance for the homeless having shifted to mainstream low-income housing programs, the budgets of programs focused on the homeless can be shifted to providing this help and dealing with their other serious problems. Existing homeless shelters will certainly be a part of the solution to dealing with temporary homelessness. Because of the time needed to determine eligibility and find regular housing, an entitlement housing assistance program for the poorest individuals will not eliminate the desirability of some short-term facilities to house people who would otherwise live on the streets. Although we might want to fund them in a different manner, existing shelters would surely be among the short-term facilities used. The current facilities should be more than adequate to handle the reduced demand for temporary shelter for quite some time.

This chapter describes the rationales for major reforms of low-income housing assistance and a politically feasible set of transitional reforms that would disproportionately benefit individuals who would otherwise be homeless. The key to understanding the benefits of the proposed reforms to homeless people is to recognize that almost all who are homeless have extremely low incomes. The median income for homeless households and single individuals is less than half of the relevant poverty threshold (Burt et al. 2001, 74–80). Reforms of mainstream programs that concentrate more assistance on the poorest individuals will disproportionately benefit those who would otherwise be homeless. Adopting all the transitional reforms would provide the long-term housing assistance needed to serve all homeless households without any increase in spending and leave more of the budgets of programs for the homeless for solving their other problems.

Rationale for an Entitlement Housing Voucher Program

Unlike other major means-tested transfer programs, housing assistance is not an entitlement despite its stated goal of "a decent home and a suitable living environment for every American family" (Housing Act of

1949, 42 USC Sec. 1441). Millions of the poorest households are not offered any housing assistance, while a smaller number of their equally poor counterparts receive large subsidies. For example, an assisted family with one child and an adjusted annual income of $10,000 living in an area with the program's average payment standard received an annual housing subsidy of $6,600 from the housing choice voucher program in 2007 if the family occupied an apartment that rented for at least the program's payment standard. The majority of households with the same characteristics in that locality received no subsidy from any low-income housing program. Furthermore, the majority of the poorest eligible households receive no assistance even as many households with considerably greater income are assisted (Olsen 2008, table 6). This is not because the poorest households do not want assistance on the terms offered. The waiting lists of most public-housing authorities consist largely of households with extremely low incomes, are very long, and would be even longer if they were open continuously for new applicants (National Low Income Housing Coalition 2004).[1]

It is difficult to reconcile these features with plausible taxpayer preferences. How would taxpayers who want to help low-income households with their housing feel about dividing a fixed amount of assistance between two households that are identical in their eyes? Surely, almost all taxpayers would divide the money equally.

Another strong argument for an entitlement assistance program for the poorest individuals is its effect on homelessness. Homeless people are the poorest of the poor. Virtually all would be eligible for a program that could be funded with the current budget for low-income housing assistance. Even without outreach, an entitlement program of housing assistance for the poorest households has the potential to eliminate homelessness except for brief periods and for the chronically homeless with serious mental illness and substance abuse. Dirk Early and Edgar Olsen (2002) show that greater targeting of low-income housing assistance to the poorest households substantially reduces homelessness.

The results of the recently completed Welfare to Work Voucher Program demonstration provide evidence of the power of regular Section 8 housing vouchers to address homelessness (Abt Associates et al. 2006), and Lisa Dasinger and Richard Speiglman (2007) show that rental subsidies much more modest than regular Section 8 voucher subsidies have a large effect on the number of very low-income people with HIV/AIDS who become homeless.[2] Housing vouchers have also proven extremely effective in getting chronically homeless people off the streets, though this requires outreach, supportive services, and willingness to house people without insisting that they solve their other problems first. Chronically homeless individuals are much more willing to live in a regular apartment than in a homeless shelter, and it is much easier to deliver other services to them when they have a fixed address than when they live on the streets. This is the thrust of the promising Housing First approach (for a summary, see Khadduri 2008; see also chapter 3, this volume). Some of the country's leading experts on homelessness have argued that "the current system of providing temporary shelter in lieu of rental assistance would appear to be relatively inefficient, since it is a less direct method of addressing the affordability gap and since, compared with independent housing, it carries such significant administrative and facility costs in addition to the social costs of disruptive shelter stays on households and children" (Culhane et al. 2007, 26).

The other serious structural shortcoming of the current system, especially from the perspective of helping the homeless, is that it relies excessively on project-based programs that serve about two-thirds of assisted individuals. Evidence indicates that tenant-based housing vouchers have a much lower total cost than any project-based assistance program, when they provide equally good housing (for a brief summary, see Olsen 2008, 9–15; for a description, critical appraisal, and detailed summary of the results, see Olsen 2009). Therefore, it would be possible to serve current recipients equally well—that is, provide them with equally good housing for the same rent—and serve many additional households by shifting resources from project-based to tenant-based assistance. This would involve terminating or phasing out current production programs, disengaging from project-based assistance to existing apartments as soon as current contractual commitments permit, and avoiding new programs of project-based assistance. The savings from these actions would make it possible to create an entitlement housing assistance program serving millions of additional individuals without spending more money, thereby avoiding the inequity of providing assistance to some and denying it to others with the same characteristics. This program would offer assistance to all the poorest individuals.

Subsidized construction is not necessary to prevent homelessness. The number of vacant units in the relevant rent range greatly exceeds the number of homeless households at each point in time. In the third quarter of 2009, the median monthly asking rent of vacant rental units in the United States was $716. About 40 percent of rental units in the country had actual or asking rents between $500 and $800 a month, and more than 12 percent of these units were vacant. Because more than 40 million rental units were either occupied or available for rent, about 2 million units were vacant in this rent range alone (U.S. Census Bureau 2006, 2009a, 2009c). Subsidized construction is not necessary even in tight housing markets because low vacancy rates and high housing prices induce increased unsubsidized construction for the middle and upper ends of the market and the movement of middle- and upper-income households into the newly built units would free existing units for other households.

In housing policy debates, it is sometimes argued that maintaining a unit of public housing is cheaper than providing a voucher to its occupant. This is based on a comparison of the per-unit amounts spent by the Department of Housing and Urban Development (HUD) on housing vouchers and operating and modernization subsidies for public housing. This is not a valid comparison of the cost-effectiveness of the two approaches because it ignores the difference in the desirability of the housing provided and the opportunity cost of the land and structure used to provide public housing. If we provide housing vouchers to public-housing tenants, the money available to fund the vouchers would be not only that which is currently spent on public-housing operating and modernization subsidies but also the money from selling public-housing projects to the highest bidders.

Tenant-based assistance has another major advantage over project-based assistance in addition to providing equally desirable housing at a lower cost. With tenant-based assistance, a recipient can occupy any vacant unit that meets the program's minimum housing standards. The program's standards reflect the interests of taxpayers who want to ensure that low-income households live in housing that meets certain minimum standards. Units that meet the program's standards and are affordable to assisted households differ greatly with respect to their condition, amenities, size, neighborhood, and location. Assisted households whose options are the same under a program of tenant-based assistance are not indifferent to the units available to them. Each family will choose the best available option for its tastes and circumstances. When its circumstances change markedly, the family will move to another unit. Because all these units are adequate as judged by the program's minimum housing standards, further restricting the family's choice serves no public purpose. Project-based assistance forces each family, if it is to receive a subsidy, to live in a particular unit. This greatly restricts recipient choice without serving any public purpose. If the subsidy is the same, it is reasonable to expect recipients of tenant-based assistance to be significantly better off than they would be with project-based assistance.

Long-Term Effects of Replacing the Current System

Replacing the current system of low-income housing assistance with an equally costly entitlement housing voucher program would ensure that all individuals who would otherwise be homeless would be offered substantial housing assistance. Although the main focus of this chapter is on how the transition to the new system could be used to eliminate homelessness within a short period, it is useful to understand the effects of a full transition to the new system.

Olsen and Jeffrey M. Tebbs have estimated the long-term effect on the number of assisted households of various types that would result from replacing a large part of the current system of low-income housing assistance with a specific entitlement voucher program with the same taxpayer cost (for the preliminary results, see Olsen 2008, 25–29). The results of this analysis should be interpreted as the difference between what the situation would be with a continuation of the current system and what it would be after the gradual replacement of the existing system with housing vouchers is completed.

Within a given locality, the Olsen-Tebbs proposed program offers assistance to all the poorest households of each size. Across localities, income limits for eligibility and the maximum subsidy are twice as high in localities where the cost of rental housing with a particular set of characteristics is also twice as high.[3] Virtually everyone who would have been homeless in the absence of this program is eligible for it.

The proposed entitlement program would replace HUD public housing, privately owned subsidized projects, and housing vouchers for families and elderly, one-person households. In 2000, the year of the Olsen-Tebbs data, these three programs served about 3.4 million households of these two types. The analysis assumes that current programs continue to serve single, nonelderly individuals, about 60 percent of whom are disabled. Olsen and Tebbs exclude single, nonelderly individuals from the analysis because they did not have a good way to predict their participation rates in the proposed program.[4] However, it is certainly not the intention to exclude them from the proposed reforms. There is every reason to believe that they would benefit greatly from them.

Olsen and Tebbs estimate that the programs replaced had a direct cost to HUD of about $21 billion in 2000 for serving these 3.4 million households. This is the amount that HUD disbursed in this year to serve these households. With minor exceptions, it does not include the initial development subsidies for public housing or HUD's privately owned subsidized projects.[5] These were disbursed in earlier years.

The proposed entitlement housing voucher program is designed to have the same cost, which eliminates the objection to it on the grounds that it would cost more. This is not to say that more should not be spent on housing assistance. If a more generous entitlement housing voucher program is funded, more people would be served and the people served would receive more help.

The Olsen-Tebbs entitlement voucher program provides a subsidy that is conditional on occupying a unit that meets certain minimum housing standards similar to those of the Section 8 housing choice voucher program. The subsidy is equal to a payment standard minus 30 percent of the recipient's adjusted income, the standard formula in HUD programs.[6] Payment standards are larger for households whose size and composition justify more bedrooms, and they are different in different localities. They are designed so that recipients who occupy units that rent for the local payment standard live in equally good housing in all locations. This is based on a much better index of differences in the rents of identical units than HUD fair market rents (FMR).

The upper income limit for eligibility is the lowest income at which the subsidy is zero. So, unlike the current system, income limits are the same in real terms in all localities. That is, the ratio of the nominal income limit to the housing price index is the same everywhere. In Washington, D.C., in 2000, the upper income limits for the proposed program analyzed ranged from about $17,500 a year for households entitled to an efficiency apartment to almost $50,000 for those entitled to eight bedrooms. For households entitled to two bedrooms, it was about $19,500.

The predicted participation rate in the entitlement program for households of each type is based on experience from the only entitlement housing assistance program that has been operated in the United States—namely, the Housing Assistance Supply Experiment (for a brief account, see Olsen 2003, 424–27; for a more detailed account, see Lowry 1983). Specifically, it is based on an estimated logit equation explaining participation among eligible households in terms of the generosity of the voucher, household size and type, minority status, and other variables. In using this equation to predict participation rates, we adjusted the generosity of the subsidy for differences in prices across time and place.

The poorest 15 percent of households would be eligible for the proposed entitlement housing voucher program. This was slightly higher than the official poverty rate at the time because the income limits exceeded the poverty threshold in many places. However, the individuals eligible for the proposed entitlement housing voucher program are a much better approximation of the poorest individuals in the country than those categorized as poor based on the official poverty line because, unlike the official poverty line, the income limits in the proposed program are adjusted for geographical price differences. It is safe to say that almost all homeless people would be eligible for the proposed entitlement program if it were expanded, as it should be, to include single, nonelderly individuals.

Our results indicate that the entitlement housing voucher program would serve 2.4 million additional households, a 69 percent increase over the number currently served. More than 1 million of these households would be in the lowest real-income decile. The proposed entitlement program would not only serve many more households in total than the HUD programs that would be replaced but also more households of each major type—white, black, and Hispanic; elderly and nonelderly; and metropolitan and nonmetropolitan areas.

The study does not predict what the increase would be for single, nonelderly people if the money devoted to them under current HUD programs were shifted to an entitlement housing voucher program. However, based on the cited results, it is reasonable to believe that the increase would be substantial.

Concerns About Relying on Tenant-Based Housing Assistance

Before considering transitional reforms of the current system, common concerns about the effectiveness of housing vouchers in certain market conditions and for serving certain types of households are worth addressing.

Some homeless people will encounter difficulties in obtaining or using vouchers under current law because of HUD eligibility rules and landlord concerns related to criminal activity, alcohol abuse, rent nonpayment, bad credit histories, and past evictions. However, they are likely to fare better under the voucher program than programs of project-based assistance.

Owners of private HUD-subsidized projects are allowed to reject tenants for these reasons and are not paid more to deal with troublesome tenants. Because these projects offer housing at below-market rents, many eligible individuals and families are eager to occupy their available units. Most landlords choose the tenants who are expected to be the least troublesome. This is surely an important reason why the majority of people served by these programs are elderly. For example, about 60 percent of the households in the HUD Section 8 New Construction and Substantial Rehabilitation Program are elderly. By statute, public-housing authorities must deny admission to public housing to individuals who have committed certain types of crimes and whose abuse of alcohol or drugs would interfere with the health, safety, or right to peaceful enjoyment of the premises by other residents (HUD 2003, 28, 48–60). Jill Khadduri presents evidence in chapter 4 of this volume that strongly suggests that the landlords of privately owned subsidized projects and public-housing authorities are disinclined to serve single, nonelderly individuals, with the exception of the physically disabled, in their housing projects.

Most public-housing authorities apply less stringent standards for receipt of housing vouchers than for occupancy in public-housing units. They must deny voucher assistance for some of the aforementioned reasons, and may deny it for other reasons, but the authorities usually leave it to owners to decide on the tenant's suitability in most respects (HUD 2001, 5.35–40, 8.20–21). Organizations that help homeless people with past behavior that makes them unattractive tenants can play an important role in gaining landlord acceptance of these potential voucher recipients by promising to continue to work with them to solve their problems, in addition to helping them with the application process and finding a unit.

It is often argued that the construction of housing projects should be subsidized because some types of individuals and families have difficulties using housing vouchers, for example, and most important for present purposes, nonelderly persons with disabilities. In fact, the tenant-based voucher program serves many people of this type. According to the HUD Picture of Subsidized Households 2000 (the latest available), about 30 percent of households with Section 8 housing vouchers had a household head or a spouse under the age of sixty-two with a disability compared with 29 percent for public housing and 29 percent for HUD's privately owned subsidized projects.

It has also been argued that economies of scale, in providing nonhousing services to the disabled, justify project-based housing assistance. Although the magnitude of these scale economies has not been studied, their existence is beyond doubt. They explain the existence of housing combined with assisted care in the unsubsidized market.

This does not, however, argue for project-based housing assistance because these economies can be achieved under a system of tenant-based housing assistance. To see why, consider the analogy of nursing homes. The scale economies involved in housing disabled people are surely smaller than those involved in providing services in nursing homes. Medicaid subsidizes low-income individuals to live in nursing homes, but not by subsidizing the construction of such facilities and requiring recipients to live in particular nursing homes to receive assistance. Instead, eligible individuals can choose any nursing home that meets the program's minimum standards for care and charges less than the program's maximum payment. Private business firms and not-for-profit organizations have built nursing homes in response to the demand created by this subsidy. A similar approach could be used to provide low-income housing assistance to individuals with special needs if congregate living is a policy that the government wants to encourage. These individuals could be offered more generous vouchers on the condition that they live in a building that provides the desired extra services. As is the case under current housing programs that provide extra services, the extra subsidy would not have to be enough to pay for them. Under the HUD Section 202 Supportive Housing for the Elderly Program, project owners are required to provide certain supportive services. However, the program places an upper limit of $15 per unit per month on the amount of the HUD subsidy and standard tenant rent that can be used for supportive services. The bulk of the money for supportive services comes from other public and private sources. HUD's Section 811 Supportive Housing for Persons with Disabilities is a similar program. As in these programs, the purpose of the more generous voucher subsidy is to pay for the staff needed to arrange and maintain the subsidies for supportive services.

Almost all housing policy analysts agree that housing vouchers work well in housing markets with high vacancy rates. However, some believe that subsidized construction is necessary to provide housing to additional recipients in the tightest housing markets. Even though the national rental vacancy rate is currently at an extraordinarily high level, it is important to understand why housing vouchers work well in even the tightest housing markets because, even today, some markets have low vacancy rates. Across the largest seventy-five metropolitan areas, the rental vacancy rate varied from 4.2 percent in Oxnard–Thousand Oaks–Ventura, California, to 21.9 percent in Orlando, Florida, with a median of 9.8 percent (U.S. Census Bureau 2009b). Furthermore, the national vacancy rate will not remain at its current high level indefinitely. High vacancy rates and depressed housing prices lead to unsubsidized construction below the expected growth in the number of households.

Some are concerned that tenant-based assistance will not work well in markets with the lowest vacancy rates because these markets do not have enough affordable vacant apartments that meet minimum housing standards to house all families that are offered vouchers. In fact, the number of vacant apartments that meet minimum housing standards and are affordable to voucher recipients need not exceed the number of available new and recycled vouchers in order to use all available vouchers. Many families offered vouchers already occupy apartments meeting the program's standards. We do not need vacant apartments for these families. They can participate without moving. Other families who are offered vouchers live in housing that does not meet Section 8 standards. These apartments can be repaired to meet the standards. Similarly, vacant apartments that do not initially meet the program's standards can be upgraded to meet them. In short, a tenant-based voucher program increases the supply of apartments that meet minimum housing standards even without stimulating the construction of new units.

The evidence from the tenant-based Section 8 Certificate and Voucher Programs illustrates these general points. One detailed analysis is based on data from a national random sample of thirty-three public-housing authorities in 1993 (Kennedy and Finkel 1994). Thirty percent of all recipients outside of New York City continued to live in the apartments that they occupied prior to participating in the program.[7] Forty-one percent of these apartments already met the program's standards and 59 percent were repaired to meet the standards. About 70 percent of all recipients outside of New York City moved to a new unit. About 48 percent of these apartments were repaired to meet the program's standards. The rest moved to vacant apartments that already met the standards. The apartments occupied by about half of the families that received certificates and vouchers outside New York City during this period were therefore repaired to meet the program's standards. The mentioned sources contain similar results for New York City. In this city, only 31 percent of the apartments occupied by recipients had to be repaired to meet the program's standards.

The Housing Assistance Supply Experiment of the Experimental Housing Allowance Program provides additional evidence on the ability of tenant-based vouchers to increase the supply of apartments that meet minimum housing standards even in tight housing markets. The supply experiment involved operating an entitlement housing allowance program for ten years in St. Joseph County, Indiana, which contains South Bend, and Brown County, Wisconsin, which contains Green Bay. About 20 percent of the families in the two counties were eligible to receive assistance (Lowry 1983). These sites were chosen to differ greatly in their vacancy rates to better determine whether the outcomes of an entitlement housing allowance program depend a great deal on this factor. At the outset of the experiment, the vacancy rates of Brown and St. Joseph counties were 5.1 percent and 10.6 percent respectively (Lowry 1983). In 2000, only 26 percent of the seventy-five largest metropolitan areas had vacancy rates less than that of Brown County, and only 20 percent had vacancy rates greater than that of St. Joseph County. Contrary to widely held expectations, the participation rate differed little between the two sites. Indeed, it was higher in the locality with the lower vacancy rate (Lowry 1983).

Data for analysis were collected during the first five years of the experiment in each site. During that period, about 11,000 dwellings were repaired or improved to meet program standards entirely in response to tenant-based assistance and about 5,000 families improved their housing by moving into apartments already meeting these standards (Lowry 1983). The dwelling improvements meant more than a 9 percent increase in the supply of apartments that meet minimum housing standards. Tenant-based assistance alone produced a greater percentage increase in the supply of adequate housing in these localities in five years than all of the federal government's production programs for low-income families have produced in the past sixty-five years (Cutts and Olsen 2002). The annual cost per household was less than $4,000 in today's prices.

Some argue that the low success rates of the Section 8 housing voucher program in areas with low vacancy rates imply that the available vouchers cannot be used in these areas and hence new construction must be subsidized to serve additional low-income households. It is important to distinguish, however, between a housing authority's voucher success rate and its voucher utilization rate. An authority's success rate is the percentage of the families authorized to search for a unit that succeed in finding a unit that meets the program's standards within the housing authority's time limit. Its use rate is the percentage of all vouchers in use.

An authority's success rate depends on many factors, including the local vacancy rate.[8] One careful study of success rates indicates that, among localities that are the same with respect to other factors, those with the lowest vacancy rates have the lowest success rates (Kennedy and Finkel 1994). Obviously, it is more difficult to locate a suitable unit when the vacancy rate is low. However, housing-market tightness does not explain most of the variation in success rates. Success rates also vary with family characteristics and program parameters. For example, families who are eligible for larger subsidies due to lower incomes or higher payment standards have a higher success rate, presumably because they have more incentive to find a unit meeting the program's standards.

For many years, public-housing authorities have overissued vouchers and thereby achieved high use rates despite low success rates. By overissuing vouchers early in the year and adjusting the recycling of vouchers returned by families who leave the program late in the year, housing authorities come close to using their voucher budget. Their ability to use the money allocated to them is further enhanced by federal regulations that allow them to exceed their voucher budgets in a given year by modest amounts using their reserves and borrowing against the following year's allotment. According to the HUD Fiscal Year 2004 Performance and Accountability Report, the voucher use rate was 98.5 percent that year.[9]

Although it is true that some families who are offered vouchers do not find housing that suits them and meets the program's standards within their housing authority's time limits, other eligible families in the same locality use these vouchers. This indicates clearly that the problem is not a lack of vacant apartments that meet program standards and are affordable to voucher recipients, or a lack of apartments whose landlords are willing to upgrade them to meet program standards. In the tightest housing markets, these apartments are more difficult to locate. Unsubsidized families also have trouble locating apartments in tight housing markets.

The real issue is not whether tenant-based vouchers can be used in all market conditions but whether it would be better to subsidize new construction in tight housing markets. The Government Accountability Office (2002, 19–20) indicates that tenant-based vouchers are more costeffective than production programs even in markets with low vacancy rates. Another key question is which type of assistance gets eligible families into satisfactory housing faster. If the choice is between authorizing additional vouchers or additional units under any construction program, the answer is clear. Tenant-based vouchers get families into satisfactory housing much faster than any construction program even in the tightest housing markets. By overissuing vouchers, housing agencies can put all their vouchers to use in less than a year in any market conditions. No production program can hope to match this speed.

Transitional Reforms of Mainstream Housing Programs

Replacing the current system of low-income housing assistance with an equally costly entitlement housing voucher program would ensure that all households that would otherwise be homeless would be offered substantial housing assistance. The current system fails to achieve this outcome because it includes many programs that are not cost-effective and serves many households at little risk of becoming homeless. About 15 percent of all households in the United States have extremely low incomes according to HUD terminology (HUD 2009b). This is the same as the percentage eligible for the Olsen-Tebbs entitlement voucher program. Few households outside this group become homeless. HUD's low-income housing programs serve many households with higher incomes—about 28 percent of those in public-housing projects or receiving tenant-based Section 8 housing vouchers and a higher percentage in privately owned HUD-subsidized projects (HUD 2009a). The Low Income Housing Tax Credit (LIHTC), the second largest and fastest-growing program, is much worse in this regard. In the early 1990s, only 39 percent of households in tax-credit projects had extremely low incomes (U.S. General Accounting Office [GAO] 1997, 136), and the owners of tax-credit projects received project-based or tenant-based Section 8 assistance on behalf of the overwhelming majority of these households.[10] Only 19 percent of the households without Section 8 assistance were in this poorest group (GAO 1997, 147). Occupants of units without Section 8 assistance had more than twice the average income of the occupants of units with this assistance (GAO 1997, 146). Recent data on the incomes of residents of tax-credit projects are not available. However, the National Council of State Housing Agencies reports that only 4 percent of the tax-credit units authorized in 2004 were targeted to extremely low-income households, and only 2 percent to homeless people (2005, 79–81).

The current system of low-income housing assistance cannot be replaced with an equally costly entitlement housing voucher program overnight. A politically feasible reform would involve a transition that does not harm, or that even benefits, the overwhelming majority of current recipients of low-income housing assistance. The key to rapidly expanding assistance to the homeless from mainstream programs is a transition that diverts money from cost-ineffective to cost-effective programs, thereby increasing the number of households served, and focuses assistance on the poorest eligible households at the expense of eligible households with higher incomes.

An obvious transitional reform is to tighten HUD income-targeting rules. The Quality Housing and Work Responsibility Act of 1998 required that at least 75 percent of new recipients of tenant-based housing vouchers have extremely low incomes—that is, incomes less than limits based on 30 percent of the local median.[11] This proportion could be increased, possibly to 100 percent of new recipients. To achieve the purpose of the tighter targeting, housing authorities should be required to reopen their waiting lists when no households with extremely low incomes remain on the list. Housing authorities often close their waiting lists to new applicants and could thwart the goal of the tighter income targeting by keeping the lists closed for long periods.

Because of concerns about concentrating large numbers of the poorest households in projects, the 1998 act set much lower targeting standards for HUD project-based assistance. Only 40 percent of new recipients of housing projects must have extremely low incomes. In my view, Congress is unlikely to change this targeting rule. Furthermore, income-targeting rules do not apply to the LIHTC program.

The greater opportunity for eliminating homelessness through reforms of project-based housing assistance involves providing less assistance through publicly and privately owned projects. The money saved could be diverted to the voucher program better targeted to the poorest households and hence the households most likely to become homeless in the absence of assistance.

One proposal to phase out project-based assistance is that contracts with the owners of private subsidized projects not be renewed. The initial agreements that led to the building or substantial rehabilitation of these projects called for their owners to provide housing that met certain standards to households with particular characteristics at certain rents for a specified number of years. At the end of the use agreement, the government must decide on the terms of the new agreement, and the private parties must decide whether to participate on these terms. A substantial number of projects have come to the end of their use agreement in recent years, and many more will do so over the next decade. When use agreements are not renewed, current occupants are provided with other housing assistance, usually tenant-based vouchers.

Up to this point, housing policy has leaned heavily toward providing owners with enough of a subsidy to induce them to continue to serve the low-income households in their projects. This has been the primary goal of the Section 8 Loan Management Set-Aside, the preservation incentives, and the Mark-to-Market program (Abt Associates et al. 2004, 1–2). We should reverse course, not renew any contracts with owners, and instead give portable vouchers to project tenants, as is current practice when owners decide to leave the program. Because of the excessive cost of subsidizing these projects, this approach will free money to serve additional households, and when current occupants leave the program, the new households that have been offered recycled vouchers will have to meet the tighter income-targeting rules of the voucher program.

It is often argued that the failure to renew use agreements on privately owned subsidized projects reduces the number of affordable housing units. Because the occupants of these projects are offered portable vouchers, this objection is misguided. Terminating use agreements does not change the number of households or the number of dwelling units. It has no effect on the overall vacancy rate. When use agreements are extended, the only unit that is made affordable to an assisted family living in the project is its current unit. If that family is offered a portable voucher, many units become affordable.

Another transitional proposal to benefit the homeless is to stop subsidizing the construction of additional public or private projects. This involves terminating or phasing out current production programs and avoiding new ones. Such a move would free money to expand the better targeted housing voucher program.

The Low Income Housing Tax Credit is the largest active production program and subsidizes more units than all the other active production programs combined. The taxpayer cost of all the subsidies associated with its projects was about $10 billion in 2006. This program is excessively costly for the housing provided, and it serves relatively few extremely low-income households who do not also have Section 8 project-based or tenant-based assistance. A modest reform is to rescind the indexing of the tax credit for inflation. This would lead to a gradual reduction in the number of units produced under this program over time. The savings could be channeled to the housing choice voucher program, which is more cost-effective and more heavily targeted to the poorest people.

Similar remarks apply to other active production programs. For example, no additional money should be allocated to HOPE VI except possibly for demolition. This has been HUD's major production program over the past decade. It is an initiative within the public-housing program under which some of the worst public-housing projects have been torn down and replaced by new housing built at lower density on the same site. It is an improvement over traditional public housing in that it avoids concentrating the poorest families at high densities in projects. It is also, however, highly cost ineffective compared with tenant-based vouchers that also avoid these concentrations (U.S. Government Accountability Office 2001, 2002). Therefore, the money that would have been spent on HOPE VI is better allocated to the much more cost-effective housing choice voucher program. This shift in the budget for housing assistance would allow us to provide all the families who would have lived in HOPE VI projects with rental units that meet minimum housing standards and would allow us to assist tens of thousands of other families who would otherwise live in deplorable conditions.

Finally, production programs should stop. Launching a new construction program is particularly inappropriate when rental vacancy rates are at historically high levels. In the third quarter of 2009, median rent was $716 per month, and the rental vacancy rate exceeded 12 percent in every $100 rent range between $400 and $1,000 (U.S. Census Bureau 2006, 2009c). However, as explained earlier, housing vouchers outperform subsidized construction programs even in the tightest markets. Any additional money for housing assistance should be used to expand the housing choice voucher program that is more cost-effective and better targeted to the poorest households.

A final transitional reform that would have a significant benefit for the homeless involves a simple change in the housing choice voucher program—namely, offering *new* recipients smaller subsidies in the interest of serving more households. The simplest reform would reduce the program's payment standard.

A common objection to this proposal is that no one would be able to find housing that meets the program's standards with the lower subsidies. This objection is logically flawed. With current subsidy levels, many more people want to participate than can be served with the existing budget (for information on voucher waiting lists, see HUD 2009c). If we reduce subsidy levels slightly, more people will still want to participate than can be served. If we decrease the subsidy levels so much that no one wants to participate, we have decreased them more than the proposed amounts.

A more sophisticated argument against the preceding proposal is that the poorest households will be unable to participate. The proposal calls for reducing the guarantee under the voucher program, called the payment standard, which is the subsidy received by a household with no income. If the payment standard is less than the rent required to occupy a unit that meets the program's minimum housing standards, then a household whose income and assistance from other sources is just enough to buy subsistence quantities of other goods would be unable to participate.

Previous studies have shown that a considerable reduction in the payment standard could occur without precluding participation by the poorest of the poor. Olsen and William Reeder (1983) and Cutts and Olsen (2002) find that the payment standard exceeds the market rent of units just meeting the program's minimum housing standards in all of the many metropolitan areas and bedroom configurations (one or two bedroom, for example) studied. The median excess varied between 33 to 80 percent between 1975 and 1993. Although refined estimates have not been made with more recent data, a rough estimate is that the median excess over all combinations of metropolitan area and number of bedrooms was 68 percent in 2001 (Cutts and Olsen 2002, 224–25). As mentioned earlier, Dasinger and Speiglman (2007) have shown that rental subsidies much more modest than regular Section 8 voucher subsidies have a large effect on the number of very low-income people with HIV/AIDS who become homeless.

If the preceding proposal leads to a particularly low participation rate by the poorest households, the rate could be counteracted by a smaller reduction in the payment standard combined with an increase in the fraction of adjusted income that tenants are expected to contribute to their rent. This tactic would result in a smaller decrease in the subsidies offered to the poorest households and a larger decrease for the eligible households with the largest income. For a given program budget, this would yield a higher participation rate by the poorest of the poor and a lower participation rate by other eligible households.

Conclusion

The failure to offer assistance to all individuals who become homeless is a fundamental failure of the current system of low-income housing assistance. But reforming the current system by replacing it with an equally costly entitlement housing voucher program would ensure that housing assistance is available to all those who would otherwise be homeless.

Because more than 600,000 households give up their housing assistance each year, the transition to an entitlement housing voucher program could be structured to eliminate homelessness within a short time without reducing benefits for current recipients of low-income household assistance or spending more money. Targeting recycled and new assistance to the poorest individuals would ensure that housing assistance is available to everyone who would otherwise be homeless.

The reforms proposed in this chapter would concentrate more assistance on the poorest individuals and thereby disproportionately benefit those who are at the highest risk of becoming homeless. Adopting all the transitional reforms would provide the long-term housing assistance needed to serve all homeless households without any increase in spending and leave more of the budgets of programs that are targeted to homeless people for solving their other problems.

Notes

1. This information is in the annual plans that public-housing authorities submit to the U.S. Department of Housing and Urban Development (HUD) each year (see HUD 2009c).
2. In the last year of the study, the maximum housing subsidy was $225 a month in Alameda County, California, for a single person entitled to a one-bedroom unit. The maximum subsidy for a household of this type under the Section 8 housing choice voucher program was $921 a month.
3. It has been suggested that low-income housing assistance be limited to low-income households with what HUD calls worst-case housing needs. These are households with incomes less than limits that are based on 50 percent of the local median income and that live in housing classified as severely inadequate or spend more than half their income on housing. The rationale for limiting assistance to this subset of the poorest households is unclear. Among households of the same size and composition with the same income living in the same area, some occupy units that do not meet the minimum housing standards specified. These households devote small fractions of their income to housing or occupy units that are better in other respects. Others occupy better housing in better neighborhoods by devoting more than 50 percent of their income to housing. Why should we give preferential treatment to these households compared with other households in the same economic circumstances? The reason for giving a preference for housing subsidies to families that devote the largest fraction of their income to

housing is especially puzzling. To the best of my knowledge, no evidence supports the proposition that among housed families with the same income and demographic characteristics living in the same housing market, those who spend the largest fractions of their incomes on housing are the most likely to become homeless. There is no clear theoretical reason to think that this correlation should be found. Much economic theory suggests that the relationship should be the opposite. Among households of the same size with the same income, those who spend the largest fraction of their income on housing may have the strongest preference for housing versus other goods, or the greatest accumulation of financial assets.

4. Because many homeless people are single, nonelderly households, it is important to find a credible method for predicting their participation in an entitlement housing voucher program. For people who would be homeless in the absence of the entitlement program, this will depend heavily on the assistance that they receive in getting assistance and finding an apartment.

5. The exceptions are disbursements to fund some HOPE VI projects and a few newly built Section 202 or 811 projects.

6. Ignoring exceptions, the payment standard in the Section 8 certificate and voucher programs has been the HUD fair market rent (FMR). HUD's current income adjustments were used to the extent possible with the data available.

7. The authors analyzed New York City separately from the other housing authorities.

8. Voucher success rates have varied from place to place and time to time (Finkel and Buron 2001). In the mid-1980s, the national average was 68 percent. In 1993 it was 81 percent, and in 2000, 69 percent. In each period, it varied considerably across the areas in the sample.

9. Although housing authorities could achieve a voucher use rate close to 100 percent each year by adjusting the extent to which they overissue vouchers, they have not always done so. Like most people, directors of housing authorities respond to incentives and disincentives. In recent years, they have faced disincentives that have led to lower voucher use rates. Barbara Sard and Martha Coven (2006) analyze the effect of proposed changes in federal regulations that are intended to induce housing authorities to use all their vouchers.

10. Many tax-credit projects involve renovations of Section 8 projects.

11. Specifically, four-person households must have incomes less than 30 percent of the local median to be in the targeted group. The limits are lower for smaller families and higher for larger families and are obtained by multiplying the four-person limit in the locality by nationally uniform constants.

References

Abt Associates Inc., Joanne Anderson, Econometrica Inc., Meryl Finkel, Charles Hanson, Richard Hilton, Jill Khadduri, Ken Lam, and Michelle Wood. 2004. *Evaluation of the Mark-to-Market Program.* Washington: U.S. Department of Housing and Urban Development, Office of Policy Development and Research.

Abt Associates, Gregory Mills, Daniel Gubits, Larry Orr, David Long, Judie Feins, Bulbul Kaul, Michelle Woods, Amy Jones and Associates, Cloudburst Consulting, and the QED Group. 2006. *Effects of Housing Vouchers on Welfare Families.*

Washington: U.S. Department of Housing and Urban Development, Office of Policy Development and Research.

Burt, Martha, Laudan Y. Aron, Edgar Lee, and Jesse Valante. 2001. *Helping America's Homeless: Emergency Shelter or Affordable Housing?* Washington, D.C.: Urban Institute Press.

Culhane, Dennis P., Stephen Metraux, Jung Min Park, Maryanne Schretzman, and Jesse Valante. 2007. "Testing a Typology of Family Homelessness Based on Patterns of Public Shelter Utilization in Four U.S. Jurisdictions: Implications for Policy and Program Planning." *Housing Policy Debate* 18(1): 1–28.

Cutts, Amy Crews, and Edgar O. Olsen. 2002. "Are Section 8 Housing Subsidies Too High?" *Journal of Housing Economics* 11(3): 214–43.

Dasinger, Lisa K., and Richard Speiglman. 2007. "Homelessness Prevention: The Effect of a Shallow Rent Subsidy on Housing Outcomes Among People with HIV or AIDS," *AIDS and Behavior* 11(Supp 2): S128–39.

Early, Dirk W., and Edgar O. Olsen. 2002. "Subsidized Housing, Emergency Shelters, and Homelessness: An Empirical Investigation Using Data from the 1990 Census." *Advances in Economic Analysis & Policy* 2(1): 1–34.

Finkel, Meryl, and Larry Buron. 2001. *Study on Section 8 Voucher Success Rates, vol. 1: Quantitative Study of Success Rates in Metropolitan Areas.* Washington: U.S. Department of Housing and Urban Development, Office of Policy Development and Research.

Kennedy, Stephen D. and Meryl Finkel. 1994. *Section 8 Rental Voucher and Rental Certificate Utilization Study.* Washington: U.S. Department of Housing and Urban Development, Office of Policy Development and Research.

Khadduri, Jill. 2008. "Housing Vouchers Are Critical for Ending Family Homelessness." Washington, D.C.: Homelessness Research Institute, National Alliance to End Homelessness.

Khadduri, Jill, and Raymond J. Struyk. 1982. "Housing Vouchers for the Poor." *Journal of Policy Analysis and Management* 1(Winter): 196–208.

Lowry, Ira S. 1983. *Experimenting with Housing Allowances: The Final Report of the Housing Assistance Supply Experiment.* Cambridge, Mass.: Oelgeschlager, Gunn & Hain.

National Council of State Housing Agencies. 2005. *State HFA Factbook: 2004 NCSHA Annual Survey Results.* Washington: National Council of State Housing Agencies.

National Low Income Housing Coalition. 2004. "A Look at Waiting Lists: What Can We Learn from the HUD Approved Annual Plans?" NLIHC Research Note #04–03. Washington, D.C.: National Low Income Housing Coalition.

Olsen, Edgar O. 1982. "Housing Policy and the Forgotten Taxpayer." *Public Interest* 66(Winter): 97–109.

———. 2003. "Housing Programs for Low-Income Households." In *Means-Tested Transfer Programs in the U.S.*, edited by Robert Moffitt. Chicago: University of Chicago Press.

———. 2008. "Getting More from Low-Income Housing Assistance." *Hamilton Project* discussion paper 2008–13. Washington, D.C.: Brookings Institution. Available at: http://www.brookings.edu/~/media/Files/rc/papers/2008/0923_housing_olsen/0923_housing_olsen.pdf (accessed April 28, 2010).

———. 2009. "The Cost-Effectiveness of Alternative Methods of Delivering Housing Subsidies." Presented at the Thirty-First Annual APPAM Research

Conference. Washington, D.C. (November 5–7, 2009). Available at: http://www.virginia.edu/economics/Workshops/papers/olsen/CESurvey2009.pdf (accessed February 18, 2010).

Olsen, Edgar O., and William Reeder. 1983. "Misdirected Rental Subsidies." *Journal of Policy Analysis and Management* 2(Summer): 614–20.

Quigley, John M. 2008. "Just Suppose: Housing Subsidies for Low-Income Renters." In *Revisiting Rental Housing: Policies, Programs, and Priorities,* edited by Nicolas P. Retsinas and Eric Belsky. Washington, D.C.: Brookings Institution Press.

Sard, Barbara, and Martha Coven. 2006. "Fixing the Housing Voucher Formula: A No-Cost Way to Strengthen the Section 8 Program." Washington, D.C.: Center on Budget and Policy Priorities. Available at: http://www.cbpp.org/files/11-1-06hous.pdf (accessed February 18, 2010).

U.S. Census Bureau. 2006. "Median Asking Rent and Sales Price of the U.S. and Regions: 1988 to Present." Housing Vacancies and Homeownership (CPS/HVS), Historical Table 11A. Available at: http://www.census.gov/hhes/www/housing/hvs/historic (accessed January 12, 2010).

———. 2009a. "Estimates of the Housing Inventory." Housing Vacancies and Homeownership (CPS/HVS), Third Quarter, Detailed Table 4. Available at: http://www.census.gov/hhes/www/housing/hvs/qtr309/q309tab4.html (accessed February 18, 2010).

———. 2009b. "Rental Vacancy Rates for the 75 Largest Metropolitan Areas: 2005–2008." Housing Vacancies and Homeownership (CPS/HVS), Annual Statistics 2008 Table 6. Available at: http://www.census.gov/hhes/www/housing/hvs/annual08/ann08t6.xls (accessed February 18, 2010).

———. 2009c. "Vacancy Rates by Selected Characteristic." Housing Vacancies and Homeownership (CPS/HVS), Third Quarter, Detailed Table 3. Available at: http://www.census.gov/hhes/www/housing/hvs/qtr309/q309tab3.html (accessed February 18, 2010).

U.S. Department of Housing and Urban Development (HUD). 1995. *HUD Reinvention: From Blueprint to Action.* Washington: Government Printing Office.

———. 2001. *Housing Choice Voucher Program Guidebook.* Publication 7420.10G, Washington: Government Printing Office. Available at: http://www.hud.gov/offices/pih/programs/hcv/forms/guidebook.cfm (accessed February 18, 2010).

———. 2003. *Public Housing Occupancy Guidebook.* Washington: Government Printing Office. Available at: http://www.hud.gov/offices/pih/programs/ph/rhiip/phguidebook.cfm (accessed February 18, 2010).

———. 2009a. "Form-50058 Tenant Reporting: Resident Characteristics Report (RCR)." Public and Indian Housing, Public Information Center (PIC). Available at: http://www.hud.gov/offices/pih/systems/pic/50058/rcr/index.cfm (accessed February 18, 2020).

———. 2009b. "Housing Affordability Data System." Office of Policy Development and Research. Available at: http://www.huduser.org/portal/datasets/hads/hads.html (accessed February 18, 2010).

———. 2009c. "Public Housing Agency (PHA) Plans." Public and Indian Housing, Public Information Center (PIC). Available at: http://www.hud.gov/offices/pih/pha (accessed February 18, 2010).

U.S. General Accounting Office (GAO). 1997. *Tax Credits: Opportunities to Improve Oversight of the Low-Income Housing Program*. GGD/RCED-97-55. Washington: Government Printing Office.

U.S. Government Accountability Office (GAO). 2001. *Federal Housing Programs: What They Cost and What They Provide*. GAO-01-901R. Washington: Government Printing Office.

———. 2002. *Federal Housing Assistance: Comparing the Characteristics and Costs of Housing Programs*. GAO-02-76. Washington: Government Printing Office.

Weicher, John. 1997. *Privatizing Subsidized Housing*. Washington, D.C.: American Enterprise Institute for Public Policy Research.

Chapter 6

Housing Market Regulation and Homelessness

STEVEN RAPHAEL

Local housing markets throughout the United States are subject to a host of regulations that tend to increase the cost of housing. Minimum lot-size requirements, quality standards, density restrictions, and other such municipally imposed regulation tend to limit the overall stock of available housing, increase average as well as minimum quality, and shift the overall distribution of housing prices toward higher levels. For the lowest income households, such factors will increase the proportion of household resources that one would need to devote toward housing. For the poorest of the poor, excessive regulation may push the price of even the minimum-quality units beyond the level of household income. To the extent that homelessness is in part driven by local housing affordability, local regulatory practices may be an important contributor to homelessness in the United States.

Of course, the importance of regulation will depend on the degrees to which local regulatory stringency increases housing costs and high housing costs affect homelessness. Although housing is definitely more expensive in more regulated local markets, it is not immediately obvious that regulation is the causal source of higher prices. Limited developable land and disproportionate economic growth may coincide with more local regulation, creating the impression of an impact of regulation on local housing markets. One thus needs to consider the specific mechanisms through which local regulation affects housing costs as well as the available empirical evidence in investigating this linkage.

In addition, clearly there are personal determinants of the individual risk of experiencing homelessness that lie outside the realm of housing economics. The incidence of severe mental illness, substance abuse, and domestic abuse is relatively high among the homeless. Many might argue that these underlying personal issues are the more important causes of homelessness in the United States and that housing affordability plays only a secondary role. Thus, the importance of local regulation of housing market in determining homelessness depends on the relative importance of housing affordability.

Housing Affordability and Homelessness

Homelessness is an extremely complex social problem with root causes in both the personal traits of those most likely at risk of a spell of homelessness and the institutional factors that influence the housing options available to the poorest of the poor. The incidence of substance abuse, mental illness, extreme poverty, and income insecurity is certainly higher among those who experience homelessness than among those who do not. Moreover, since the mid-twentieth century, the total resources devoted to inpatient treatment of the severely mentally ill have declined dramatically, with the absolute numbers institutionalized in state or county mental hospitals declining from more than half a million in the 1950s to less than 70,000 today (Raphael and Stoll 2008). Certainly, being mentally ill and a substance abuser elevates the risk of experiencing homelessness in the United States.

Nonetheless, many individuals and families among those who experience homelessness are neither substance abusers nor severely mentally ill. These individuals tend to be extremely poor, are disproportionately from a minority group, and generally have difficulty affording the lowest-quality housing units offered by their local housing markets. As we know from the seminal work of Dennis Culhane and his colleagues (1999) and the 2008 *Third Annual Homeless Assessment Report* (AHAR) *to Congress* (U.S. Department of Housing and Urban Development 2008), the proportion of the population experiencing homelessness over the course of a year is two to three times single-night counts. This suggests that homelessness is much broader and perhaps more common than the lower one-night counts suggest. Moreover, point-in-time snapshots tend to disproportionately capture those who experience long spells, those who in turn are arguably more likely to be chronically homeless and have particularly high incidence of mental illness and substance abuse problems. Hence point-in-time empirical snapshots may lead us to overemphasize the primacy of personal problems in determining homelessness.

The potential theoretical connection between homelessness and housing prices is straightforward. To the extent that minimum-quality housing is either priced such that it would consume an extremely high proportion of one's income or that it comes at a price that exceeds one's income, a person may become homeless. When one can afford the minimum-quality housing unit but have little income left over for all else (such as food, clothing, and the like), one might rationally choose to forgo conventional housing and try one's luck doubling up with relatives and friends or temporarily using a city's shelter system. In the latter case, where the price of the minimum-quality unit exceeds income, homelessness is the only option. In either case, homelessness results from decisionmaking that is subject to extreme income constraints and perhaps minimum-quality thresholds in the housing offered in private markets.

A key puzzle in understanding the causes of homelessness lies in understanding why it increased so much during the 1980s and the apparent stability at the higher levels since the early 1990s. Brendan O'Flaherty (1995, 1996) offers a theoretical model of housing markets that, when combined with the increase in income inequality commencing in the early 1980s, provides insight into the changing incidence of homelessness. His argument is built around a model of housing filtering. New housing construction occurs above a certain quality threshold, and housing units filter down through the quality hierarchy and, in turn, the rent distribution through depreciation. Below a minimum quality, rents do not justify maintenance costs, leading to abandonment by landlords or conversion of units to other uses. Most relevant to our discussion later on, the rate at which housing filters down through the quality distribution will depend on new construction rates at higher quality levels. With abundant new housing at higher levels, higher-income households will be more likely to abandon older housing that then filters down to lower-income households. Thus the supply of lower-cost affordable housing is linked dynamically to the supply of higher-quality housing through filtering and depreciation.

Changes in the distribution of income affect the level of homelessness through the price of lowest-quality housing. An increase in income inequality around a stable mean, corresponding roughly to the course of incomes during the 1980s in the United States, reduces the demand for middle-quality housing and increases the demand for low-quality housing. Households whose incomes have declined reduce their demand for housing, enter the lower-quality housing market, and bid up prices at the bottom of the market. Higher rents for the lowest-quality housing imply a higher cutoff-income level below which homelessness is likely to result.

Empirically, point-in-time counts of the incidence of homelessness as well as period-prevalence counts are generally higher in regions of the country where housing is more expensive (see, for example, the number of studies cited in O'Flaherty 2004). John Quigley, Steven Raphael, and Eugene Smolensky (2001) demonstrate this positive association using several data sets that count the homeless during the mid-1990s and earlier. Using data from the 1990 census S-night enumeration, an earlier enumeration of metropolitan-area homelessness by Martha Burt (1992), Continuum of Care counts for California counties pertaining to the mid-1990s, and

Figure 6.1   Homeless on a Single Night Against Median Monthly Rent (2007)

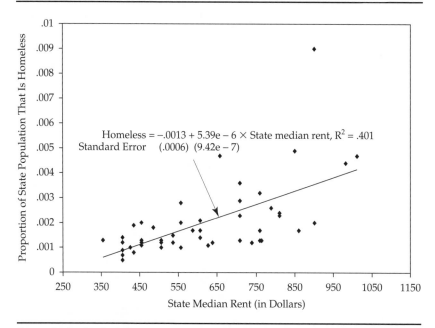

Homeless = −.0013 + 5.39e − 6 × State median rent, $R^2 = .401$
Standard Error   (.0006) (9.42e − 7)

Source: Author's calculation.

longitudinal data on annual caseloads for the California Homeless Assistance program, the authors find consistent evidence of higher levels of homelessness in areas with high rents and low rental vacancy rates.

This empirical relationship is also readily observable in more recent counts of the homeless population. Figures 6.1 and 6.2 are scatter plots of the proportion of a state's population that is homeless on a given night in January 2007 against two measures of housing affordability: median monthly contract rents and the ratio of rent to income for the median renter household in the respective state. In each figure, each data point marks the state's homelessness level as well as the cost of housing. A positive relationship between these two variables would take the form of an upward sloping data cloud. The measure of homelessness comes from the 2008 AHAR and is based on the figures provided in Continuum of Care applications. I tabulated median rents and rent-to-income ratios using data from the 2007 American Community Survey (ACS). The association between the incidence of homelessness across states and the variation in median rents and median rent-to-income ratios is clear and positive, as is evident in the general shape of the scatter plots as well as in the linear bivariate regressions fit to the data. Interstate variation in rents explains

Figure 6.2   Homeless on a Single Night Against Median Rent-to-Income Ratio (2007)

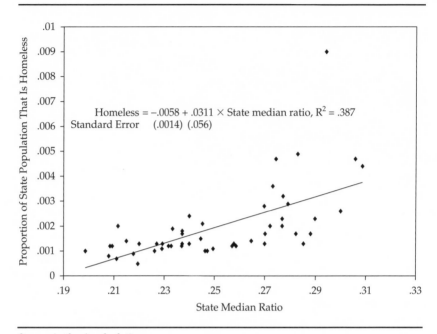

Source: Author's calculation.

roughly 40 percent of the variation in homelessness across states, while the comparable figure for rent-to-income ratios is approximately 39 percent.[1]

Regulation and Housing Costs

Thus, both theoretical arguments and empirical evidence suggest that homelessness is in part a housing-affordability problem. This of course offers only a partial explanation for the rise and persistence of homelessness in the United States, but recent trends in income as well as in housing prices suggest that the housing market itself may be a particularly important determinant of homelessness. The extent to which local regulation of housing markets affects homelessness will depend on the extent to which it affects the price of housing consumed by those likely to experience homelessness. Moreover, through filtering and competition between income groups in the housing market, the cost of such low-quality housing will depend on the prices of housing further up the quality distribution as well as the determinants of housing supply at all quality levels, factors likely to be affected by the local regulatory regime. Here, we discuss this particular theoretical link in the chain—the impact of local regulation on housing supply and housing affordability.

Theoretical Connections Between Regulation and Housing Costs

Local regulation may affect the operation of local housing markets and, ultimately, the price and minimum quality of the lowest-quality units available, in a number of ways. Minimum habitation standards generally preclude building new dwellings without basic amenities, such as private kitchens, complete plumbing, and multiple exits. Such regulations are most likely to have a direct impact on the supply of housing that people at high risk of homelessness are likely to occupy.

Zoning regulation often restricts the amount of land within a municipality available for residential development and then dictates the density and quality of the housing that can be built. Growth controls, growth moratoria, exaction fees leveled on new development, and lengthy and complex project approval processes tend to discourage new housing construction and the nature of new housing that is ultimately supplied to the local market. Although such regulations may not prohibit construction of minimum-quality housing, they do constrain production processes and likely restrict supply.

These alternative forms of housing-market regulation impact housing costs by increasing production costs, restricting housing supply, and increasing housing demand. All three factors will ultimately be reflected in an area's housing prices. Moreover, existing research indicates that the impacts of such regulation are greatest on the supply and price of housing for low- and moderate-income families.

The impact of regulation on production costs operates directly through the added costs of winning approval for a project as well as indirectly by constraining the manner in which the developer must construct new units. The direct costs include but are not limited to the time devoted to preparing permit applications, legal fees associated with application and in some instances appealing zoning-board decisions, and the increased uncertainty associated with potential delays in the progress of a project. The indirect costs are more subtle and perhaps best illustrated with an example. The common practice of large-lot zoning entails municipalities requiring minimum lot sizes per unit of single-family housing. To the extent that a minimum lot-size requirement constrains the building plans of housing providers, builders are being forced to use more land per unit than they otherwise would.

In a competitive housing market, builders provide housing using a mix of land, capital (such as building materials, machinery, and the like), and labor that minimizes the costs of a given quality and quantity of housing. Moreover, through competition in the housing market, such cost-conscious behavior is passed onto consumers in the form of lower prices. When producers are constrained to use more land per unit of housing, land preparation or acquisition costs per unit constructed will be higher. These increased costs will ultimately be passed on to the consumer in the form of higher housing prices.

Several regulatory practices also restrict and constrain the amount of land available to the housing sector, thus in turn restricting the supply of new units. Large-lot zoning, for example, artificially constrains how much housing is permitted on a given number of acres. With limited zoning for residential development, any requirement that increases the minimum lot size per housing unit reduces the number of units that can be built. Other common practices, such as zoning disproportionate amounts of land for industrial use, restrict the overall supply of land for housing and by extension the supply of housing. As with all markets, artificially restricting supply in such a manner will drive up housing prices, if all else is held equal.

In addition to its effects on production costs and housing supply, restricting density is also likely to increase demand for housing in the area. If consumers prefer low over high density, a regulatory environment that decreases the overall residential density of a community is likely to increase the attractiveness of that community to outsiders. This increased attractiveness generates increased demand for housing in the regulated community, which in turn drives up housing prices.

What Does Empirical Research Show?

There is ample empirical evidence finding that regulatory restrictions tend to increase the price of housing and, in turn, to make communities less affordable for low- and moderate-income households. Since the mid-1970s, several studies published in scholarly journals have assessed whether local land-use regulations affect housing supply and prices. The general finding in this line of research is that indeed, land-use constraints are associated with higher housing prices. William Fischel (1990) provides a review of early research on the effects of land-use regulation and growth control measures, in particular on housing and land markets. This extensive review of the extant literature, as of 1990, concluded that growth and density controls have significant and substantial effects on land and housing markets. Specifically, Fischel points out that housing market regulations increase home prices in the municipalities that impose such restrictions, have spillover effects on home prices in neighboring municipalities without such restrictions, and reduce the value of undeveloped land that has become subject to restrictive regulation.

A recent nationwide assessment of the effects of housing regulation on housing costs is provided in a study by Edward Glaeser and Joseph Gyourko (2003). The authors attempt to estimate the size of the regulatory tax imposed on the suppliers and consumers of housing in various metropolitan areas and assess whether the tax is larger where land markets are more heavily regulated. In measuring the tax per housing unit, the authors note that in a competitive housing market the price of a house should be no greater than the cost of supplying the house new. The costs of supplying a new unit of housing can be broken down into three components: land costs, construction costs (labor, materials, equipment rental, and so on), and the costs associated with negotiating the regulatory process (in the language of the authors, the regulatory tax). For a number of metropolitan areas, the authors estimate land costs by comparing the price of otherwise similar homes situated on lots of different sizes, with the difference in price providing an estimate of how much consumers pay for slightly more land. Construction cost estimates are readily available from a number of sources. With the first two components and data on housing values from the American Housing Survey, the authors are able to estimate the regulatory tax by subtracting land costs and construction costs from housing values. They find quite large regulatory taxes embodied in the price of housing. They also find that in most areas, land costs explain only one-tenth of the difference between housing prices and construction costs, and the remaining nine-tenths by the price effects of land-use regulation.

Glaeser and Gyourko then use this estimate of the regulatory tax to first characterize the degree to which housing is overvalued in metropolitan areas and assess whether such overvaluation is greater in cities with more regulated land markets. Specifically, they measure the proportion of each metropolitan area's housing stock that is more than 40 percent overvalued by the regulatory housing tax. They characterize the degree of local regulatory stringency using data from the Wharton Land Use Control Survey of sixty metropolitan areas. Indeed, they find that cities with the most regulated land markets have the greatest proportion of housing overvalued by their measure of the regulatory tax.

In a follow-up study, Glaeser, Gyourko, and Raven Saks document the overall increase in this regulatory tax nationwide and that housing suppliers have become less responsive in terms of new supply to overvalued housing (2005a, 2005b). The authors show that the ratio of housing prices to construction costs has increased considerably since 1970. In addition, new construction rates have declined despite extreme price pressures in more regulated areas, such as those on the East Coast and the West Coast. Finally, the authors demonstrate that in earlier decades, new construction tended to be higher in metropolitan areas with relatively high price-cost ratios, whereas in later decades this relationship has disappeared.

In an analysis of California housing markets, John Quigley and Steven Raphael (2005) assess the importance of local land-use regulation in explaining the evolution of housing prices and building in California cities between 1990 and 2000. The study uses a survey conducted during the early 1990s to gauge land-use regulation and constructs an index of the regulatory environment based on fifteen measures.[2] The study demonstrates three facts. First, housing is more expensive in California cities where land markets are more heavily regulated. Second, growth in the housing stock was slower over the 1990s in more regulated cities. Finally, housing supply is much less responsive to increases in price in more regulated cities. The last finding is perhaps the most significant, as it indicates that housing suppliers are less able to respond to increases in housing demand in more regulated areas.

Further evidence of the effect of housing regulation on the responsiveness of housing supply to changes in demand is provided in a study by Christopher Mayer and Tsuriel Somerville (2000). The authors measure the regulatory environment of more than forty metropolitan areas and characterize the regions based on the degree of regulatory stringency as pertaining to land use. They then assess whether the supply of housing is less responsive to increases in demand in more regulated metropolitan areas. They find evidence suggesting that this is the case.

Finally, Steven Malpezzi and Richard Green (1996) study how the degree of regulatory stringency affects the price of rental housing at various points in the rental-housing quality distribution—low, medium, and high. To the extent that regulations have an impact on the supply of relatively low-quality housing, one might expect larger impacts on low- and moderate-income households. Their results indicate that moving from a relatively unregulated to a heavily regulated metropolitan area increases rents among the lowest-income renters by one-fifth and increases home values for the lowest-quality single-family homes by more than three-fifths. The largest price effects of such regulations occur at the bottom of the distribution in units that are disproportionately occupied by low- and moderate-income households.

Thus, the existing research on the effects of land-use regulatory stringency on housing prices and supply consistently documents several findings. First, housing is more expensive in regulated markets, which cannot be explained by higher land values. Second, the supply of housing is less responsive to changes in demand in more regulated markets, suggesting that demand pressures result in greater price increases the more stringent the regulatory environment is. Finally, the effect of land-use regulation on prices is greatest on the housing units that are most likely to be occupied by low- and moderate-income households.

Impacts of Specific Regulatory Practices

The studies discussed thus far assess the effect of the overall regulatory environment on housing prices and supply. Other studies investigate the effects of specific forms of density control and land-use regulation on housing outcomes. One of the most extensive analyses is provided by Rolf Pendall (2000). This study uses an original survey of local land-use practices to assess the effect of specific zoning and growth management regulations on housing market outcomes and the representation of racial and ethnic minorities among the residential populations of the localities. Pendall surveyed 1,510 cities, towns, and counties in the twenty-five largest metropolitan areas in the country, with a final response rate of 83 percent and observations on 1,169 jurisdictions. In the mailed questionnaire, municipal-planning directors were asked whether the locality uses the following land-use controls in their planning processes:

- low-density zoning only: defined as gross residential-density limits with no more than eight dwellings per acres

- building permit caps: controls that place annual limits on new building permits

- building permit moratorium: total stoppage of residential building permits in effect for at least two years

- adequate public-facilities ordinances: ordinances that require levels of services be set for more than two urban infrastructures or public service systems

- urban-growth boundaries: restrictions that permanently or temporarily limit expansion on the urban edge

- boxed-in status: urban expansion precluded by political boundaries or water bodies

The author extracted data from the 1980 and 1990 U.S. Censuses of Population and Housing on the housing stock of each municipality and the racial composition of the municipalities' residents in both years and matched these data to the survey data pertaining to land-use practices. Regarding the operation of the housing market, the study reports that communities that employed low-density-only zoning had lower growth in their housing stock between 1980 and 1990 and experienced a decline in the proportion of housing that was multifamily and an increase in the share that was single family. Such communities also experienced a decline in the proportion of the housing stock that was rental housing, all factors that tend to reduce rental affordability.

Low-density-only zoning is the only one of the six land-use practices investigated that consistently affects housing market outcomes. None of the other practices appeared to reduce growth in the housing stock, with one practice (boxed-in status) actually positively associated with growth. Similarly, none of the other practices restricted the share of multifamily dwellings, restricted the share of rental housing, or increased the share of single-family housing. Several of the practices, however, did exert significant negative effects on the fraction of rentals that were affordable.

In a study of thirty-nine municipalities in Waukesha, Wisconsin, in 1990, Richard Green (1999) investigates the effect of various land-use regulations on the minimum land or service requirements for new housing, on the supply of affordable housing. He uses a detailed regulation land-use survey of the county's municipalities and estimates the effect of the measured provisions on housing prices, rents, and the proportion of housing that would be affordable to a low- or medium-income household. The zoning-requirement measures include required street width, minimum front setbacks, minimum lot width, storm-sewer and sanitation requirements, and water, curb, gutter, and sidewalk requirements. Green finds significant and substantial negative associations between more stringent regulations regarding minimum land requirements (that is, street width, front setback, and lot width) and the proportion of housing that is affordable.

Glaeser, Gyourko, and Saks (2005c) investigate the contribution of regulatory stringency to high housing prices in Manhattan. The study first assesses the degree to which the price per square foot of residential housing in New York City exceeds the marginal construction costs for multifloor buildings. In a competitive housing market, prices should be equal to the marginal costs of constructing housing, given that housing suppliers would compete away any supranormal profits in the process of competing for buyers. The extent to which prices exceed marginal construction costs therefore provides an indication of the extent to which regulatory barriers are increasing the costs of supplying housing. The authors demonstrate a steep increase in the ratio of housing prices to marginal construction costs. The authors also demonstrate that at the close of the twentieth century, housing supply in New York was considerably less sensitive to increases in condo prices. The authors also show that despite the high demand and the unprecedented prices of housing in Manhattan, building heights on new projects began a steep decline beginning during the 1970s. The authors attribute part of the run-up in New York housing prices to density restrictions that limit the size of buildings.

To summarize, although few studies estimate the effects of specific forms of land-use regulations on housing market outcomes, the existing studies do suggest that policies that reduce density—minimum lot size as in Pendall, minimum lot width and setback requirements as in Green, or height restrictions as in Glaeser, Gyourko, and Saks—increase housing costs and diminish the supply of affordable housing. Combined with the consistent cross-sectional relationship between measures of housing costs and homelessness, the existing research on housing market regulation suggests that such regulation may be responsible in part for the rise of homelessness in the United States.

Local Housing Markets in Regulated and Unregulated Markets

The preceding discussion suggests that in more regulated markets, housing is more expensive and the quantity of housing supplied is less sensitive to shifts in housing demand. It also suggests that housing supplies of various qualities are linked to one another by depreciation through the quality hierarchy and competition for units between households of different income groups. In this section, I document the empirical correlations between a measure of the degree of local regulation and various indicators of the evolution of housing supply, housing costs, and housing competition among households.

Gyourko, Albert Saiz, and Anita Summers (2006) present a new measure of the local regulatory environment in U.S. housing markets, presenting indices of regulatory stringency at the level of both metropolitan areas as well as states. The indices are based on responses to a survey of 2,600 communities across the country querying local-planning directors about the use of various regulatory practices, typical approval times for residential projects, the influence of various pressure groups in approval and zoning decisions, and a number of other such practices. The indices also take into account state-level policy with regards to land use and the degree to which the state's judicial system defers to local land-use decisions. Table 6.1 reproduces the Wharton Residential Land Use Regulation Index (WRLURI) tabulated at the state level. The indices are based on a number of subindices of regulatory practices and outcomes. The index values are standardized to have a mean of zero and a standard deviation of one.[3]

In what follows, I stratify states into the five groups of ten listed in table 6.1, ranked from the most to the least restrictive regulatory environments, and compare the evolution of state housing-market outcomes between 1970 and 2007 across these groupings. To characterize state housing markets, I draw on data from the 1970 1 percent Public Use Microdata Sample of the U.S. census and the 2007 American Community Survey (Ruggles et al. 2009). Unless otherwise noted, all the comparisons pool the owner-occupied and rental housing stock.

To be sure, the simple comparisons presented here do not establish a causal relationship between more stringent regulations and the outcomes analyzed. It is entirely possible that the stringency of regulation may be shaped by unobserved factors that also affect the housing outcomes that I analyze in this section. For example, high housing prices may beget growth controls in an attempt to limit changes to the character of a local housing market. Nonetheless, this empirical profile does reveal sharp contrasts between more and less regulated housing markets that, when combined with the studies discussed, suggest a potentially important role for regulation in determining housing costs and, by extension, homelessness.

Regulation and the Composition of Housing Stock

Table 6.2 compares the frequency distributions of the housing stock across the number of rooms, the number of bedrooms, and the age of the unit for the five groups of states that were defined by the degree of regulatory

Table 6.1 Ranking of U.S. States by the WRURLI Land Use Regulation Index

Most Regulated		Second Most Regulated		Medium Regulation		Second Least Regulated		Least Regulated	
Hawaii	2.32	Colorado	.48	New York	-.01	Nevada	-.45	Arkansas	-.86
Rhode Island	1.58	Delaware	.48	Utah	-.07	Wyoming	-.45	West Virginia	-.90
Massachusetts	1.56	Connecticut	.38	New Mexico	-.11	North Dakota	-.54	Alabama	-.94
New Hampshire	1.36	Pennsylvania	.37	Illinois	-.19	Kentucky	-.57	Iowa	-.99
New Jersey	.88	Florida	.37	Virginia	-.19	Idaho	-.63	Indiana	-1.01
Maryland	.79	Vermont	.35	Georgia	-.21	Tennessee	-.68	Missouri	-1.03
Washington	.74	Minnesota	.08	North Carolina	-.35	Nebraska	-.68	South Dakota	-1.04
Maine	.68	Oregon	.08	Montana	-.36	Oklahoma	-.70	Louisiana	-1.06
California	.59	Wisconsin	.07	Ohio	-.36	South Carolina	-.76	Alaska	-1.07
Arizona	.58	Michigan	.02	Texas	-.45	Mississippi	-.82	Kansas	-1.13

Source: Author's compilation using data from Gyourko, Saiz, and Summers (2006).

Table 6.2   Comparison of the Distributions of Housing Units for States, Grouped by Degree of Regulatory Stringency

	Most Regulated			Second Most Regulated			Medium Regulation			Second Least Regulated			Least Regulated		
	1970	2007	Change	1970	2007	Change	1970	2007	Change	1970	2007	Change	1970	2007	Change
Panel A. Number of Rooms															
1	2.05	1.32	−.73	1.72	.63	−1.09	1.83	.84	−.99	.97	.35	−.62	1.14	.40	−.74
2	4.16	4.15	−.01	3.03	2.57	−.46	3.50	2.75	−.75	2.50	1.93	−.57	2.85	2.08	−.77
3	12.34	10.44	−1.90	9.25	7.86	−1.39	12.10	8.91	−3.19	9.08	6.52	−2.56	10.04	6.90	−3.14
4	20.08	17.13	−2.95	18.15	15.79	−2.36	20.90	16.04	−4.86	22.93	16.49	−6.44	22.43	15.79	−6.64
5	23.85	20.03	−3.82	24.79	20.81	−3.98	24.51	21.47	−3.04	29.72	25.13	−4.59	29.17	24.22	−4.59
6	19.83	18.28	−1.55	23.03	20.33	−2.70	19.75	19.16	−.58	20.23	20.72	.49	19.47	20.56	1.09
7	9.59	12.46	2.87	10.68	13.86	3.18	9.31	12.73	3.42	8.60	13.02	4.42	8.63	13.29	4.46
8	4.84	8.15	3.31	5.63	9.05	3.42	4.88	8.63	3.75	3.52	7.83	4.31	3.94	8.32	4.38
9+	3.26	8.04	4.78	3.72	9.10	5.38	3.23	9.48	6.25	2.44	8.01	5.57	2.34	8.44	6.10
Panel B. Number of Bedrooms															
0	3.14	1.81	−1.33	2.21	.82	−1.39	2.48	1.12	−1.36	1.24	.51	−.74	1.53	.57	−.96
1	17.79	13.16	−4.81	14.09	9.97	−4.12	17.21	11.51	−5.70	11.93	7.86	−4.07	13.86	8.59	−5.27
2	32.15	27.28	−4.87	31.59	27.21	−4.39	33.42	25.02	−8.42	39.18	25.54	−13.64	37.74	26.24	−11.50
3	33.78	35.77	1.99	38.48	41.82	3.34	35.16	41.15	5.99	38.54	47.26	8.72	36.93	45.77	8.84
4	10.65	17.49	6.84	10.99	16.42	5.43	9.57	16.81	7.24	7.69	15.32	7.63	8.29	15.44	7.15
5+	2.30	4.50	2.21	2.64	3.76	1.12	2.17	4.41	2.23	1.42	3.52	2.10	1.89	3.39	1.51
Panel C. Age of Housing Units in Years[a]															
0–1	3.00	1.65	−1.35	3.41	2.01	−1.40	3.04	2.21	−.83	4.46	2.93	−1.53	3.45	2.17	−1.28
2–5	10.26	5.51	−4.75	10.23	7.18	−3.05	9.67	7.64	−2.03	12.68	10.78	−1.91	10.49	8.04	−2.45
6–10	14.92	7.17	−7.75	11.41	7.48	−3.93	12.00	7.18	−4.82	14.64	9.10	−5.54	11.62	7.31	−4.31
11–20	24.91	16.42	−8.49	22.86	16.00	−6.86	22.05	15.27	−6.78	22.24	17.38	−4.86	21.79	14.70	−7.09
21–30	13.51	18.79	5.29	11.72	18.74	7.02	12.97	17.30	4.33	14.73	20.96	6.23	13.83	19.49	5.66
30+	33.39	50.46	17.07	40.36	48.59	8.23	40.26	50.40	10.14	31.25	38.85	7.60	38.82	48.29	9.47

Source: Author's calculations based on the 1970 Public Use Microdata Sample of the U.S. Bureau of the Census and the 2007 American Community Survey (Ruggles et al. 2009).
Note: States are grouped into regulatory groups based on the survey analyzed in Gyourko, Saiz, and Summers (2006).
a. For the age of the housing units, the end year is 2000. Data taken from the 1 percent Public Use Microdata from the 2000 census.

stringency. For each group and for each outcome, the table presents the distribution in 1970, the distribution in 2007, and the changes occurring over these thirty-seven years. Across all three outcomes, differences that vary systematically with the degree of local regulatory stringency are notable. In the most regulated states, the proportion of housing units with seven or more rooms increases from approximately 18 percent to 29 percent, a change of approximately 11 percentage points. By contrast, the comparable figures for the least regulated states are 15 percent in 1970 and 30 percent in 2007, an increase of 15 percentage points. Similarly, the proportion of housing units with three or more bedrooms increases by 11 percentage points in the most regulated states in contrast to the 15 percentage point change in the least.

To the extent that newer housing is larger and offers more bedrooms, these differential shifts suggest that new housing construction occurs at a slower rate in more regulated states relative to less regulated states. Indeed the patterns in panel C of table 6.2 indicate that this is the case. Interestingly, the distribution of the housing stock in the least regulated states is more skewed toward older units in 1970, with 52.65 percent of the units twenty-one years or older and nearly 39 percent of these units thirty years or older, and the comparable figures for the most regulated states being 46.9 percent and 33.39 percent. Over the subsequent thirty-seven years, however, these patterns reverse. The proportion of the housing stock more than twenty years old increases by more than 22 percentage points in the most regulated states, in contrast with a 15 percentage point increase in the least regulated.

Table 6.3 presents similar comparisons for the distribution of housing units across structure type. Although the empirical relationships between these outcomes and regulatory stringency are less salient, several patterns across these groupings are nonetheless interesting. First, the proportion of units accounted for by mobile homes increases by more in less regulated than in more regulated states, with the change in the percentage of units increasing with near uniformity across the five state groups. Second, although the relationship between regulatory stringency and the change in the proportion of units in multifamily structures is less pronounced, there does appear to be a relationship with this variable, albeit a weak one. For example, the proportion of the housing stock in multifamily structures declines by 3.45 percentage points in the most regulated states and by 2.81 percentage points in the second most regulated. For the least regulated, this proportion declines by 2.81 percentage points, and among the second least regulated states, it increases by 1.71 percentage points.

These simple comparisons suggest important differences in housing construction patterns between regulated and less regulated housing markets. The rate of new construction appears to be lower in regulated states, reflected in the lower-quality housing and older housing stock at

Table 6.3   Distribution of Housing Stock Across Structure Types

	1970	2007	Change
Panel A. Most Regulated States			
Mobile home	2.38	3.82	1.44
Single-family detached	60.05	58.45	−1.6
Single-family attached	3.89	7.51	3.62
Two to four units	15.36	9.87	−5.49
Five to nine units	5.51	5.64	.13
Ten or more units	12.81	14.71	1.91
Panel B. Second Most Regulated States			
Mobile home	3.25	5.77	2.53
Single-family detached	64.12	62.78	−1.34
Single-family attached	6.71	8.34	1.63
Two to four units	13.89	7.32	−6.57
Five to nine units	3.35	4.16	.81
Ten or more units	8.69	11.64	2.95
Panel C. Medium Regulated States			
Mobile home	2.37	5.93	3.56
Single-family detached	58.53	61.52	2.99
Single-family attached	1.82	4.63	2.81
Two to four units	15.65	9.03	−6.62
Five to nine units	4.67	4.90	.23
Ten or more units	19.96	14.00	−2.96
Panel D. Second Least Regulated States			
Mobile home	4.91	10.79	5.88
Single-family detached	79.03	69.19	−9.84
Single-family attached	.56	2.80	2.24
Two to four units	8.78	5.79	−2.99
Five to nine units	2.15	4.62	2.47
Ten or more units	4.56	6.80	2.24
Panel E. Least Regulated States			
Mobile home	3.95	8.62	4.67
Single-family detached	74.97	71.46	−3.51
Single-family attached	1.28	2.92	1.64
Two to four units	12.03	6.49	−5.54
Five to nine units	2.92	3.90	.98
Ten or more units	4.85	6.60	1.75

Source: Author's calculations based on the 1970 Public Use Microdata Sample of the U.S. Bureau of the Census and the 2007 American Community Survey (Ruggles et al. 2009).
Note: States are grouped into regulatory groups based on the survey analyzed in Gyourko, Saiz, and Summers (2006).

the end of the period studied. Moreover, the proportional importance of multifamily units and mobile homes diminishes by more in the most regulated states. Taken together, these patterns are consistent with a relatively restricted housing supply in more regulated local markets.

Regulation, Housing Costs, and Housing Price Inflation

Is housing more expensive in more regulated markets? Moreover, has housing appreciated more slowly in less regulated markets?

I begin to explore these questions by documenting the simple cross-sectional relationships between alternative measures of housing costs and the WRLURI regulation index. Figure 6.3 is a scatter plot of median monthly contract rents against the regulation-index values measured at the state level. Figure 6.4 is a comparable scatter plot in which the dependent variable is now the median rent-to-income ratio among the renter households for each state. Both figures measure the housing outcomes with data from the 2007 ACS. The data reveal a strong and statistically significant relationship between these two variables. The quality of the

Figure 6.3   Median Monthly Rent at State Level Against Local Land-Use Regulation Index (2007)

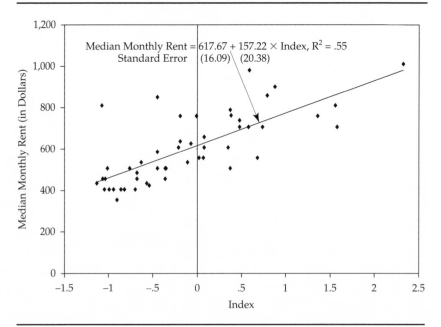

Source: Author's calculation.

Figure 6.4   Median Rent-to-Income Ratio Among Renters Against Index of Regulatory Stringency (2007)

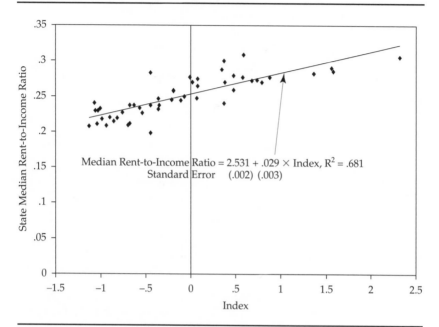

Source: Author's calculation.

fits of the underlying trend lines are such that the regulatory stringency index explains 55 percent of the cross-state variation in median rents and nearly 68 percent of the cross-state variation in median rent-to-income ratios. Interestingly, Gyourko, Saiz, and Summers (2006) document that population density is actually higher in the least regulated states, suggesting that the positive association between housing prices and regulations observed in figures 6.3 and 6.4 are likely to reflect in part a restriction on supply (rather than a demand-induced increase in regulatory stringency).

It is also the case that housing prices have climbed at a faster rate in more regulated states on a quasi-quality adjusted basis. To demonstrate this pattern, using 1970 data for the nation as a whole, I first calculated average housing prices for housing units defined by the interaction of the number of rooms, the number of bedrooms, and the unit structure types (categories used in tables 6.2 and 6.3). I then used these average housing prices to allocate each housing type into one of five quality quintiles, where the lowest-quality quintile comprises those housing units in the lowest fifth of the 1970 price distribution and the highest-quality quintile are those units in the highest fifth.[4] Next, I calculated average housing prices within each of the quality quintiles defined with the 1970 price

Table 6.4   Estimated Price Appreciation by 1970 Quality Quintiles, All U.S. Housing Units

	1970 Price (thousands of dollars)	2007 Price (thousands of dollars)	P_{2007}/P_{1970}	Nominal[a]	Real[b]
Quintile 1	11.202	144.227	12.88	.072	.025
Quintile 2	14.405	177.488	12.32	.070	.024
Quintile 3	16.811	198.273	11.79	.069	.023
Quintile 4	19.329	214.519	11.10	.067	.021
Quintile 5	26.244	308.852	11.77	.069	.023

Source: Author's calculations based on the 1970 Public Use Microdata Sample of the U.S. Bureau of the Census and the 2007 American Community Survey (Ruggles et al. 2009).
Notes: Housing quality quintiles are defined relative to the 1970 distribution of housing units across price groups defined by number of rooms, number of bedrooms, and structure type. Average prices in 2007 are weighted average within 1970 defined quality quintiles using the 1970 within group frequency distribution as weights.
a. Figures provide the annual nominal appreciation rate implied by the documented price levels.
b. Figures subtract the annual inflation rate implied by the starting and ending price levels for 1970 and 2007 (.0463) from the annual nominal price appreciation rate.

distribution but for 2007, where the distribution of units across groups within a quintile for 1970 is used to weight the price estimate.[5] Finally, I used these averages to gauge the overall growth in housing prices, the implied annual nominal appreciation rate and the implied annual real housing-price appreciation rate.

Table 6.4 presents figures for the national housing stock. The first column presents estimates of average nominal housing prices within a quintile for 1970 in thousands of dollars, the second column presents comparable estimates for similar quality housing in 2007, and the third column presents the ratio of average nominal prices in 2007 to the average nominal house price in 1970. Nationwide, the data indicate price appreciation is higher for lower-quality housing: average prices increase nearly thirteenfold among bottom-quintile housing in contrast with twelvefold among top-quintile housing. In nominal terms, the price appreciation observed over these thirty-seven years is consistent with a constant annual nominal appreciation rate of roughly 7 percent with a higher value for the lowest-quality housing (7.2 percent) and a lower value for the highest-quality housing (6.9 percent).[6] In real terms, average annual appreciation is roughly 2.5 percent for the lowest-quality housing and 2.3 percent of the highest-quality housing.

Repeating these tabulations for the five state groups defined by the WRLURI, using constant quality definitions across all states, reveals stark differences in these pricing patterns. Table 6.5 presents the results from these more detailed tabulations. Over the period, housing price appreciation is considerably greater in more regulated states than in less regulated

Table 6.5   Estimated Price Appreciation for Housing Units by 1970 Quality Quintiles, All U.S. Housing Units

	1970 (thousands of dollars)	2007 (thousands of dollars)	P_{2007}/P_{1970}	Nominal[a]	Real[b]
Panel A. Most Regulated States					
Quintile 1	14.358	215.962	15.04	.076	.030
Quintile 2	17.590	271.520	15.44	.077	.030
Quintile 3	20.370	303.729	14.91	.076	.029
Quintile 4	23.594	334.348	14.17	.074	.028
Quintile 5	28.517	463.573	16.26	.078	.032
Panel B. Second Most Regulated States					
Quintile 1	11.917	146.947	12.33	.070	.024
Quintile 2	14.595	161.611	11.07	.067	.021
Quintile 3	17.883	198.170	11.08	.067	.021
Quintile 4	19.320	240.920	12.47	.071	.024
Quintile 5	25.831	298.241	11.55	.068	.022
Panel C. Medium Regulated States					
Quintile 1	12.137	124.725	10.28	.065	.019
Quintile 2	15.530	170.233	10.96	.067	.021
Quintile 3	17.459	157.205	9.00	.061	.015
Quintile 4	19.800	179.366	9.06	.061	.015
Quintile 5	27.909	281.259	10.08	.064	.018
Panel D. Second Least Regulated States					
Quintile 1	7.405	95.834	12.94	.072	.025
Quintile 2	10.340	102.136	9.88	.064	.018
Quintile 3	13.446	125.251	9.32	.062	.016
Quintile 4	15.785	152.449	9.66	.063	.017
Quintile 5	22.384	204.876	9.15	.062	.015
Panel E. Least Regulated States					
Quintile 1	8.962	88.206	9.84	.064	.017
Quintile 2	11.487	90.132	7.85	.057	.011
Quintile 3	14.407	112.938	7.84	.057	.011
Quintile 4	16.351	129.168	7.90	.057	.011
Quintile 5	22.835	186.518	8.17	.058	.012

Source: Author's calculations based on the 1970 Public Use Microdata Sample of the U.S. Bureau of the Census and the 2007 American Community Survey (Ruggles et al. 2009).
Notes: Housing quality quintiles are defined relative to the 1970 distribution of housing units across price groups defined by number of rooms, number of bedrooms, and structure type. Average prices in 2007 are weighted average within 1970 defined quality quintiles using the 1970 within group frequency distribution as weights.
a. Figures provide the annual nominal appreciation rate implied by the documented price levels.
b. Figures subtract the annual inflation rate implied by the starting and ending price levels for 1970 and 2007 (.0463) from the annual nominal price appreciation rate.

Table 6.6   Key Percentiles of the Distribution Rent-to-Income Ratios Among Renter Housing in 1970 and 2007 by the Stringency of Housing Regulation Practices

Percentile	10th	25th	50th	75th	90th
Panel A. Most Regulated States					
1970	.085	.124	.187	.320	.590
2007	.130	.200	.300	.514	.973
Change	.045	.076	.113	.194	.383
Panel B. Second Most Regulated States					
1970	.076	.112	.176	.310	.615
2007	.119	.179	.277	.461	.960
Change	.043	.067	.101	.151	.345
Panel C. Medium Regulated States					
1970	.074	.108	.168	.286	.546
2007	.106	.163	.258	.440	.871
Change	.032	.055	.090	.154	.325
Panel D. Second Least Regulated States					
1970	.063	.097	.153	.262	.506
2007	.096	.150	.237	.398	.773
Change	.033	.053	.084	.136	.267
Panel E. Least Regulated States					
1970	.070	.099	.157	.270	.536
2007	.092	.144	.231	.400	.800
Change	.022	.045	.074	.130	.264

Source: Author's calculations based on the 1970 Public Use Microdata Sample of the U.S. Bureau of the Census and the 2007 American Community Survey (Ruggles et al. 2009).
Note: Rent-to-income ratios are for renter households only.

states. Among the most regulated states, housing prices increase fourteen- to sixteenfold depending on the quality group. Among the least regulated states, housing prices increase approximately eight- to tenfold. Among the most regulated states, the implied real annual price appreciation defined by the beginning- and end-year housing values are around 3 percent. In contrast, annual real price appreciation for the least regulated states hovers around 1.1 percent, although the value is somewhat higher, 1.7 percent, for the lowest-quality quintile.

The impact of housing regulation on the affordability of housing most likely to be occupied by those who face the highest risk of homelessness is perhaps best illustrated by comparing the evolution of rent-to-income ratios in more and less regulated states, because lower-income households are more likely to rent than to own. Table 6.6 compares select percentiles of the distribution of rent-to-income ratios in 1970 and 2007 for states grouped according to the stringency of local land-use regulation.

**Figure 6.5   Median Rent-to-Income Ratios for Renter Households
in Bottom Quartile**

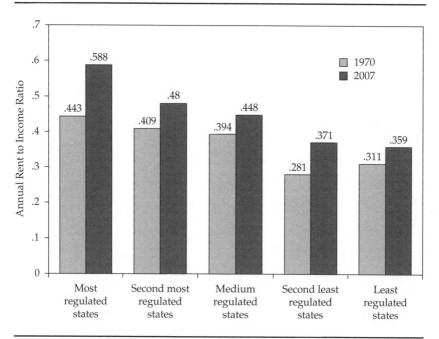

Source: Author's calculation.

Renters in the most regulated states experience the largest increase in rent-to-income ratios at all points in this distribution. For example, the ratio at the 10th percentile increases by .045 in the most regulated states but by .022 in the least regulated. The comparable figures for the change in the median are .113 for the most regulated and .074 for the least regulated. The largest increases (as well as the largest disparities in growth) are observed in the highest percentiles of the rent-to-income distributions. Among renters in the most regulated states, the rent-to-income ratio at the 90th percentile of the distributions increases by .383. The comparable increase among renters in the least regulated states is .264.

Of course, the homeless are most likely to be drawn from among the poorest of the population of renter households. Thus we must also discuss the relationship between budget shares devoted to housing and regulation among particularly low-income renters. Figure 6.5 makes this comparison. The figure presents the median rent-to-income ratio among renter households in the bottom quartile of the national family income distribution in 1970 and 2007 for each of the five groups of states. Again, we see a striking empirical relationship with the degree of housing regulation that mirrors that presented in table 6.6. However, the changes here are more pronounced. Among low-income renters in the most regulated states, the median ratio of rent to income increases .443 to .588, a 14.5 percentage point increase. The comparable figures for low-income renters in the least regulated states are .311 and .359, a 3.9 percentage point increase.

Thus housing is more expensive in more regulated markets. In addition, housing prices have appreciated at much faster rates in regulated housing markets relative to unregulated housing markets. Finally, these differences appear to have a particular impact on low-income households in the most regulated states, where the median rent-to-income ratio among this group now exceeds .5.

How Important Is Regulation in Determining Homelessness?

I have thus far presented a series of indirect arguments that, when taken together, suggest that local regulation of housing markets may be in part responsible for the rise of homelessness during the past few decades. I have yet to directly link local regulatory stringency to the incidence of homelessness. More important, I have yet to address the relative culpability of land-use regulation in explaining homelessness in the United States.

Of course, answering these questions convincingly is difficult. Assessing the importance of regulation requires properly measuring the impacts of regulation on housing costs and then the causal effects of housing affordability on homelessness. One encounters several measurement and methodological problems when trying to draw such inferences. First, data on homelessness and regulation are scarce and often afford researchers little variation beyond what can be observed in a cross section. The few efforts at measuring variation in regulatory stringency have been herculean tasks that generally provide us with snapshots only at a given time for only a few geographic areas. Moreover, one would strongly suspect that the impact of introducing such regulations on housing outcomes, both homelessness as well as affordability more generally, should occur with a lag. That is to say, new regulations should not affect the existing durable stock but instead the path of new construction. Unfortunately, most surveys of land-use regulation policy measure current practices, with little information on the timing of new regulatory innovations. With regard to homelessness, methods for counting the homeless at a given time, as well as period-prevalence estimation methods, have improved greatly. However, it will be a few years before current ongoing efforts yield data amenable to longitudinal analysis.[7]

A second important challenge concerns the ability to infer causality from the currently available cross-sectional data sets. For example, in estimating the effects of regulation on housing costs with cross-sectional data, one might suspect that areas experiencing rapid growth in housing demand endogenously enact more strict regulation in an attempt to control

Figure 6.6   State Population Homeless on a Single Night Against Local Regulation Index (2007)

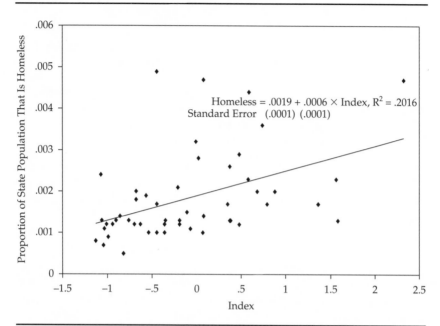

Homeless = .0019 + .0006 × Index, R² = .2016
Standard Error   (.0001) (.0001)

Source: Author's calculation.

growth—that is, high housing prices may cause a more stringent regulatory environment rather than a reverse. Although some evidence suggests that this is not the case and, in particular, that more regulated areas are less dense than less regulated areas (Gyourko, Saiz, and Summers 2006), one can never be certain in a nonexperimental setting.

With these caveats in mind, I present a series of simple regression models relating variation in the incidence of homelessness across states to variation in a single gauge of housing affordability and, in turn, housing affordability to the state-level WRLURI variable. Specifically, I present a series of ordinary least squares (OLS) models that regress single-night homeless rates for 2007 on state-level median rent-to-income ratios estimated from the 2007 ACS along with several other state-level covariates that may explain variation in homelessness. I then present a series of two-stage-least-squares (2SLS) models where rent-to-income ratios are instrumented with the WRLURI. Using preferred estimates of these models, I explore a few simple simulations in which I reduce regulation in specific states and tabulate the effect on national homelessness implied by the model estimates.

Before presenting the model estimation results, I document the reduced form relationship between homelessness and regulation. Figure 6.6 is a

Table 6.7   OLS Estimates of the Effects of Rent-to-Income Ratios on Homelessness, Unweighted

	OLS Estimation, Dependent Variable = Proportion Homeless			Instrumental Variables Estimation, Dependent Variable = Proportion Homeless, Instrumental Variable = Regulatory Stringency		
Rent-to-Income Ratios	.025	.026	.020	.020	.019	−.001
	(.004)	(.005)	(.006)	(.005)	(.007)	(.011)
Black	—	−.001	−.004	—	−.001	−.004
		(.001)	(.001)		(.001)	(.002)
Hispanic	—	.001	−.000	—	.002	.003
		(.001)	(.002)		(.002)	(.002)
Poor	—	.006	.007	—	.003	−.001
		(.005)	(.005)		(.005)	(.006)
Prison release rate	—	.004	−.059	—	−.027	−.091
		(.134)	(.128)		(.137)	(.148)
Under eighteen	—	—	−.016)	—	—	−.040
			(.012)			(.015)
Over sixty-five	—	—	−.031)	—	—	−.045
			(.012)			(.015)
Average January Temperature/1000	—	—	.032	—	—	.043
			(.011)			(.013)
R^2	.452	.503	.613	.435	.481	.487
N	50	50	50	50	50	50
First stage t (p-value)	—	—	—	10.14	7.85	5.40
				(.000)	(.000)	(.000)

Source: Author's compilation.
Note: Standard errors in parentheses.

scatter plot of the proportion of a state's population that is homeless on a single night in 2007 against the WRLURI. The relationship between these variables is clear, positive, and statistically significant. In what follows, the 2SLS results permit decomposing this reduced form effect into the product of the effect of regulation on housing costs and the effect of housing costs on homelessness.

Tables 6.7 and 6.8 present a series of regression models in which the dependent variable is the proportion of the state's population that is homeless and the key explanatory variable is the median rent-to-income ratio in the state. The first three models present OLS results, and the next three 2SLS results in which the WRLURI variable is used as an instrument for the rent-to-income ratio. Table 6.7 presents unweighted regression results, and table 6.8 presents estimation results in which the models are weighted by state population in 2007. Beginning with the OLS

Table 6.8   OLS Estimates of the Effects of Rent-to-Income Ratios on Homelessness, Weighted by State Population

	OLS Estimation, Dependent Variable = Proportion Homeless			Instrumental Variables Estimation, Dependent Variable = Proportion Homeless, Instrumental Variable = Regulatory Stringency		
Rent-to-Income Ratios	.032	.037	.035	.027	.031	.019
	(.003)	(.005)	(.005)	(.004)	(.007)	(.010)
Black	—	−.002	−.004	—	−.002	−.004
		(.001)	(.001)		(.001)	(.002)
Hispanic	—	−.000	−.001	—	.000	.002
		(.001)	(.001)		(.001)	(.002)
Poor	—	.014	.016	—	.011	.008
		(.005)	(.004)		(.006)	(.006)
Prison release rate	—	.071	−.018	—	.062	.001
		(.119)	(.116)		(.121)	(.132)
Under eighteen	—	—	−.020	—	—	−.041
			(.012)			(.018)
Over sixty-five	—	—	−.031	—	—	−.039
			(.009)			(.012)
Average January Temperature/1000	—	—	.015	—	—	.021
			(.010)			(.012)
R^2	.652	.750	.804	.635	.743	.757
N	50	50	50	50	50	50
First stage t (p-value)	—	—	—	9.13	5.81	4.09
				(.000)	(.000)	(.000)

Source: Author's compilation.
Note: Standard errors in parentheses.

results, there is a robust partial correlation between the rent-to-income ratio and homelessness. Although I cannot control for an extensive set of covariates, given that there are only fifty observations, controlling for the proportions that are black, Hispanic, poor, under eighteen years of age, and over sixty-five, as well as the prisoner release rate in 2006, does not alter the coefficient on the housing-affordability measure.[8] The OLS results are somewhat sensitive to a measure of average temperature in January, though the coefficient on the regulatory index is still significant when this covariate is added to the specification. The instrumental variables models are generally consistent with the OLS estimates except for the model including January temperature, where the coefficient on regulation falls to zero. Note that the regulatory stringency variable is a fairly strong instrument, in terms of statistical significance, in all models and always has the proper—that is to say, positive—sign in the first-stage regressions.

The weighted regression results in table 6.8 are similar, although the rent-to-income effects are somewhat larger than the corresponding OLS coefficients from the unweighted models. In addition, the rent-to-income variable is significant in all three 2SLS specifications—at the 1 percent level in the first two specifications and 10 percent in the last.

I use these estimation results to assess the relative importance of regulation in determining current homelessness levels in the following manner. The instrumental variables models estimated in tables 6.7 and 6.8 can be expressed by the equations

$$homelessness_i = \alpha + \beta \, Rent/Income_i + \varepsilon_i$$

$$Rent/Income_i = \gamma + \delta \, Regulation_i + \eta_i,$$

where the second-stage dependent variable is the proportion of a state's population that is homeless, and where for simplicity I have ignored other covariates that may enter the model specification. As written, regulation affects homelessness only indirectly through its impact on the rent-to-income ratio. In particular, the change in the proportion homeless in a given state caused by a change in the degree of regulatory stringency would be given by the expression $dhomelessness_i = \beta\delta*dRegulation_i$. Thus, if we define the variable pop_i as the population of a given state, the predicted effect on the overall homelessness count for the nation for a given vector of state-level regulatory changes would be given by the equation

$$dhomelessness_i = \sum_{i=1}^{50} \beta\delta \quad pop_i d \, Regulation_i.$$

I simulate the effects of two alternative changes in the distribution of the state-level WRLURI. First, I calculate the implied change in total single-night homelessness that we would observe were we to reduce the degree of regulatory stringency in states with above median WRLURI values to the median value, holding all other state values (for those at or below the median) constant. Second, I calculate similar changes implied by reducing the WRLURI values of all states to the minimum value of this variable.

Table 6.9 presents the results from this exercise. For both simulations, I use the smallest of the 2SLS estimates of these parameters from the weighted regressions. Since the smallest estimates from the unweighted models yields a structural coefficient of zero, these simulations should be thought of as upper-bound estimates of the impact of housing market regulation on homelessness.[9] Relative to a base homelessness count of 645,273 persons,[10] reducing regulatory stringency above the median to the median value would result in a decline in homelessness of 46,246, roughly 7.2 percent of total homelessness. Reducing all state-level regulatory

Table 6.9   Simulated Effects of Reducing Regulatory Stringency

	For States Above Median Level to Median Level	In All States to Level of Least Regulated State
Base homeless count[a]	645,453	645,253
Simulated homeless count	599,005	500,960
Difference	46,246	144,294

Source: Author's compilation.
Note: Estimates based on the 2SLS estimates from the final specification of the weighted models in table 6.8.
a. Total homeless count is tabulated by applying state-level homeless rates from AHAR to state-level population estimates from the American Community Survey.

stringency values to the minimum value results in even larger declines—144,294 persons, roughly 22 percent.

Of course, reducing the degree of regulatory stringency is unlikely to result in such large declines in homelessness. Regulated states have pursued development paths governed by their regulatory regimes, and housing patterns are, to a certain extent, locked in by the consequent land-use patterns and the durability of the existing housing stock. Nonetheless, these simulations suggest that the regulatory environment in which many local housing markets have developed may indeed have contributed to homelessness by increasing housing prices and rents.

Conclusion

This chapter has made several arguments and presented several basic stylized facts that hint at a potentially important role of local housing market regulation in driving homelessness. First, the theoretical link between regulation and housing affordability—and, in turn, affordability and homelessness—is straightforward, with the second link in this causal chain well established in nonexperimental analysis relating homelessness to variation in housing costs. Second, a large and growing body of empirical literature demonstrates higher housing costs in more regulated local markets, with particularly large price disparities between more and less regulated markets for low-quality, low-income housing. Third, the empirical evidence presented here suggests that more regulated housing markets experienced relatively greater housing price appreciation and slower growth in the stock of housing. Finally, the correlation between one measure of regulatory stringency and a recent single-night enumeration of the homeless is direct and positive. The strength of this relationship, as mediated through the effect of regulation on housing costs, suggests that regulation may be a substantial contributor to U.S. homelessness levels.

Of course, finding that local housing market regulation contributes to homelessness does not necessarily imply that combating homelessness requires that we first and foremost eliminate local control of land-use planning. Given the historical deference to local land-use decisions that characterizes most housing markets in the United States, such a proposal is politically and practically infeasible. Presumably, incumbent residents (homeowners in particular) benefit from local land-use control practices, both in terms of housing values as well as in terms of minimizing externalities through the close colocation of deemed-incompatible land uses. Hence, it is hard to imagine a feasible homelessness-reduction policy agenda centered around limiting local-government involvement in land-use planning.

Nonetheless, the likely contribution of such policies to housing price appreciation and homelessness makes salient some of the extreme unintended distributional consequences of local housing-market regulation. It also provides strong support for either income-support efforts or housing cost subsidies that would render decent minimum-quality housing affordable to extremely low-income individuals.

Notes

1. The outlier data point with a very high proportion of homeless and high median rent is Washington, D.C. Dropping this observation from the scatter plot does not appreciably alter the regression coefficients, although discarding this observation does increase the R^2 in each model.
2. The land-use regulations considered include restriction on residential building permits issued in a given time frame, limits on population growth in a given time frame, adequate service levels required for residential development, adequate service levels required for nonresidential development, rezoning of residential land to agricultural open space, reduction in density permitted by the general plan, voter approval required for residential upzoning, a supermajority council vote required for residential upzoning, restrictions on commercial building within a given time frame, restriction on industrial building within a given time frame, commercial industrial land rezoned to less intense uses, height restrictions on nonresidential buildings, growth management elements in the general plan, and urban-limit lines.
3. Based on the survey results and a legislative- and case-history analysis of each state, the authors construct the aggregate index from a factor analysis of the following subindices: an index measuring the degree of local political pressure in the development process, an index gauging the extent of state political involvement in local land-use measures, an index measuring the degree of state court involvement, a local zoning-approval index indicating the number of public bodies that must approve a given residential project, a local project-approval index gauging the number of local organizations that must approve a project, a local assembly index indicative of the opportunity for community involvement in approval meetings, a supply-restriction

index, a density-restriction index, an open-space index, an exactions index, and finally an approval-delay index.

4. These tabulations combined rental and owner-occupied housing. For the price of owner-occupied housing, I use the respondent's estimate of the value of the unit. For rental units, I convert monthly contract rents into housing values by multiplying by twelve and then dividing by the average mortgage interest rate on a thirty-year fixed-rate fully amortizing loan. Although this ignores the role of physical depreciation, anticipated price appreciation, and tax policy on housing valuation, several of these ignored factors offset one another. This imputation thus provides a rough proxy on the value of rentals.

5. Weighting in this manner eliminates any quality enhancements occurring via a shift in the distribution across the joint rooms-bedrooms–unit structure distribution that may have occurred within defined quality quintiles.

6. For a thirty-seven-year period, the constant annual nominal appreciation rate, a, consistent with an N-fold increase in nominal prices is given by the equation $a = N^{1/37} - 1$.

7. Thankfully, future annual homelessness assessment reports will provide additional years of data from both Continuum of Care applications as well as homelessness-management information systems that may facilitate longitudinal analysis of the determinants of homelessness.

8. With the exception of the prisoner release rate, I measure all the explanatory variables with data from the 2007 ACS. The prisoner release rates at the state level come from the Bureau of Justice Statistics.

9. The first-stage coefficient on the regulation variable does not change much from specification to specification, although the coefficients in the fullest specifications (the one I use in each instance) are generally slightly smaller. The first-stage results are available on request.

10. This total comes from applying the AHAR proportion estimates to noninstitutionalized population totals estimated from the 2007 ACS.

References

Burt, Martha. 1992. *Over the Edge: The Growth of Homelessness During the 1980s*. New York: Russell Sage Foundation.

Culhane, Dennis P., Edmund F. Dejowski, Julie Ibanez, Elizabeth Needham, and Irene Macchia. 1999. "Public Shelter Admission Rates in Philadelphia and New York: The Implications of Turnover for Sheltered Population Counts." *Housing Policy Debate* 5(2): 107–39.

Fischel, William A. 1990. *Do Growth Controls Matter? A Review of the Empirical Evidence on the Effectiveness and Efficiency of Local Government Land Use Regulation*. Cambridge, Mass.: Lincoln Institute of Land Policy.

Glaeser, Edward L., and Joseph Gyourko. 2003. "The Impact of Building Restrictions on Housing Affordability." *Federal Reserve Bank of New York Economic Policy Review* June: 21–39.

Glaeser, Edward L., Joseph Gyourko, and Raven Saks. 2005a. "Why Have Housing Prices Gone Up?" *American Economic Review* 95(2): 329–33.

———. 2005b. "Why Is Manhattan so Expensive? Regulations and the Rise in House Prices." *Journal of Law and Economics* 48(2): 331–69.

———. 2005c. "Why Have Housing Prices Gone Up?" NBER working paper 11129. Cambridge, Mass.: National Bureau of Economic Research.

Green, Richard K. 1999. "Land Use Regulation and the Price of Housing in a Suburban Wisconsin County." *Journal of Housing Economics* 8(2): 144–59.

Gyourko, Joseph, Albert Saiz, and Anita Summers. 2006. "A New Measure of the Local Regulatory Environment for Housing Markets: Wharton Residential Land Use Regulatory Index." Wharton School working paper. Philadelphia: University of Pennsylvania.

Malpezzi, Stephen, and Richard K. Green. 1996. "What Has Happened to the Bottom of the U.S. Housing Market?" *Urban Studies* 33(1): 1807–20.

Mayer, Christopher J., and Tsuriel Somerville. 2000. "Land Use Regulation and New Construction." *Regional Science and Urban Economics* 30(6): 639–62.

O'Flaherty, Brendan. 1995. "An Economic Theory of Homelessness and Housing." *Journal of Housing Economics* 4(1): 13–49.

———. 1996. *Making Room: The Economics of Homelessness.* Cambridge, Mass.: Harvard University Press.

———. 2004. "Wrong Person and Wrong Place: For Homelessness, the Conjunction Is What Matters." *Journal of Housing Economics* 13(1): 1–15.

Pendall, Rolf. 2000. "Local Land Use Regulation and the Chain of Exclusion." *Journal of the American Planning Association* 66(2): 125–42.

Quigley, John, and Steven Raphael. 2005. "Regulation and the High Cost of Housing in California." *American Economic Review* 95(2): 323–28.

Quigley, John, Steven Raphael, and Eugene Smolensky. 2001. "Homeless in America, Homeless in California." *Review of Economics and Statistics* 83(1): 37–51.

Raphael, Steven, and Michael A. Stoll. 2008. "Why Are So Many Americans in Prison?" In *Do Prisons Make Us Safer? The Benefits and Costs of the Prison Boom,* edited by Steven Raphael and Michael Stoll. New York: Russell Sage Foundation.

Ruggles, Steven, Matthew Sobek, Trent Alexander, Catherine A. Fitch, Ronald Goekan, Patricia Kelly-Hall, Miriam King, and Chad Ronnander. 2009. Integrated Public Use Microdata Series: Version 4.0 [Machine-readable database]. Minneapolis, Minn: Minnesota Population Center [producer and distributor]. Available at: http://usa.ipums.org/usa (accessed February 18, 2010).

U.S. Department of Housing and Urban Development (HUD). 2008. *The Third Annual Homeless Assessment Report to Congress.* Washington: Government Printing Office.

PART III

MANAGING RISK

Chapter 7

Homelessness as Bad Luck: Implications for Research and Policy

BRENDAN O'FLAHERTY

Sometimes bad things happen to people. They lose their jobs; companions walk out on them; their health—physical or mental—deteriorates; they get evicted; prices of goods they rely on rise; they lose their benefits. Sometimes they are blameless in these calamities; sometimes they are not. Good things happen to people, too.

Stochastic processes are a major consideration in the study of homelessness. Individual narratives of how people become homeless emphasize bad luck, and good luck often figures in how people leave homelessness. More objective studies support this subjective view. Predicting who will become homeless on the basis of observable characteristics is extremely difficult, and even the most thorough studies end up with large errors of both type 1 and type 2.

Unobservable characteristics are therefore hugely significant in what leads to homelessness. These characteristics are either persistent or transient. If they were persistent, spells of homelessness would be very long—years or decades long. But most spells of homelessness are measured in days or months, not decades. Homelessness is not an indelible characteristic like a birthmark or a Social Security number. Almost everyone who will be homeless two years from today is housed now, and almost everyone who is homeless today will be housed two years from now. Homeless spells are more like semesters than careers. Some homeless spells are many years long, but these are rare. What is important about these spells is that at their starts they are unpredictable. Bad luck can be decades long as well as days long.

143

Transient unobservable characteristics, then, are responsible for a large proportion of homelessness. Luck is the colloquial term for transient unobservable characteristics (and it is appropriate to use this term even when the probability of becoming homeless is not the same for every person at every time[1]).

Looking at homelessness as part of the stochastic variation in people's lives has many implications; this chapter elucidates a few of them. I show that transitions to homelessness are inherently unpredictable; services cannot be well targeted at people likely to become homeless, no matter how diligently and resourcefully researchers and service providers try. Current housing conditions are the best predictor of future homelessness, although housing market shocks are probably not the major immediate precursor to homelessness. Reducing real income volatility may be more effective in reducing homelessness than raising people's average level of well-being. Smoothing may work better than uplifting.

In paying attention to how individuals experience homelessness, I am not implying that the environment in which they find themselves is unimportant or unchanging. Changes in that environment imply changes in individual probabilities of experiencing homelessness and so changes in the aggregate volume of homelessness. How environment affects aggregate homelessness has been studied extensively (for instance, see Raphael, this volume). The question this chapter addresses is how, in any given environment, homelessness can be prevented or reduced. It is not a question of why so many fires occur, but rather how the fire trucks should be deployed. Both questions are worth studying. I do not examine what sort of shocks poor people face and what sort of shocks precipitate homelessness (see O'Flaherty 2009a).

The chapter also examines institutions and programs that might reduce volatility. Reforms in the private housing market do not appear promising, with the possible exception of shared-equity mortgages, partly because housing price shocks are not a major problem. Subsidized housing programs are good at reducing volatility among their recipients but are not designed as insurance programs for the wider community. Aid does not generally flow to those who need it most when they need it most.

Shelters, on the other hand, work well as part of the safety net and would work better if they applied some lessons from the theory of optimal unemployment insurance. Post-shelter subsidies should be widespread rather than targeted and most easily available early in shelter spells. The chapter also looks at the nascent field of homelessness prevention.

Why Does Risk Matter?

Risk matters because homelessness is a transient state for which onset cannot easily be predicted in advance. If some people were fated to be homeless and stay homeless for most of their lives, or if one could anticipate well in advance who would become homeless and when, then analysts could ignore risk. Abundant empirical work indicates that neither of these conditions holds. Homelessness is a fairly unpredictable event in some people's lives. It is like unemployment. Three strands of literature support this picture.

The first is the finding that most shelter spells are short—a few days—and very few shelter spells last more than two years (see, for example, Culhane et al. 2007). Comparably accurate data on spells of street homelessness are not available, for obvious reasons. The significance of this literature is not the length of the spells by itself, but that almost everyone who is homeless eventually stops being so.

The second strand finds that many people go through homelessness at some point in their lives; the many short spells represent a large group of people, not a small group of people cycling repeatedly (see, for instance, Link et al. 1994; Culhane and Metraux 1999).

The final strand shows that predicting in advance who will become homeless and when is very hard for skilled statisticians with abundant data and so presumably hard too for the people involved themselves. A status can be transient and widespread without being random—enrollment in third grade, for instance—and so unpredictability does not follow from the first pieces of the picture. A study by Marybeth Shinn and her colleagues (1998), which was elaborated upon in another study by Shinn and Jim Baumohl (1998), is probably the best-known paper that tries to forecast homelessness.

Shinn and her colleagues look at welfare families in New York City in 1988. Using a rich set of both survey and administrative data, they fit a logistic regression for the probability of requesting shelter within several years of the first interview. They derive a relative operating characteristic (ROC) curve from this regression, and discuss the point on the ROC curve where the *false-alarm rate* is 10 percent: that is, 10 percent of the families who did not request shelter are predicted to request shelter. At the corresponding cutoff, the *hit rate* is 66 percent: that is, 66 percent of the families who did request shelter are predicted to request it. This 10 percent rate is arbitrary; for any false-alarm rate, the ROC curve gives the corresponding hit rate. I concentrate on this point, though, to simplify exposition (it is also the only point on the ROC curve that the paper describes explicitly).

Let us say that the families predicted to request shelter at this point on the ROC have characteristic X, and families predicted not to request shelter have characteristic Y at some time slightly before they either do or do not request it. Call this time 0 and the time of shelter request time 1. From the findings of Shinn and Baumohl (1998), we can infer that the welfare population could be approximately described by table 7.1.

Thus a family with characteristic X at time 0 had an 18 percent (six in thirty three) chance of requesting shelter at time 1, and an 82 percent chance of not requesting shelter. Nothing in the rich data set that Shinn and her colleagues worked with explains what made the 18 percent who

Table 7.1   Distribution of New York City Welfare Population, 1988

	At Time 0		
	Characteristic X	Characteristic Y	Total
At Time 1			
Request Shelter	6	3	9
Don't Request	27	244	271
Total	33	247	280

Source: Author's compilation based on Shinn and Baumohl (1998).
Note: Numbers represent thousands of families.

requested shelter different from the 82 percent who did not request shelter. Nor is there anything in the data set that explains why the 1 percent of characteristic Y families who requested shelter were different from the 99 percent who did not. Perhaps there was some measurement error that resulted in these divergent experiences, or perhaps there was some persistent unobservable characteristic that triggered homeless spells beginning at just this time (although it may be difficult to explain why a persistent characteristic did not trigger homelessness earlier). In that case, better econometric work may be able to make predicting easy work. Or perhaps the families that became homeless were just unlucky. Theory tells us that the latter may be a better explanation.

Economic Theory

The role of risk in transitions to homelessness is clear from economic theory. Several simple and well-known results in consumption theory are powerful and novel when applied to homelessness. Consumption theory is the part of macroeconomics that tries to explain what determines the total amount that people spend buying rather than saving. Essentially, it uses models with only one composite consumption good, which can be used as food, clothing, carpet cleaner, or anything else.

How can we apply these results to housing, which is actually only one of many consumption goods? For now, I assume that housing is the only good, and that the only problem consumers face is how to spread their consumption of different qualities of housing over the various periods of their lives: for instance, should they live in a high-quality house now and a poor-quality house when they are old, or should they do the opposite? Thus I ignore the problem of how to allocate wealth between housing at any time and other goods at that time. This simplification turns out to be innocuous.[2]

To simplify further, I assume that life has only two periods, which I call *today* and *tomorrow*. Most but not all of the questions we are interested in can be addressed in this framework.

I think of homelessness as a set of very poor and very cheap qualities of housing. No qualities are worse or cheaper than those called homelessness.

Several interesting results can be seen in this stark setting.

First is that transitions into homelessness are impossible unless the future is uncertain or saving is extremely difficult. That implies that the study of homelessness requires explicit consideration of risk.

To see why, suppose consumers today know perfectly what tomorrow will be like, and they can save, though maybe they cannot borrow. They will not plan to be worse off tomorrow than they are today. Why? If they were going to be worse off tomorrow, a dollar tomorrow would be more valuable to them than a dollar today, and by increasing saving they could move a dollar from today's consumption to tomorrow's. Therefore they will always consume at least as much housing tomorrow as they consumed today. Because a transition into homelessness means consuming less housing tomorrow than today, transitions into homelessness will not occur under these conditions.

Thus, with perfect foresight, people are homeless either none of the time or all of the time; there are no transitions. Because we do see many transitions, however, we need to think about them in a model in which either the future is uncertain or saving is notably difficult.

Suppose saving is difficult. Then even with perfect foresight, people could enter homelessness. They would know that something bad was going to happen to them tomorrow, but they would not be able to transfer resources from today to tomorrow to deal with it.

If homelessness were of this variety, it could easily be averted by finding people who knew they were going to be homeless next period and offering them savings accounts, which could be done essentially without cost. Because individuals could know whether they were destined to be homeless, econometricians could know as well, and predicting who would become homeless would be easy.

The intuition is fairly simple. For most people, homelessness is very bad, and all homeless spells represent a small fraction of their lifetime. Thus, with perfect foresight and perfect capital markets, no one would ever be homeless: everyone could and would reduce consumption in good times enough that they could stay out of homelessness in bad times. Just as no one plans to have a fire, no one plans to become homeless. If you knew your home would catch on fire tomorrow afternoon, you would take effective steps to prevent it. Similarly, if you knew you would be homeless next month, and everything else relevant about next month, you would take effective steps to prevent it.

Even without perfect capital markets, people who were old enough would not become homeless: they would save up enough resources in good times to avoid the predicament. The standards for *old enough* are pretty low. Hence for people who are old enough and have some way of saving something, homelessness can happen only by surprise; otherwise they would have set aside resources to avoid it. Surprises, by definition, cannot be anticipated or forecast by an outside econometrician.

With uncertainty, the situation is quite different and corresponds more closely to the transitions we see. To be concrete, suppose tomorrow's income is not known today, but there are no market imperfections. Empirically, income shocks seem to be the most important of those that lead to homelessness (see O'Flaherty 2009a).

The most striking result about this situation is from a study by Robert Hall (1978). In the special case of quadratic utility, in which people act as if they maximize the expected value of a quadratic function of consumption, actual consumption is a martingale: the expected value of consumption tomorrow is the same as consumption today. The intuition is that consumers try to keep consumption constant over time, and so all the information that they have today is incorporated in the level of consumption that they choose for today. Because they cannot forecast perfectly, they will almost certainly have to adjust their consumption tomorrow, but the expected size of the adjustment is zero, accounting for the possibility of both positive and negative adjustments. Consumption changes because of surprises, and the expected size of the response to consumption because of surprises is zero. Surprises, of course, cannot be predicted, by either the consumer or the observing econometrician.

This result does not in any way depend on subjective discount rates or taste for savings. These parameters affect consumption today, but not the relationship between consumption today and consumption tomorrow.

Thus, under these conditions, the business of predicting housing consumption tomorrow is fairly easy, even if the predictions are not especially accurate: all we have to know is housing consumption today. Housing consumption today is a sufficient statistic for housing consumption tomorrow. No other information today can improve this prediction: not the consumer's demographics, not the consumer's medical or psychological state, not any risk factors that might apply, not any characteristics of the housing market. The prediction based on housing consumption today may carry a great deal of uncertainty, and it will almost certainly be wrong, but no information today can improve it.

The situation is somewhat different, however, if we are interested in predicting transitions into and out of homelessness, rather than housing consumption. Consider transitions into homelessness. A consumer who is not homeless today becomes homeless tomorrow if and only if she receives a large enough negative shock tomorrow—her income is unexpectedly very low, for example. The better her level of housing consumption today, the larger the negative shock tomorrow she can withstand without being driven to homelessness. Thus within a homogeneous population, meaning a population facing the same distribution of shocks, today's housing consumption will contain all available information about the probability of homelessness tomorrow. The better today's housing, the smaller the probability of being homeless tomorrow.

But within a heterogeneous population, meaning a population in which some identifiable groups face different distributions of shocks, today's housing consumption will not contain all available information about the probability of homelessness tomorrow. Consider two individuals consuming the same housing today but with different distributions of income tomorrow. The individual with the greater variance in income tomorrow is more likely to be homeless tomorrow. Thus information about the variance and higher moments of future income, as well as information about consumption today, is useful in predicting transitions to homelessness. More risky income will be associated with greater probability of becoming homeless, ceteris paribus.

The situation with transitions out of homelessness is symmetrical. Within a homogeneous population, people who are homeless today have a higher probability of being homeless tomorrow than anyone who is not homeless today—and indeed, in a multiperiod extension, a person who is homeless today has a higher probability of being homeless on any day arbitrarily far into the future than anyone not homeless today. But within a heterogeneous population, homeless people with riskier incomes are more likely to escape homelessness tomorrow than their counterparts with less risky incomes. Variables positively associated with the probability of transitioning into homelessness, conditional on today's housing consumption, will also be positively associated with the probability of leaving homelessness.

How are these results affected by dropping the assumptions of quadratic utility and perfect capital markets? For our purposes, quadratic utility makes little difference. In general, consumers try to keep the marginal utility of consumption constant over time, rather than consumption, and so marginal utility is a martingale, not consumption. But because the correspondence between marginal utility and consumption is one to one, all the qualitative results carry over: housing today is a sufficient statistic for housing tomorrow, housing today is a sufficient statistic for homelessness tomorrow in a homogeneous population, and housing today and income risk predict homelessness tomorrow in a heterogeneous population.

Imperfect capital markets are easy to incorporate. Consumers who face binding borrowing constraints consume less today than they would otherwise want to and more tomorrow. Their expected consumption tomorrow is therefore greater than today's consumption, assuming quadratic utility. Information about borrowing constraints is similarly useful in predicting future consumption and homelessness.

Savings constraints work the opposite way. People who cannot save as much as they want to will plan to consume less tomorrow than they do today. An individual whose savings are constrained is more likely to be homeless tomorrow than an unconstrained counterpart who consumes the same quality of housing today.

Thus, for research purposes, information about capital-market imperfections is useful in predicting homelessness.

For policy purposes, encouraging saving and making it easier for poor people to save are likely to be effective homelessness-prevention tools. The saving that needs encouragement is unrestricted saving, not saving restricted to one or more meritorious purposes, as in most current programs to encourage saving by poor people. Whether relaxing borrowing constraints reduces homelessness is not clear. It would increase homelessness in the two-period model that I use here but might not have that effect in a multiperiod model, in which allowing someone who would otherwise be homeless to borrow against future income would cause an immediate first-order reduction in homelessness. More work needs to be done on this question.

An Illustration

We can illustrate this way of looking at homelessness with a crude reinterpretation of the results of Marybeth Shin and her colleagues (Shinn et al. 1998; Shinn and Baumohl 1998). Those results were consistent with our theoretical prediction for a relatively homogeneous population with few constraints on saving or borrowing: current housing consumption was just about the only predictor of future homelessness.

To get a rough idea of how important risk was in the lives of families who became homeless, I assumed that consumption followed a particular stochastic pattern called a first-order autoregressive process. In such a process, consumption oscillates around an average value, with the oscillations driven by random shocks every period.[3] This kind of stochastic process is not exactly the same kind that Hall's model in the previous section implies, but it is a little easier to work with. Clearly more work needs to be done on this topic.

I take the characteristics X and Y to be levels of housing consumption. From the results of Shinn and her colleagues about the probabilities of transition from X and Y to homelessness, from the proportions of families at X and Y originally, and from the probability of being homeless in five years, I can solve for all parameters of the autoregressive process and for the values of X and Y.[4] This calibration produces plausible values.

With these parameter values in hand, we can get a rough idea of how policies that changed these parameters would affect homelessness. That will allow us in turn to have an idea of whether risk has a major effect or whether the average level is the main thing that matters.

First consider what would happen to the transitions from X and Y if σ, the standard error of the shocks, fell from 1 to .5: in table 7.1, the number of homeless families would fall from 9,000 to 1,137. Most of the fall is in the number of families entering homelessness from X. Reducing risk has a major impact on immediate homelessness. To accomplish the same reduction by raising the average consumption of the population would require an increase in α, which is proportional to steady state consumption, from .5431 to 1.5191, approximately a tripling.

Asymptotically, the contrast is not so great: cutting σ from 1 to 0.5 reduces homelessness from 8 percent to .25 percent. The same decrease in homelessness could be achieved by doubling α, from .5431 to 1.0862.

Of course, which kind of policies are better to use depends on cost and feasibility; whether we know any policies that could either halve σ or double α is unclear. The point of the exercise has been to show that policies that reduce volatility are worth exploring; they can be just as effective in reducing homelessness as those that raise expected housing consumption. Smoothing works just as well as uplifting. This chapter looks at a variety of policies for smoothing housing consumption.

Saving, Borrowing, and Family Contributions

One traditional way that people smooth consumption in the face of uncertainty is by saving and borrowing, through either market institutions, such as banks and insurance companies, or the help of families and friends. Sometimes assistance from families and friends is in kind rather than in cash—a hot meal, a place to spend the night, or information about a job. We will see that poor people use many mechanisms to smooth consumption, but all of them have weaknesses. Poor people do manage to smooth consumption, but they cannot do so fully.

I begin by considering saving, which seems easy in principle. Poor people do save. In 2003 and 2004; MetroEdge conducted a survey on financial behavior and attitudes in twenty-one low- and moderate-income census tracts in each of three cities—Los Angeles, Chicago, and Washington. Median household income in this survey was $18,552. In this sample, 49 percent said that they had savings. Of households with annual income below $10,000, 28 percent had savings (Seidman, Hababou, and Kramer 2005). But saving is not easy.

The obvious way to save is to use a checking account or a savings account at a bank. Many poor people, however, lack such accounts: 29.6 percent in the entire MetroEdge sample. Of households with annual income below $10,000, 48.1 percent lacked accounts. Of households with income between $10,000 and $20,000, 43.4 percent lacked them (Seidman, Hababou, and Kramer 2005, table 1). Ellen Seidman and her colleagues found that "consumers who are unable to build up and maintain minimum balances and who cash a limited number of relatively small checks each month may well pay less for transactional services by using a check casher rather than having a checking account" (2005, 4). Part of the reason is that many vendors in low-income neighborhoods do not accept checks. About 20 percent of landlords, for instance, wanted to be paid by currency or money order.

One alternative to using a bank for saving money is to hold currency. About 21 percent of savers in the MetroEdge survey did not use a bank account. Currency, of course, pays no interest. It is also subject to theft and loss, especially for those whose housing is precarious or scant.

Buying durable goods—cars, furniture, electronics, jewelry—is in principle another way of saving, and the availability of installment plans and rent-to-own stores removes some of the lumpiness that might otherwise discourage these investments. But interest rates on installment plans are high, the goods themselves usually deteriorate over time, transactions costs are high, and adverse selection difficulties are probably present in the market for secondhand durable goods. As investments, durable goods are far from secure, and they are most likely to lose value at times when other things are going poorly for their owners. Because these investments are illiquid, they will lose value when their owners experience a liquidity crisis: in the best-case scenario, they will lose only part of their value when sold quickly on the thin secondhand market; in the worst case, they will be repossessed. These investments are also in danger of being lost, stolen, forfeited, or stolen when a household is forced to relocate or to become homeless.

Cars are an exception to this last problem. But especially in densely populated cities, cars are expensive to keep. Liability insurance costs are high, and cars are exposed to the dangers of theft, collision, and parking tickets.

A final way to save is to invest in human capital—to acquire skills and credentials. Aside from liquidity problems, however, the Thirteenth Amendment makes this a poor way of accumulating precautionary savings, given that the principal can never be converted into cash.

Thus, though precautionary savings are certainly one way that poor people can smooth consumption, none of the available ways of saving have attractive interest rates or attractive correlations with the rest of a household's portfolio.

Government assistance programs also reduce precautionary savings (Engen and Gruber 1995; Gruber and Yelowitz 1997; Hubbard, Skinner and Zeldes 1995; Powers 1998; Neumark and Powers 1998). First, they reduce the need for precautionary savings by increasing consumption in poor times; the need to save for a rainy day is less pressing if rainy days are merely misty. Second, asset limits for eligibility in various means-tested programs require that households liquidate most of these assets and spend most of the proceeds before they can receive benefits (Carney and Gale 2001). Asset limits do not discourage precautionary savings per se because in the absence of government programs, these assets would be spent down anyway when bad shocks occurred. Asset limits may discourage life-cycle savings because life-cycle savings may not have been spent down so completely in a transitory bad shock. Because precautionary and life-cycle savings are hard to distinguish, asset limits could discourage some precautionary savings.

In the other direction, borrowing is also hard for poor people. Many poor people have bad credit histories, because of either previous unfortunate incidents, like medical bills or scams or relationships that fell apart (Edin 2001), or having no credit histories at all.

Borrowing is not impossible, however. From 1983 to 1995 the proportion of poor households with at least one credit card rose from 17 percent to 36 percent, and the average balance of a poor household grew 3.8 times (Sullivan 2005). Credit cards and other unsecured debt (unsecured loans from financial institutions, outstanding bills including medical bills, loans from individuals, and education loans), however, do not seem to be used much to smooth consumption. Sullivan (2005) found that among households with low or no assets, unsecured debt did not expand when households experienced transitory negative income shocks; instead, consumption contracted. Credit cards were not particularly useful in smoothing consumption: the average interest rate was about 15 percent, and the available credit for the average low-asset household with a card was only about $800 (Sullivan 2005).

Payday lending has also grown tremendously since the turn of the century, from a volume of about $8 billion in 1999 to $40 to $50 billion in 2004 (Stegman 2007).

> [In a typical payday loan,] the borrower writes a postdated check for $300 and receives $255 in cash—the lender taking a $45 fee off the top. The lender then holds on to the check until the following payday, before depositing it in his own account. . . . The entire transaction can take place in less than an hour. All that a prospective borrower . . . needs is a home address, a valid checking account, a driver's license and Social Security number; a couple of pay stubs to verify employment; wages and pay dates; and minimum earnings of at least $1,000 a month. (Stegman 2007, 169)

We know little about whether payday loans are used to smooth consumption. Clearly they cannot insure against unemployment shocks, and the requirements of a checking account and a job may rule out many people who are down on their luck. Only 4.2 percent of residents in the MetroEdge survey had taken at least one payday loan in the previous year, about the same number that had used a pawnshop. Sullivan's results on unsecured debt suggest that payday loans may not be used for smoothing consumption either, especially by poor people, who probably qualify only during what for them are good times. Empirical work on this question is well worth pursuing.

Families can also help smooth consumption. Laurence Kotlikoff and Avia Spivak (1981) compare a family to an incomplete annuity market.

Families can overcome adverse selection problems if participation in family insurance networks is almost mandatory and outsiders are excluded. Family members can also often monitor one another well and thereby reduce moral-hazard problems. Family insurance contracts, however, are not legally enforceable, risk is not well disseminated, and often members are subject to correlated shocks—especially if they are close enough to monitor one another.

Most empirical work has looked at how family transfers respond to unemployment shocks. In the United States, the response appears to be small (Dynarski and Gruber 1997; Bentolila and Ichino 2008). It is thus not surprising that a number of studies (Shinn et al. 1998, for instance) have found that strong family ties do not appreciably reduce the risk of entering homelessness, ceteris paribus.

All these reasons indicate that consumption-smoothing is hard for poor people, and so they do not smooth consumption perfectly. But some does take place, which is why transitions to and from homelessness are hard to predict.

Mitigating Risk in the Rental Market

Several institutions mitigate tenants' risks in the rental housing market.

Leases

Probably the most important risk-mitigation institution is the lease. Leases transfer several important risks associated with the occupancy of an apartment from the tenant to the landlord. Landlords thus act as tenants' insurers. But they do so at a price.

One risk that landlords insure tenants against is nominal, or unanticipated nominal, rent increases during the term of the lease. Rent the tenant pays does not go up during the term of the lease even if market rents go up and a potential tenant is willing to pay more; rent theoretically does not go down if the market softens. Because renegotiation of rent between consenting parties cannot be prevented, the protection against rent increases that landlords offer is probably more meaningful than the protection against rent decreases that tenants offer.

Because individual tenants can do little to influence the rental market or inflation, this aspect of leases appears to carry with it no moral-hazard problems. Ex ante, it induces tenants to make larger irreversible investments in the apartment and neighborhood, but that is part of the purpose.

The other important risk is physical damage to the apartment and system failure. Repairs can be quite expensive, well beyond the means of many tenants. Unlike insurance against market risk, insurance against damage risk carries with it serious moral-hazard problems. Careless or malicious tenants can create huge repair bills. Landlords can reduce their exposure by insisting on deposits and by promulgating rules of tenant behavior. But deposits cannot be extremely large, and landlords cannot verifiably observe a great deal of important tenant behavior—how closely children are supervised, for instance.

Landlords do not always provide the damage insurance that they have promised. Sometimes they are unwilling to do so; sometimes they are unable, because of financial resources or borrowing constraints. Landlords can reinsure, but not against every risk: they can insure against fires that tenants start, but not against repeatedly broken elevators or roach infestations. Insurance companies, too, worry about landlord moral hazard: fully insured landlords could become lax about tenant selection, preventive maintenance, and rule enforcement in ways that insurance companies could not verifiably observe at any reasonable cost.

Finally, landlords insure tenants against liquidity shocks. Tenants with leases may be several months in arrears before they can be evicted; thus landlords are obligated to extend a certain amount of credit. For tenants without credit cards, this ability to borrow can be valuable. Rent is often the single largest item in the budgets of low-income households, and grocery stores and gasoline stations are not legally obligated to extend credit.

This credit facility has obvious moral-hazard implications. Tenants may take bigger financial risks than they would have in its absence and may walk away from their apartments when the back rent gets too high.

Because leases obligate the landlord to provide three types of insurance, two of which are subject to moral hazard, they are expensive. In equilibrium, rent has to cover not just the normal costs of space, utilities, and maintenance but also the premiums for the insurance.

Because leases are expensive, not everyone has a lease. On one hand, some people have nonlease tenancies: they share housing with a friend or a relative, or they live in hotels, rooming houses, or some other kind of accommodation legally exempt from lease requirements. On the other hand, some people (in the United States, most people) occupy housing that they own. Households also live in subsidized apartments, where the rent does not have to cover the implicit insurance premiums.

Because the housing market is segmented in this way, adverse selection is possible. Ownership provides no comparable damage insurance to households who encounter physical problems and usually provides no comparable liquidity insurance to households that encounter financial problems. The era of subprime mortgages may have been an exception. Nonlease tenancies carry no financial insurance but almost completely insure tenants against paying the costs of physical damage. Subsidized apartments are like lease tenancies, but cheaper and rationed.

Because sorting occurs, changes in rules for one variety of occupancy can have ramifications for other types of occupancy. For instance, if municipalities place restrictions on nonlease tenancy by shutting down single-room occupancies (SROs) and rooming houses, the mix of prospective tenants seeking lease tenancy will include more people who tend to damage property, and the premium that all lease tenants have to pay may rise. This could move some lease tenants to opt for owner-occupancy. If these tenants are the most physically and financially responsible, leased rents could rise further, and the market could implode. With some parameters, lease tenancy may be viable only if enough nonlease housing is available.

Rent Control

Just as leases are designed to protect tenants from rent increases within their temporal boundaries, rent control is designed to protect tenants from rent increases between leases. As Richard Arnott (1995) emphasizes, rent control comes in many forms, but the common elements are that covered landlords are restricted in the amount that they can raise a continuing tenant's rent between leases and in their ability to deny new leases to continuing tenants. Some forms of rent control also limit the increases that landlords can impose when an apartment changes hands. Rent control usually applies only to a proper subset of apartments in a city.

For covered tenants, rent control acts like a very long lease and so reduces their exposure to rental price risk. The major moral-hazard problem associated with this insurance is that tenants may stay in their apartments too long. Edward Glaeser and Erzo Luttmer (1997), for instance, found that rent control in New York City resulted in substantial misallocation of apartments for this reason.

Insurance for covered tenants, however, may pass some risk to uncovered tenants. Uncovered tenants (or would-be tenants) could face enhanced risks from rent control: in particular, short-run rental price risk and search risk. To understand short-run price risk, suppose the supply of apartments is fixed and all rent volatility arises from shocks to demand. To be precise, assume that there are one hundred identical apartments. Without rent control, the market-clearing rent will equal the 101st highest-bid rent (willingness to pay). Thus the volatility of market rent is the volatility of the 101st highest-bid rent.

Now suppose that rent control has just been implemented and covers fifty of the apartments and their current tenants. Because the control has only just been implemented, all those fifty rent-controlled tenants are among the top one hundred bidders. Now let a positive but heterogeneous demand shock hit: everyone's bid rent rises, but not by the same amount. In general, some number—say, $x > 0$—of the rent-controlled tenants will fall out of the top one hundred bidders. Thus the new market-clearing rent with rent control will be the $(101 - x)th$ highest-bid rent from the new distribution of bid rents. This is greater than the 101st highest-bid rent in the new distribution, which would be the new rent in the absence of rent control. Rent control in this situation then, when it starts with no misallocation of apartments, exacerbates short-run rent increases for uncovered tenants.

Because rent control would not be binding if the demand shock were negative, it does not affect uncovered rent decreases. Under rent control, uncovered rents are therefore both higher in mean and more volatile.

On the other hand, if rent control originally causes a large misallocation of apartments, uncovered rents will be higher than they would be in the absence of rent control but not necessarily more volatile. At the extreme, suppose that originally and always the fifty rent-controlled tenants are never among the top one hundred bidders. Then the uncovered market rent is always the fifty-first highest-bid rent. This is always greater than the 101st highest, but it is not necessarily more volatile.

On the search issue, because rent control reduces turnover in controlled apartments, vacancy rates in these apartments will be low. To the extent that intertenant rent increases are also regulated, prospective tenants will also queue for these apartments, and entry into the rent-controlled sector will be rationed.

There is no reason for lower turnover in the rent-controlled sector to be offset by higher turnover in the uncontrolled sector to the extent that moral hazard, not selection, is causing the lower turnover. Indeed, turnover in the uncontrolled sector may actually fall as a result of rent control. Without rent control, some households would move every month from apartments in the uncontrolled sector to others in what would be the controlled sector. With rent control, there are fewer vacancies in the rent-controlled sector for these households to move to. Some households will extend their tenures in the uncontrolled sector, and uncontrolled-sector turnover will fall.

Less turnover and fewer vacancies mean that households have a tougher problem adjusting to shocks of all kinds; that is, shocks hit harder. If vacancies are plentiful, people who lose wealth or break up with their partners can easily find apartments appropriate to their new circumstances; they are worse off, but they can adjust. If vacancies are scarce, they may not be able to find a new and more appropriate place to live before they have to leave the old one. Thus they will need to spend a few weeks on a friend's couch or in a homeless shelter before they can resettle. Adjustment is more costly and painful.

Rationing in the rent-controlled sector also has implications for risk and homelessness. Rightly or wrongly, landlords may believe that some prospective tenants will be more expensive for them, either because those tenants will not pay on time or in full or because they will cause physical damage or disturb other tenants. When rent-controlled apartments are rationed, indulging these beliefs costs landlords nothing; they can deny entry to tenants whom they don't like without losing money, even if their beliefs are ill founded. Groups of people believed to be expensive—mentally ill people or single parents with small children, for instance—will therefore be concentrated in the uncontrolled sector. Because uncontrolled rents are either higher or more volatile or both because of rent control, these groups will face higher or more volatile rents. Because mentally ill people and single parents with small children are among the groups most likely to be homeless, rent control could thus increase homelessness.

Rent control could also have long-run effects on the housing market, although most ordinances try to mitigate these effects. Rent-control ordinances with poorly administered provisions for hardship rent increases could lead landlords to hasten abandonment of aging buildings, and ordinances that control rents in new buildings can reduce construction. Even ordinances that exempt new buildings from rent control can reduce construction, because cities can never credibly promise not to subject those buildings to rent control in a decade or two, and developers may take current rent-control conditions as a forecast of future rent-control conditions.

The risk that the building they now live in will be abandoned is probably the major issue of low-income tenants, and it is not rent control per se that affects this. Administration and inflation are more important.

Rent control thus reduces risk for some people and increases it for others. The net effect of rent control on homelessness is an empirical question and has been the subject of a large body of empirical literature.

The consensus in this literature is that rent control's effect on homelessness is small, but there is no consensus on whether this effect is positive or negative. The early studies on this topic used the 1984 estimates of rates of homelessness in sixty cities from the Department of Housing and Urban Development (HUD) and ran single-equation models (Tucker 1987; Quigley 1990; Appelbaum et al. 1991; Bohanon 1991; Honig and Filer 1993; Gissy 1997). Except for William Tucker (1987), who used almost no controls, the authors found that rent control had no significant effect on homelessness.

These models suffered from five problems, several of which the later literature tried to address.

Heterogeneity of Rent Control.   Rent control takes many forms, and details can have important effects, as we have seen. Old rent control should also be different from new rent control. Yet all these studies model rent control as a single dummy variable. Because the papers use a noisy measure of actual rent control, the coefficient on rent control should be biased toward zero.

Cross-Sectional Aggregate Misspecification.   The consensus on homelessness is that it results from a conjunction of individual circumstances and market conditions (like rent control). Yet all these studies fit an equation with homelessness as a linear function of both aggregated individual circumstances and market conditions. Brendan O'Flaherty (2004) shows why this procedure produces biased coefficient estimates. The bias, however, is not toward overestimating the effects of market conditions.

Poor Data Set.   HUD estimates of 1984 homelessness are both highly suspect and based on nothing more than so-called expert guesses.

Endogeneity of Rent Control.   Establishing and maintaining rent control is a political decision. Some of the factors affecting this decision could be correlated with homelessness. Cities with a lot of homelessness, for instance, might keep rent control because their citizens fear (rightly or wrongly) that de-control would exacerbate it. With regard to the 1984 estimates, Christopher Jencks (1994) suggests that officials in cities with rent control were likely to give higher estimates of homelessness because people who like rent control are likely to be more sympathetic to the homeless, which was true especially during the Reagan years. In general, cities with a more liberal culture may be more likely to have rent control and to have policies that treat homeless people more leniently—both in policing and in sheltering. More lenient policies probably result in higher homeless counts (for time-series evidence that shelter policies affect shelter population, for example, see Cragg and O'Flaherty 1999; O'Flaherty and Wu 2006, 2008).

Effects of Rent Control.   Rent control changes the distribution of rents and the equilibrium vacancy rate. In equations that include rent and vacancy variables on the right-hand side as well as in a rent-control dummy, the effect of rent control is not estimated cleanly.

The second generation of rent-control studies (Grimes and Chressanthis 1997; Early and Olsen 1999; Troutman, Jackson, and Ekelund 1999) tried to correct some of these problems. All used a better data set, the 1990 census, although William Troutman and his colleagues emphasized results with the 1984 HUD data set, and all did something about endogeneity. But none addressed the heterogeneity of rent control, and each had idiosyncratic weaknesses.

The Dirk Early and Edgar Olsen study (1999) is probably the strongest. It models the effects of rent control on rents and vacancy rates explicitly and attempts to handle endogeneity by controlling directly for the quality and availability of shelter beds. It uses individual observations and so does not use a misspecified aggregate equation. The conclusion is that rent control may reduce homelessness, but the effect is not significant at conventional levels.

Although this study is the strongest, it still has some serious weaknesses. The coefficients on shelter availability and shelter quality have the wrong sign, possibly because the variables are calculated using observed homelessness. O'Flaherty (2004) shows that a linear equation for homelessness estimated with individual observations is also misspecified: coefficients on market variables, like rent control, are biased toward zero in such equations. Because the poor measurement of rent control already introduces attenuation bias, the combination of biases reduces confidence in the conclusion of no-effect.

Paul Grimes and George Chressanthis (1997) and Troutman and his colleagues (1999) both find that rent control increases homelessness and that the effect is statistically significant. Grimes and Chressanthis, however, find that the magnitude is small in practical terms. Both studies use aggregate cross-sectional linear equations, and neither tries to account for the effects of rent control on rents and vacancy rates. Both recognize the problem of endogeneity, but neither has a convincing strategy to deal with it. Troutman and his colleagues estimate a two-equation system where the key identifying assumption is that a city's liberal political culture affects measured homelessness only through rent control. Grimes and Chressanthis use a recursive system of equations without any particular instrumental variable; Early and Olsen (1999) find that this procedure leads to less efficient estimation.

Thus we have no reason to think that rent control has a big effect on homelessness, one way or another. Although the literature is far from definitive, there is no reason to think that expanding or introducing rent control is a good strategy for reducing the risks that renters face and reducing homelessness.

Ownership

Ownership reduces one set of risks that renters face, but increases several other sets. Many institutions mitigate these risks, and several new institutions to do so have been proposed. Traditionally, poor people—people at risk of being homeless—have rented rather than owned, but traditions need not always be maintained eternally.

The great insurance advantage of owning a house is that it is a hedge against certain types of rental price risk (see Sinai and Souleles 2005; Ortalo-Magne and Rady 2002). If rents go up, owners don't have to pay any increase. Formally, when the implicit market rent an owner pays herself goes up, the value of the asset she holds also goes up. Todd Sinai and Nicholas Souleles show that people pay more for ownership as opposed to rentals in metropolitan areas where average rents are more volatile; the authors interpret this as showing a premium that people are willing to pay for the insurance that ownership provides (2005).

On the other hand, owners face risks that renters do not. The obvious example is physical risk: when the furnace breaks or the roof leaks, the owner has to pay for the repair. Homeowners' insurance and flood insurance cover a limited group of large disasters but, probably because of moral hazard, do not cover the normal problems of decay and deterioration. In a sense, maintenance is a way of insuring against these costs, but it is highly imperfect: furnaces all break down sooner or later, and children and pets can do great damage in even the best-maintained houses.

Owners also face risks from price deterioration. Leaving a declining area is a lot easier for tenants than for owners. Price depreciation is not a problem for owners who do not intend to move or who intend to move to another house whose price is also depreciating. But when the shock to prices comes from an idiosyncratic reduction in the attractiveness of the house, there is nothing to hedge the loss. An owner in a neighborhood where crime is escalating loses no matter what she does: if she moves, she loses financially; if she stays, her quality of life deteriorates.

Price-depreciation shocks are sometimes correlated with shocks to human capital. This happens most frequently when the demand for a region's output falls. People lose their jobs at the same time that their home value plummets. Andrew Caplin and his colleagues (1997, 74) find a significant positive correlation between changes in house prices and changes in average weekly wages across forty-two metropolitan areas between 1975 and 1994.

Traditional Mortgages

By traditional mortgages I mean self-amortizing thirty-year mortgages with a down payment and no prepayment penalties, even though such mortgages are less than eighty years old. These mortgages give home-owners what is called a put option: they can trade the house for the out-standing principal on the mortgage at any point. Traditional mortgages thus insure homeowners against big losses in house value from either physical or market causes.

Such insurance, of course, comes at a price in higher interest rates. Moreover, default carries stigma and generally precludes further borrowing for at least several years; thus the home value must be well below the mortgage principal for even the most ruthless homeowner to find default advantageous. Finally, in traditional mortgages the principal starts well below the original home value, because of the down payment, and decreases monotonically over time. Except in the early years of a mortgage, the protection is useful only for very large drops in home value.

On the other hand, this insurance raises only small moral-hazard problems. The possibility of returning the house to the mortgage holder reduces the homeowner's incentive to maintain the house, but because people maintain their houses in part for their own enjoyment and because the probability of default is often small, the maintenance disincentive is usually small. Owner-occupied houses are probably usually better maintained than apartments (see Wang et al. 1991).

Mortgages can also help homeowners insure against liquidity shocks. Homeowners can take out home equity loans or second mortgages and can also refinance. These instruments often allow homeowners much more access to ready cash than renters usually have—provided that their homes have not lost value. Because this sort of borrowing reduces a homeowner's equity, it also makes the put option more valuable. The more borrowed against a house, the less the loss in value required before default becomes attractive.

These opportunities to borrow and default thus make homeownership especially attractive to financially irresponsible people—more attractive than renting. The traditional response to this adverse selection problem has been to require large down payments and high FICO scores and to deny second mortgages and home equity loans that would produce high loan-to-value ratios. This goes far to explain why poor people were not often homeowners. Like credit cards, traditional mortgages were such good insurance against the risks poor people face that they rarely held them.

Subprime Mortgages

Suppose house prices are always rising at a healthy clip. The user cost of living in an owner-occupied house for a year is then almost nothing, and everybody should therefore be able to live in a house. Mortgage holders cannot lose money either, no matter whom they lend to, because if the homeowner defaults, the mortgage holder will be left with a house worth more than the amount it originally lent. In such a world, lending to poor people to buy houses makes a lot of sense. It isn't the real world, but it is approximately the world investors saw when they expanded subprime lending.

I define subprime loans as loans to borrowers with relatively low FICO scores where equity is not designed to grow rapidly, with small down payments and with prepayment penalties for the first several years. Exploding ARMs (adjustable rate mortgages) and other loans with low initial teaser rates are examples. The design of these loans was for the homeowner to live cheaply for a few years as house value rose. The mortgage would then be renegotiated when the high monthly payments were due to kick in because the owners were not capable of making these new payments. The renegotiation would raise the principal to the new higher house value, and the cycle would start again, but with investors claiming the appreciation in house value in return for lowering the monthly payments. The prepayment penalties made it hard for the owner to sell to a third party before renegotiation and realize the value of house appreciation.

Thus, in this arrangement, as long as house prices kept rising, the homeowners were essentially tenants but with some responsibility for repairs. They did not realize the actual price appreciation, though the anticipated price appreciation made the low user cost possible. They did not accumulate equity to borrow against in liquidity emergencies. Indeed, because mortgage servicers were famously opaque, subprime homeowners probably had less ability to borrow by delaying payments than landlords usually give their tenants. Moreover, in the Northeast, many subprime loans financed two- and three-family houses, and so their owners probably had more financial emergencies than ordinary tenants did, given that they were responsible for more units than an ordinary tenant was.

Because in a rising market subprime homeowners had less insurance than ordinary tenants, lenders faced no adverse selection problem and so did not need to screen out financially irresponsible borrowers. This allowed homeownership to expand, but in name only. It also allowed subprime lenders to expand into second mortgages.

In a falling market, however, subprime mortgages appear to be different from tenancy contracts. Tenants don't lose their apartments when the market price declines. If we use the same terms applied to traditional mortgages, subprime homeowners are well protected against falling house prices because they can trade the house for the full amount of the loan at any time. But they lose a place to live and they acquire the stigma of default.

Subprime loans thus do not seem to be a good way to mitigate the risks that poor people face.

Shared-Equity Mortgages

The idea of shared-equity mortgages is for outside investors to take an equity rather than a debt position in a house. The occupant and the investor own the house jointly and share risks. Right now, shared-equity mortgages are a reform proposal, not an operating institution, though shared equity plays a role in the Hope for Homeowners program: the federal government shares in the price appreciation of houses that it rescues from foreclosure. Andrew Caplin and his colleagues (1997) provide the most detailed description of how shared-equity mortgages would work and why they would be better than traditional mortgages.

By slicing the occupant's equity, these mortgages reduce the physical and housing-market risk that occupants face. There would be some moral-hazard issues with maintenance, but Caplin and his colleagues argue that these would be small. Shared equity would not insure against a housing price disaster as traditional mortgages do, but it does insure against smaller risks and the occupant's loss is limited to the occupant's share. Shared equity also does not impose default stigma as readily. Occupants, like subprime owners, give up reaping the full rewards of price appreciation, but these gains do not provide insurance, and occupants do not lose them completely.

The remaining question is the extent to which shared-equity mortgages can provide insurance against liquidity shocks. In theory, occupants could reduce their equity in the house at any time. With third parties they could borrow against or sell some of their equity. They could do the same with the original investor rather than a third party.

However, the original investor might be more averse to such arrangements than traditional mortgage holders usually are. Traditional mortgage holders don't care what happens to the house as long as they can eventually reclaim their principal. But shared-equity investors lose money if anything goes wrong with the house. In reducing equity, the occupant has less incentive to maintain and improve the place; the shared investor loses as a result. If the occupant borrows against equity, the shared investor could face two problems if the loan becomes large relative to the collateral. The first is moral hazard again: the occupant will see some probability that all the equity will go to the outside lender and so reduce maintenance and improvement effort. The second problem is interference: the third-party lender will now aggressively try to minimize the shared investor's proceeds when the house is eventually sold.

These problems probably do not imply that occupants will be absolutely and totally unable to use their stakes in the house as a source of emergency cash. But they will not be able to use them as freely as ATMs, the way many owners with traditional mortgages did. And they will have only a fraction of the equity to borrow against as well.

On the positive side, though, occupants may have slightly better liquidity in declining markets, when they are likely to need it most.

More important, because the temptations to use the mortgage as a source of cash will be smaller, the barriers against homeownership will be smaller.

Housing Market Futures

Robert Shiller (1993) has proposed that homeowners could use housing market futures to hedge against a loss in the market value of their homes. Essentially, homeowners could bet that the value of homes in their area would go down; if that happened, they would be compensated for some of their loss. Since housing futures markets have recently been established, it is plausible that homeowners can now concoct their own insurance against price risk. Housing futures markets, however, are recent creations, and liquidity is still low.

If housing futures markets became thick and liquid, many parts of the housing market would work differently. Because defaults are tied to house prices, investors in mortgage-backed securities and insurers of mortgages would be able to hedge their risks more easily; mortgage rates could fall as a result.

Renters could also use housing futures markets. Rents are somewhat correlated with house prices, and renters who were worried about rent increases could therefore hedge by betting that house prices would rise. This would also be an attractive strategy for renters hoping to buy a first home, although it may be difficult for poor people. Taking a long position in housing futures is a way of buying insurance against gentrification.

Futures markets have some drawbacks, however, especially as a vehicle for reducing homelessness. Many of these drawbacks are tied to how housing prices can be measured. The markets now use repeat sales indices, and there is good reason to think that no other method can create indicators that are both credible to the market because they are hard to manipulate and pretty well correlated with the actual price changes that homeowners experience (for a discussion about why other types of published indices are not viable, see Shiller 2008). Repeat sales are relatively rare: about 5.6 million existing single-family homes were sold in 2002, for instance, out of a stock of about 63 million, and some of those sales were not arm's-length transactions (U.S. Bureau of the Census 2003, tables 959, 948). Hence the regions for which price changes can be reliably estimated are large. If the index is noisy, it is not good for hedging because it will introduce noise into the portfolio. Housing futures are now traded for the national as a whole and nine large metropolitan areas.

But intrametropolitan variation in house-price change is considerable (Brehon 2007). Gentrification, for instance, is usually seen as a neighborhood issue, not a metropolitan one. Resale indices for neighborhoods can be computed, but will be noisy and infrequent, and so will not be good vehicles for hedging. Sales volume is lowest in real estate markets when prices are going down, and resale indices will therefore be least reliable when owners need them most.

Futures markets also provide no insurance against physical risks such as furnace breakdowns.

Still, the combination of shared-equity mortgages and housing futures markets could reduce the risks of homeownership among people who are not wealthy. Taking a short position in housing futures induces no moral-hazard problems, and outside investors in shared-equity mortgages would probably place no restrictions on occupants' ability to do so. Similarly, renters with long positions in housing futures would be better protected than they are today.

Subsidized Housing

Subsidized housing in the United States insulates its beneficiaries from numerous risks. This is probably a major reason that subsidy recipients are much less likely than other similarly situated people to become homeless, even when the expected value of the subsidy is treated as income (see, for instance, Mills et al. 2006; Shinn et al. 1998). Recipients get an insurance policy along with an apartment. It is less clear, however, whether this method of distributing insurance policies in fact reduces risk for the average person or the average poor person.

I begin by looking at how federal housing subsidy programs insure their participants against some risks, and then at how these programs affect risk for the entire population.

How Subsidized Housing Affects People Who Get Subsidies

Four main federal housing programs are available for low-income people: public housing, the Low Income Housing Tax Credit (LIHTC), other project-based housing, and housing choice vouchers (for an overview, see Quigley 2000). Entry into all these programs is rationed: many more people are eligible and want to participate than are allowed to participate.

In most of these programs, tenants pay 30 percent of their eligible income for rent. This provides partial insurance against income shocks and (almost) complete insurance against rent shocks. Except for housing choice vouchers under some circumstances, the market rental for an apartment has no effect on how much a tenant herself pays. For housing choice vouchers, the tenant pays 30 percent of her income, plus any positive difference between the apartment's actual rent and HUD's fair market rent (FMR), but no more than 40 percent of her income. Thus some housing choice voucher tenants are exposed to some market risk, especially since the lag between the surveys on which FMR is based and the end of administrative use is more than a year. In practice, HUD often allows local authorities to use rent standards higher or lower than the FMR and allows adjustments in how the FMR is calculated. About two-fifths of housing choice voucher recipients pay more than 31 percent of their income in rent. Such tenants are concentrated in low-rent localities, mainly in the South. It appears that they pay more than 30 percent because of income losses and because they have big families and the corrections for family size in calculating the FMR are faulty—not because they live in hot housing markets (see McClure 2005).

The income insurance is somewhat enhanced because local authorities often reduce the income they count in order to take hardships into account. The New York City Housing Authority (NYCHA), for instance, allows deductions for certain medical, dental, disability assistance, and childcare expenses (2008a, 6).

Both types of insurance, of course, present moral-hazard problems. Partial income insurance is a work disincentive, and complete rental insurance is a mobility disincentive that produces a misallocation of housing resources, such as rent control. Several scholars have studied the work-disincentive effects of partial rent insurance and found them to be modest (Ludwig and Jacob 2008; Susin 2005; Tatian and Snow 2005; Olsen, Davis, and Carillo 2005) or nonexistent (Shroder 2002). I am aware of no attempts to estimate the cost of misallocations caused by subsidy programs.

Federal subsidies do not buffer their recipients so well from other types of shocks. For example, administrative time lags make these programs a very poor tool for mitigating liquidity problems. In the normal course of events, a tenant's income is reported every year—retrospectively. NYCHA, for instance, begins gathering retrospective income information five months before lease renewal, and thus income for seventeen months before lease renewal influences rent for twelve months after lease renewal, but contemporaneous income does not. Procedures are often in place to deal with emergencies, but even the emergency procedures are slow. If a tenant loses a job, rent can be reduced during the term of a lease, but only after a thirteen-week waiting period (NYCHA 2008b, FAQ 6).

Project-based programs, that is, all programs other than housing choice vouchers, provide no insurance against neighborhood deterioration. When a neighborhood becomes less attractive, unsubsidized tenants may see relative rent reductions. They have the option of moving. Tenants with project-based subsidies, however, do not see rent reductions and cannot move without losing their subsidies. Thus they are at greater risk from neighborhood deterioration than unsubsidized tenants.

Tenants with housing choice vouchers are in between. They can move without losing their subsidies, but their rent will not necessarily go down. Moving with a housing choice voucher, moreover, is not always easy. In New York City, for example, routine transfers take nine to fourteen months (NYCHA 2008b, FAQ 9). It appears that many transfer requests do not come to fruition. NYCHA states that 40 percent of tenants request transfers when their leases expire, but in 2007 the number of transfers processed was only 5.4 percent of leased units.

The risk of physical damage to their apartments is probably at least as great for subsidized tenants as it is for their unsubsidized counterparts. In all cases, landlords are legally responsible for making repairs; the risk for the tenants is that the landlords fail to do so. No theory indicates that public-housing authorities and other subsidized project-based landlords will be any more diligent at making repairs than private unsubsidized landlords are. Housing choice voucher recipients are probably at least as well insured against physical damage as unsubsidized tenants because they have regular leases and might be somewhat better insured because the government inspects these units on a regular basis.

Subsidized housing tenants are probably at greater risk than most low-income tenants of losing their apartments for the presence of a family member because of a criminal conviction. With certain exceptions, people who have been convicted of a violent or drug-related crime, excluding a DWI, cannot live in subsidized housing.

Finally, as far as relationship shocks are concerned, the picture is complex. The surplus in a relationship must clear a higher bar if one of the members lives in subsidized housing because relationships are taxed through higher rent. Thus we would expect to see less sharing among subsidized tenants. This finding has been confirmed in a number of empirical studies (Mills et al. 2006; Susin 2005; Ellen and O'Flaherty 2007; Sinai and Waldfogel 2005).

Whether this higher bar makes the relationships that do form more precarious depends on the stochastic process under which the surplus in relationships evolves. If it evolves according to a random walk, then where the bar is will make no difference to the probability that a relationship that has formed will continue. But if the surplus is a mean-reverting process, the higher bar makes a difference, and relationships with subsidies are more likely to fall apart. This process seems somewhat more likely than a random walk, but the empirical work is silent on the question. It does not show whether subsidized households are smaller because additions are less frequent, or subtractions are more frequent, or both.

Thus subsidized housing reduces income risk and rent risk but has little positive effect on liquidity risk, relationship risk, neighborhood risk, or physical-damage risk. The first two effects are probably more important than the others, since subsidies greatly decrease the probability of becoming homeless. This is the effect of subsidized housing conditional on receiving subsidized housing.

How Subsidized Housing Affects Poor People in General

Our second question is the unconditional effect of public-housing programs rather than their effect that is conditional on receipt. Why is this an interesting question? Even insurance policies can make life riskier if they are awarded to their recipients at the wrong times or under the wrong circumstances.

Suppose the government is going to award a fixed number of valuable insurance policies. If these policies are awarded to people following good events, and the premiums are paid by people who realize bad events, then the insurance policies may make the average person's life less secure, not more secure. To understand whether something perverse like this might be happening with subsidized housing, we must look at who receives subsidies and when those subsidies begin and end.

Eligibility rules place some limits on who lives in subsidized housing and when they live there. For entry, the housing choice voucher program requires that a household be very low income (VLI), that is, have a combined income below 50 percent of the median in its metropolitan area. Three-quarters of entering families must be extremely low income (ELI), or below 30 percent of the area median. HUD also adjusts the VLI and ELI limits to take history into account (they cannot be reduced and so made more stringent) and to reflect what it considers to be abnormally high housing costs. As with most subsidized housing variables, these numbers are lagged, so that 2005 income reported in 2006 is used to determine eligibility in 2007. The ELI in most big cities is close to the poverty level, and the VLI is about 1.6 times the poverty level, for a family of four.

These national eligibility and targeting rules are often supplemented by local rules. For instance, since March 2007 in New York City, only victims of domestic violence and participants in witness protection programs have been eligible for new housing choice vouchers.

The other housing subsidy programs are not as focused on poor people as housing choice vouchers are. Basic eligibility is that families are low income (LI) and have incomes less than 80 percent of median income, thus roughly 2.5 times the poverty level. The targeting provisions are also less strict: 40 percent of new tenants must be ELI in public housing and other project-based programs, and 75 to 85 percent must be VLI in the project-based programs. With the LIHTC, 20 percent of units must be for VLI applicants, and the rest can be market rate, but because LIHTC projects are chosen competitively and the subsidy depends on the number of VLI units, many have higher percentages of units set aside for households that are VLI when they enter. Most LIHTC projects are now almost completely VLI.

In all programs, applicants must apply and wait, sometimes for a very long time, before they can enter the program, and many eligible applicants never do so. They are not designed as safety-net programs; they are a fire department that requires appointments. Entry into these programs is not likely to be correlated with bad luck, but especially with housing choice vouchers, because the income limits are lower, it is probably not correlated with good luck either.

Participants leave these programs because they are evicted for serious rule infractions or because they find a better alternative apartment. Usually there is no income requirement for continued participation, and no one is forced to leave because his or her income is too high. But as a household's income rises, its rent rises, and so continued participation in the program becomes less attractive. This is most explicit with housing choice vouchers. The subsidy goes to zero when household income is about forty times the FMR, where FMR is multiplied by twelve months and divided by .30. In most big cities, this amount is around the VLI limit. In the project-based programs, the relationship is not so explicit, but because the FMR is supposed to be a rent at which decent apartments are available in the private market, households with annual income more than forty times the FMR should start noticing that they can find better apartments at lower rent outside their subsidized projects.

Empirically, households are more likely to exit subsidy programs when their income is higher and when private-housing markets are looser (Hungerford 1996; Olsen et al. 2005; Ambrose 2005).

In general, these rules probably make these programs function more or less as a very poorly timed safety net on most occasions, especially when negative shocks are likely to lead to homelessness. This is conjecture on my part, however. Researchers have studied the consumption-smoothing benefits of unemployment insurance (Hamermesh 1982; Gruber 1997), cash welfare (Gruber 2000), income taxes (Auerbach and Feenberg 2000), and food stamps (Gundersen and Ziliak 2003), but as far as I know, no similar work has been done for housing subsidy programs.

Entry into subsidized housing does seem to be more likely following idiosyncratic negative income or relationship shocks, in part because of the eligibility rules and priorities and in part because the subsidies are greater for households whose incomes are lower. Entry requires application and application is not without cost; thus those who value entry the most are most likely to apply and to gain entry. A negative income or relationship shock makes a household more likely to apply and so more likely to gain entry. By the same sort of reasoning, the availability of subsidized housing also provides some insurance against idiosyncratic housing-price shocks, even though these are not mentioned in the eligibility criteria: idiosyncratically higher rents for a household mean greater gain from entry and greater willingness to apply.

Exit rates also smooth consumption. Good events are likely to lead to exit and the end of subsidy: higher income, a new partner, discovery of a cheap and inviting place to live.

But there are many exceptions to this pleasant picture. The major exceptions are area-wide income and rent shocks, as opposed to idiosyncratic shocks. Consider an area-wide income shock—a recession, say. Because income standards are lagged, the recession makes more people eligible and targeted for entry and makes more people apply. Fewer current tenants exit because their incomes are not rising. Thus the probability that any particular needy person will gain entry falls. Subsidized housing is like an emergency room that is empty except when you need it.

The situation is similar for a general rent shock. More people want subsidized housing, but fewer vacancies become available and the probability of entry for an eligible person falls. In the housing choice voucher program, the FMR falls relative to market rent, and even those who receive vouchers may not find a landlord to accept them. The administrative authority to raise the payment standard may make it easier to get landlords to accept vouchers, but this easing may exacerbate the problem of high demand: the local authority must cut the number of vouchers available when it raises the cost of each voucher. Once again, assistance is least available when it is needed the most.

Even for some idiosyncratic shocks, bad news reduces the probability of entry and raises the probability of exit. The most obvious shock like this is conviction for a violent or drug-related offense. Some symptoms of mental illness work the same way: they make it harder to clear the bureaucratic hurdles required for entry and easier to get evicted for failing to meet the requirements to maintain assistance.

The aggregate effect of subsidized housing programs is thus not clear.

Shelters

Shelters are an insurance policy: they place a floor under the consumption of housing. To the extent that some people prefer streets to the quality of shelters that are available, streets rather than shelters are the insurance policy. When I say *shelters* I mean *the more preferred of streets and shelters*. In a world where people suffer stochastic shocks, shelters are a great way to smooth housing consumption.

Like all other forms of insurance, of course, shelters create moral-hazard problems. Shelters reduce precautionary savings and induce some people who would otherwise be conventionally housed and pay rent to move to a shelter and pay no rent. They also induce people to search less assiduously for new housing than they should and possibly to hold out for better or less expensive re-housing than they should.

In the absence of moral hazard and adverse selection problems, shelters that provide the right kind of safety net would replicate the quality of housing that their residents would consume in better times. Rent would be set at a level that would allow their residents to consume the same bundle of nonhousing commodities that they consumed in good times.

Intertemporal optimization requires that the marginal utility of income in good times equal the marginal utility of income in bad times. Intratemporal optimization requires that the marginal utility of housing, per dollar, equal the marginal utility of nonhousing, per dollar, in both states of the world, and that the marginal utility, per dollar, of both goods equal the marginal utility of income. Thus the consumption of housing must be the same in both states of the world, and so too must the consumption of nonhousing.

Shelters are like unemployment insurance. People get unemployment insurance when they lose their jobs, and they get a bed in a shelter when they lose their homes. People continue to receive unemployment insurance until they find a new job or reach an administrative limit; people stay in shelters until they find a new place to live or reach an administrative limit.

But there are important differences. First, shelters are in-kind whereas unemployment benefits are cash. Moreover, living in a shelter precludes living anywhere else (by the laws of physics); receiving cash from unemployment insurance does not preclude receiving cash from other sources (including concealed employment). Thus people who try to enter shelters self-select more than those who try to collect unemployment insurance. Shelters, in this regard, are more like an employer of last resort than unemployment insurance benefits.

Looking at shelters as unemployment insurance—a way to smooth consumption when people are down on their luck—has many important implications for shelter management. I derive some of them elsewhere (O'Flaherty 2009b, 2009c). In those papers I show that a system of small subsidies for everyone who leaves the shelter are superior to an equally costly system of subsidies for a proper subset of families—that if the shelter authorities are constrained to give selective subsidies and can measure time in shelter, some exit subsidies should be offered immediately on shelter entrance, and that under some conditions, shelter quality should deteriorate as a spell lengthens. I also show how optimal shelter quality can be thought about.

These same techniques also hint at answers to the thorny question of how to treat people who sleep in railroad terminals, parks, and other public spaces. Formally, these places are the same as shelters, only with probably a very high social cost for each night a homeless person spends in one. The same trade-off between insurance—if things were so bad that I had to sleep in Penn Station, I would not want somebody making life even worse by rousting me and sending me to jail—and moral hazard dictates the optimal policing approach.

Homelessness Prevention

Homelessness-prevention programs try to provide cheaper services than shelters to people who might become homeless; the goal in doing so is that they not become homeless. Since picking which individuals will become homeless next month is almost the same sort of hopeless exercise as picking which stocks will beat the market next month, temptations to dismiss such programs are strong (for a review of these programs and associated research, see Apicello 2008). But the impossibility of stock-picking does not preclude wise investment, and the unknowability of who will become homeless does not imply that supports cheaper than shelters cannot be part of a good social-insurance system. Health insurance treats colds as well as cancer.

Homelessness prevention should thus be seen as a way of darning holes in the safety net. Safety-net programs are in part substitutes for each other: people with good medical insurance are more likely to be able to buy food, and people with good access to food pantries are more likely to be able to fill their prescriptions. Any additional insurance that poor people have is likely to reduce shelter population (and food-stamp population, and so on), though not necessarily by a lot.

The question for design of homelessness-prevention programs is what holes in the safety net can most productively be darned: what other types of insurance are the best substitutes for shelters, and what can reasonably be offered without too much moral hazard or adverse selection. I look at each of the various shocks that could affect poor people.

Health and addiction shocks often lead to homelessness, and therefore mitigating them should reduce shelter population. Moral-hazard problems are not huge, except possibly on the provider side, since treatment, not cash, is generally offered, and treatment is usually of little value to people without these conditions. But it might be easier to expand existing institutions that treat these conditions than to establish new organizations and label them homelessness prevention.

Food-price shocks are similar: pantries and food stamps seem like a better way to insure against food shocks than separate programs.

For relationship shocks, the picture is mixed. Extreme relationship shocks—domestic violence—are probably best handled by specialized agencies and law enforcement, not a homelessness-prevention agency. The question of optimal treatment of domestic violence and the optimal population of battered women's shelters is important and well beyond the scope of this chapter (see, for instance, Dugan 2003; Farmer and Tiefenthaler 2003; Iyengar 2008).

For less extreme relationship shocks, especially those involving doubled-up families, homelessness prevention might play several roles. Mediation and conciliation of disputes could be helpful, both to the families involved and to the shelter system, and present only small moral-hazard problems: people not involved in disputes do not value mediation, but the possibility of mediation may lead some people to do less on their own to resolve disputes. Beyond conflict resolution, Renya Wasson and Ronald Hill advocate policies to lessen tensions in shared apartments: "restaurant vouchers, child care, . . . mental therapy, access to bathroom and/or cooking facilities" (1998, 339).

The parts of this recommendation that involve cash or cash substitutes—restaurant vouchers and child care—may have serious moral-hazard problems, because many people want to eat in restaurants and have their children looked after. The in-kind provisions do not have these problems and should be seriously considered. If sharing an apartment did not mean sharing everything all the time, more people might take advantage of this form of organization and those that did might do so for longer periods. Places where families could come to prepare and eat meals or clean up would in some sense be minishelters, but in some cases they might be all the safety net a family needed.

Whether free or cheap public kitchens or clean-up places could operate in a safe and sanitary manner is a more difficult question. Many cities established public bathhouses at the beginning of the twentieth century to help poor people's hygiene, but these institutions have disappeared, in some cases, amid opprobrium. On the other hand, laundromats have succeeded in making people feel comfortable performing intimate tasks in public, like folding underwear, even in the roughest neighborhoods. Perhaps laundromat operators (or beauticians) would do a good job setting up public kitchens and showers.

For income and expense shocks, agencies that specialize in income support and unemployment compensation already exist; improving their performance may be more effective than setting up new agencies.

A homelessness-prevention program, however, might have a niche in making loans or grants to relieve liquidity problems involving housing debts, such as someone facing an emergency who cannot otherwise borrow to cover that month's rent. Notice that homeowners facing such problems would be able to borrow against their equity. Perhaps homelessness-prevention agencies could take the family's leasehold interest as collateral and foreclose on the collateral by moving another family in from a shelter. On the family level, this program would look like musical chairs, but on the market level the effect might be different. The implicit rent guarantee from the homelessness-prevention agency might encourage landlords to rent to tenants that they might otherwise consider too risky.

Alternatively, the agency could make direct payments but treat them as loans with recourse. Payments for restaurants or child care to encourage sharing could also be treated as recourse loans. Governments often have databases that allow them to collect loans that would be difficult for private companies. Recourse loans reduce both moral hazard and taxpayer cost. But they do not eliminate either, especially if they are large relative to the recipient's normal income, and so should be used judiciously. People with large recourse loans can still default on them and turn to the underground economy for subsistence. Adding recourse loans on the backs of people who already have large child-support obligations and many outstanding motor vehicle tickets, for instance, may be counterproductive. We need more information about how recourse loans might work.

Homelessness-prevention activities might also mitigate some types of rent shocks. The prevention agency might make emergency repairs to apartments, bill the landlord, and place a lien on the property to ensure collection. It could offer legal and mediation assistance in disputes and evictions. It could also maintain a registry of apartments to help families quickly find available apartments, and registries of moving companies, with some information on rates and performance. Loans for moving costs are another obvious activity, but loans for security deposits are more problematic because they could reduce the family's incentive to take good care of the property and so serve as a signal to landlords. In cities where rent control sometimes makes deposits simply a way of increasing expected revenue tenancy rather than of aligning tenant and landlord incentives, the injunction against security deposits might have less force.

Because the number of people at risk of homelessness is large relative to the number who actually become homeless at any time, perhaps homelessness prevention might be most effective in providing incentives for other insurance mechanisms to do their jobs better.

For instance, homelessness-prevention agencies might encourage rent-insurance programs. In such programs, households or landlords would pay premiums on a monthly basis, and the insurance agency would pay their rents (or an agreed dollar sum) for a predetermined number of months if a well-defined event (such as job loss, disability, or major illness) prevented them from making rent payments during this time. Payments would go directly to the landlord. Such an insurance policy would allow poor people to save in a way designed to reduce their probability of homelessness.

Because people who don't pay rent for several months and then become homeless don't bear the full burden of their misfortune immediately, this insurance should be subsidized, both by the government and by landlords. Subsidies can also reduce adverse selection problems, which might be large.

This insurance would reduce homelessness in two ways. More tenants would be able to stay in the apartments they already have, and landlords might be more willing to rent to potential problem tenants and so help people without apartments and those who are trying to leave homelessness.

Perhaps private companies could offer this insurance to landlords (requiring, for instance, that landlords enroll all their tenants to mitigate adverse selection) and receive a government subsidy. Landlords would be able to recover at least part of their premium through higher rents, because the insurance would make their apartments more attractive, and they would gain from fewer missed payments, reduced eviction costs, less turnover, and lower vacancy rates. One private company, Insurent, now offers a policy something like this in the New York metropolitan area, but it acts essentially as a cosigner on the lease, in return for a large up-front fee and the right to sue for recovery of the insurance paid. For poor people, it would be better to spread the premium out over time (though it might diminish with tenure) and to limit the insurer's recourse.

The government could also run an insurance program directly with landlords mandatorily enrolled, based on the model of unemployment insurance.

Any insurance program would raise some moral-hazard concerns, because tenants would have less incentive to avoid the major adverse events that would trigger payment. These effects might not be large, however, relative to the status quo, for two reasons. Some of the costs that insurance would pick up are now being borne by landlords and the government, and the major adverse events that trigger payment generally have large impacts beyond apartment loss. Losing your apartment is far from the only thing to fear about major illness, for instance.

Moral-hazard problems probably preclude rent insurance from covering rent shocks, however. Fortunately, rent shocks are not a major precursor to homelessness (O'Flaherty 2009a).

Homelessness-prevention agencies might also want to encourage families and friendship networks to act as insurance companies, especially by sharing housing. Removing the penalties for sharing that now exist in the food stamp program, Supplemental Security Income, and assisted housing would be a good first step (for a description of these penalties, see

Ellen and O'Flaherty 2007). Homelessness-prevention agencies might also want to subsidize sharing directly. Moral hazard could be mitigated by restricting the subsidies to instances where sharing is being initiated—for instance, adult children returning to their parents' home after at least five years' absence. These initiation subsidies would supplement the in-kind encouragement that I described earlier to keep existing sharing arrangements from breaking up.

Jennifer Apicello (2008) reviews the literature and practice on many of these approaches to emergency homelessness prevention. Some have shown promise, but no rigorous evaluations have been undertaken. These programs should probably be evaluated on their ability to reduce consumption volatility, not on their ability to reduce homelessness.

Conclusion

Fire trucks are there to be used. So are safety nets, parachutes, life preservers, air bags, and seat belts. One hopes that they are never used, but realistically one knows that they will be. The exact times and places of use, however, can never be predicted. If you knew your faulty wiring was going to cause a fire truck to visit your house tomorrow, you would have it fixed today.

Shelters and street refuges are like fire trucks. In this chapter, I have tried to develop some of the implications of this analogy. Fire trucks have many substitutes—for instance, sprinkler systems, fireproof construction, and the use of electricity rather than candles. I have tried to explore a similar, large group of substitutes for shelters. More than any particular result, my goal has been to show that it can be productive to think of homelessness as a stochastic event, an unpredictable condition that some people pass through, often more slowly and more often than we would like.

Notes

1. For instance, there is nothing inconsistent in this view with the fact that a person who is poor today is more likely to be homeless tomorrow than a person who is not poor today. Probabilities can differ among people. What is important is that the probability that any person who is poor and not homeless today will be homeless tomorrow is less than one (in fact, considerably less than one).

2. Most results in consumption theory are derived from first-order conditions, and with many goods first-order conditions require that the marginal utility of each good in each period be the same, assuming units are defined so that a unit of each good costs a dollar. Thus every first-order condition for each individual good is the same as the first-order condition for the composite good. Hence we will use models where housing is the only consumption good, because these are simpler.

3. Consider a particular family, and let c_t denote its consumption of housing at time t. We assume that c_t evolves according to the autoregressive process

$$c_t = \alpha + \beta c_{t-1} + \varepsilon_t$$

where $\alpha > 0$ and β, $0 \le \beta < 1$, are time-invariant parameters, the same for everyone, and

$$\varepsilon_t \sim N(0, \sigma^2) \text{ and } E(\varepsilon_t \varepsilon_s) = 0 \text{ for } t \ne s.$$

4. We define homelessness as housing of quality 0. To reproduce the results of Marybeth Shin and her colleagues on transitions from period 0 to period 1, the parameters (α, β, X, Y) must satisfy

$$\Phi(-\alpha - \beta X) = \frac{6}{33.1}$$

$$\Phi(-\alpha - \beta Y) = \frac{3}{245.3}$$

We also impose the condition that expected housing consumption in period 0, which is

$$X + \frac{246.9}{280} Y$$

be equal to the long-run asymptotic mean housing level $\frac{\alpha}{1-\beta}$. This gives us a third condition

$$\frac{33.1}{280} X + \frac{246.9}{280} Y = \frac{\alpha}{1-\beta}.$$

These three equations imply that asymptotic mean housing is

$$\frac{\alpha}{1-\beta} = 2.0895$$

Shinn and her colleagues did a five-year follow-up and found that 4 percent of the families who used a shelter in period 1 were in a shelter at the five-year follow-up. About half of shelter families were placed in subsidized housing, and almost none of these were homeless at the follow-up. We can infer, then, that after about five years, about 8 percent of families who requested shelter and did not receive subsidized housing were homeless.

There is abundant evidence that housing consumption evolves differently over time for families who are in subsidized housing. Thus we concentrate on the remaining families.

Asymptotically, housing consumption is distributed

$$N\left(\frac{\alpha}{1-\beta}, \frac{\alpha^2}{1-\beta^2}\right).$$

Thus if 8 percent are homeless, it follows that

$$\Phi\left(\frac{2.0895}{\sqrt{1-\beta^2}}\right) = .08.$$

Hence $\beta = .7401$, $\alpha = .5431$, $X = .4963$, $Y = 2.3031$. Plausible parameter values allow us to explain the findings of Shinn and her colleagues as the evolution of an autoregressive process.

References

Ambrose, Brent W. 2005. "A Hazard Rate Analysis of Movers and Stayers in Assisted Housing Programs." *Cityscape* 8(2): 69–93.

Apicello, Jennifer. 2008. "Applying the Population and High-Risk Framework to Preventing Homelessness: A Review of the Literature and Practice." New York: Columbia University, Columbia Center for Homelessness Prevention Studies.

Appelbaum, Richard, Michael Dolny, Peter Dreier, and John Gilderbloom. 1991. "Scapegoating Rent Control: Masking the Causes of Homelessness." *Journal of the American Planning Association* 57(2): 153–64.

Arnott, Richard. 1995. "Time for Revisionism on Rent Control." *Journal of Economic Perspectives* 9(1): 99–120.

Auerbach, Alan, and Daniel Feenberg. 2000. "The Significance of Federal Taxes as Automatic Stabilizers." *Journal of Economic Perspectives* 14(3): 37–56.

Bentolila, Samuel, and Andrea Ichino. 2008. "Unemployment and Consumption Near and Far Away from the Mediterranean." *Journal of Population Economics* 21(2): 255–80.

Bohanon, Cecil E. 1991. "The Economic Correlates of Homelessness in Sixty Cities." *Social Science Quarterly* 72(4): 817–25.

Brehon, Daniel J. 2007. "Essays on the Economics and Econometrics of Urban Crime and House Price Prediction." Ph.D. diss., Columbia University.

Caplin, Andrew, Sewin Chan, Charles Freeman, and Joseph Tracy. 1997. *Housing Partnerships: A New Approach to a Market at a Crossroads.* Cambridge, Mass.: MIT Press.

Carney, Stacie, and William G. Gale. 2001. "Asset Accumulation Among Low-Income Households." In *Assets for the Poor: The Benefits of Spreading Asset Ownership,* edited by Thomas M. Shapiro and Edward N. Wolff. New York: Russell Sage Foundation.

Cragg, Michael, and Brendan O'Flaherty. 1999. "Do Homeless Shelter Conditions Determine Shelter Population? The Case of the Dinkins Deluge." *Journal of Urban Economics* 46(3): 377–415.

Culhane, Dennis P., and Stephen Metraux. 1999. "One-Year Rates of Public Shelter Utilization by Race/Ethnicity, Age, Sex, and Poverty Status for New York City (1990 and 1995) and Philadelphia (1995)." *Population Research and Policy Review* 18(3): 219–36.

Culhane, Dennis P., Stephen Metraux, Jung Min Park, Maryanne Schretzman, and Jesse Valente. 2007. "Testing a Typology of Family Homelessness Based on Patterns of Public Shelter Utilization in Four U.S. Jurisdictions: Implications for Policy and Program Planning." *Housing Policy Debate* 18(1): 1–28.

Dugan, Laura. 2003. "Domestic Violence Legislation: Exploring Its Impact on the Likelihood of Domestic Violence, Police Involvement, and Arrest." *Criminology and Public Policy* 2(2): 283–312.

Dynarski, Susan, and Jonathan Gruber. 1997. "Can Families Smooth Variable Earnings?" *Brookings Papers on Economic Activity* 1997(1): 229–303.

Early, Dirk, and Edgar O. Olsen. 1999. "Rent Control and Homelessness." *Regional Science and Urban Economics* 28(6): 797–816.

Edin, Kathryn. 2001. "More Than Money: The Role of Assets in the Survival Strategies and Material Well-Being of the Poor." In *Assets for the Poor: The Benefits of Spreading Asset Ownership*, edited by Thomas M. Shapiro and Edward N. Wolff. New York: Russell Sage Foundation.

Ellen, Ingrid, and Brendan O'Flaherty. 2007. "Do Government Programs Make Households Too Small? Evidence from New York City." *Population Research and Policy Review* 26(4): 387–409.

Engen, Eric M., and Jonathan Gruber. 1995. "Unemployment Insurance and Precautionary Saving." NBER working paper 5252. Cambridge, Mass.: National Bureau of Economic Research.

Farmer, Amy, and Jill Tiefenthaler. 2003. "Explaining the Recent Decline in Domestic Violence." *Contemporary Economic Problems* 21(2): 158–72.

Gissy, William G. 1997. "Rent Controls and Homelessness Rates." *International Advances in Economic Research* 3(1): 113–21.

Glaeser, Edward, and Erzo Luttmer. 1997. "The Misallocation of Housing Under Rent Control." *American Economic Review* 93(4): 1027–46.

Grimes, Paul W., and George A. Chressanthis. 1997. "Assessing the Effect of Rent Control on Homelessness." *Journal of Urban Economics* 41(1): 23–37.

Gruber, Jonathan. 1997. "The Consumption-Smoothing Benefits of Unemployment Insurance." *American Economic Review* 87(1): 192–205.

———. 2000. "Cash Welfare as a Consumption-Smoothing Mechanism for Divorced Mothers." *Journal of Public Economics* 75(2): 157–82.

Gruber, Jonathan, and Aaron Yelowitz. 1997. "Public Health Insurance and Private Savings." NBER working paper 6401. Cambridge, Mass.: National Bureau of Economic Research.

Gundersen, Craig, and James P. Ziliak. 2003. "The Role of Food Stamps in Consumption Stabilization." *Journal of Human Resources* 38(Supplement): 1051–79.

Hall, Robert. 1978. "Stochastic Implications of the Life Cycle Permanent Income Hypothesis: Theory and Evidence." *Journal of Political Economy* 86(5): 971–87.

Hamermesh, Daniel. 1982. "Social Insurance and Consumption: An Empirical Inquiry." *American Economic Review* 72(1): 101–13.

Honig, Marjorie, and Randall K. Filer. 1993. "Causes of Intercity Variation in Homelessness." *American Economic Review* 83(1): 248–55.

Hubbard, R. Glenn, Jonathan Skinner, and Stephen P. Zeldes. 1995. "Precautionary Saving and Social Insurance." *Journal of Political Economy* 103 (2): 360–99.

Hungerford, Thomas L. 1996. "The Dynamics of Housing Assistance Spells." *Journal of Urban Economics* 30(2): 193–208.

Iyengar, Radha. 2008. "Does the Certainty of Arrest Reduce Domestic Violence?" NBER working paper 13186. Cambridge, Mass.: National Bureau of Economic Research.

Jencks, Christopher. 1994. *The Homeless.* Cambridge, Mass.: Harvard University Press.

Kotlikoff, Laurence, and Avia Spivak. 1981. "The Family as an Incomplete Annuities Market." *Journal of Political Economy* 89(2): 372–91.

Link, Bruce G., Ezra Susser, Ann Stueve, Jo Phelan, Robert E. Moore, and Elmer Struening. 1994. "Lifetime and Five-Year Prevalence of Homelessness in the United States." *American Journal of Public Health* 84(12): 1907–12.

Ludwig, Jens, and Brian Jacob. 2008. "The Effects of Housing Assistance on Labor Supply: Evidence from a Voucher Lottery." NBER working paper 14570. Cambridge, Mass.: National Bureau of Economic Research.

McClure, Kirk. 2005. "Rent Burden in the Housing Choice Voucher Program." *Cityscape: A Journal of Policy Research and Development* 8(2): 5–20.

Mills, Gregory, Abt Associates, Daniel Gubits, Larry Orr, David Long, Judie Feins, Bulbul Kaul, Michelle Woods, Amy Jones and Associates, Cloudburst Consulting, and the QED Group. 2006. *Effects of Housing Vouchers on Welfare Families.* Washington: U.S. Department of Housing and Urban Development and Office of Policy Development and Research.

Neumark, David, and Elizabeth T. Powers. 1998. "The Effect of Means-Tested Income Support for the Elderly on Pre-Retirement Saving: Evidence from the SSI Program in the United States." *Journal of Public Economics* 68(2): 181–206.

New York City Housing Authority (NYCHA). 2008a. "Guide to the Section 8 Assistance Program." Available at: http://www.nyc.gov/html/nycha/down loads/07213N.pdf (accessed May 27, 2008).

———. 2008b. "Frequently Asked Questions." Available at: http://www.nyc.gov/ html/nycha/html/section8/lh_ten_faqs.shtml#q6 (accessed May 27, 2008).

O'Flaherty, Brendan. 2004. "Wrong Person AND Wrong Place: For Homelessness, the Conjunction Is What Matters." *Journal of Housing Economics* 13(1): 1–15.

———. 2009a. "What Shocks Precipitate Homelessness?" Department of Economics working paper. New York: Columbia University.

———. 2009b. "Managing Homeless Shelters." Department of Economics working paper. New York: Columbia University.

———. 2009c. "When Should Homeless Families Get Subsidized Apartments? A Theoretical Inquiry." *Journal of Housing Economics* 18(2): 69–80.

O'Flaherty, Brendan, and Ting Wu. 2006. "Fewer Subsidized Exits and a Recession: How New York City's Family Homeless Shelter Population Became Immense." *Journal of Housing Economics* 15(2): 99–125.

———. 2008. "Homeless Shelters for Single Adults: Why Does Their Population Change?" *Social Service Review* 82(3): 511–50.

Olsen, Edgar O., Scott E. Davis, and Paul E. Carillo. 2005. "Explaining Attrition in the Housing Voucher Program." *Cityscape* 8(2): 95–113.

Olsen, Edgar O., Catherine A. Taylor, Jonathan W. King, and Paul E. Carillo. 2005. "The Effects of Different Types of Housing Assistance on Earnings and Employment." *Cityscape* 8(2): 163–87.

Ortalo-Magne, Francois, and Sven Rady. 2002. "Tenure Choice and Riskiness of Nonhousing Consumption." *Journal of Housing Economics* 11(3): 266–79.

Powers, Elizabeth T. 1998. "Does Means-Testing Welfare Discourage Savings? Evidence from a Change in AFDC Policy in the United States." *Journal of Public Economics* 68(1): 33–53.

Quigley, John. 1990. "Does Rent Control Cause Homelessness? Taking the Claim Seriously." *Journal of Policy Analysis and Management* 9(1): 89–93.

———. 2000. "A Decent Home: Housing Policy in Perspective." *Brookings-Wharton Papers on Urban Affairs* 1(1): 53–88.

Seidman, Ellen, Moez Hababou, and Jennifer Kramer. 2005. "A Financial Services Survey of Low- and Moderate-Income Families." Paper presented at Promises and Pitfalls: As Consumer Finance Options Multiply, Who Is Being Served and at What Cost? Washington, D.C. (April 7–8, 2005). Available at: http://www.chicagofed.org/cedric/files/2005_conf_paper_session_2_seidman.pdf (accessed June 1, 2008).

Shiller, Robert. 1993. *Macro Markets: Creating Institutions for Managing Society's Largest Risks.* New York: Oxford University Press.

———. 2008. "Derivatives Markets for Home Prices." NBER working paper 13962. Cambridge, Mass.: National Bureau of Economic Research.

Shinn, Marybeth, and Jim Baumohl. 1998. "Rethinking the Prevention of Homelessness." Presented at the National Symposium on Homelessness. Washington, D.C. (October 28–29, 1998). Available at: http://www.aspe.os.dhhs.gov/ProgSys/homeless/symposium/13-Preven.HTM (accessed June 3, 2008).

Shinn, Marybeth, Beth Weitzman, Daniela Stojanovic, James R. Knickman, Lucila Jiminez, Lisa Duchon, Susan James, and David Krantz. 1998. "Predictors of Homelessness Among Families in New York City: From Shelter Request to Stability." *American Journal of Public Health* 88(11): 1651–57.

Shroder, Mark. 2002. "Does Housing Assistance Perversely Affect Self-Sufficiency? A Review Essay." *Journal of Housing Economics* 11(4): 381–417.

Sinai, Todd, and Nicholas S. Souleles. 2005. "Owner-Occupied Housing as a Hedge Against Rent Risk." *Quarterly Journal of Economics* 120(2): 763–89.

Sinai, Todd, and Joel Waldfogel. 2005. "Do Low-Income Housing Subsidies Increase the Occupied Housing Stock?" *Journal of Public Economics* 89(11–12): 2137–64.

Stegman, Michael A. 2007. "Payday Lending." *Journal of Economic Perspectives* 21(1): 169–90.

Sullivan, James X. 2005. "Borrowing During Unemployment: Unsecured Debt as a Safety Net." Paper presented at Promises and Pitfalls: As Consumer Finance Options Multiply, Who Is Being Served and at What Cost? Washington, D.C. (April 7–8, 2005). Available at: http://www.chicagofed.org/cedric/files/2005_conf_paper_session_2_sullivan.pdf (accessed June 1, 2008).

Susin, Scott. 2005. "Longitudinal Outcomes of Subsidized Housing Recipients in Matched and Survey Data." *Cityscape* 8(2): 189–218.

Tatian, Peter A., and Christopher Snow. 2005. "The Effects of Housing Assistance on Income, Earnings, and Employment." *Cityscape* 8(2): 135–61.

Troutman, William H., John D. Jackson, and Robert B. Ekelund Jr. 1999. "Public Policy, Perverse Incentives, and the Homeless Problem." *Public Choice* 98(1–2): 195–212.

Tucker, William. 1987. "Where Do the Homeless Come From?" *National Review* 39(September 25): 32–43.

U.S. Bureau of the Census. 2003. *Statistical Abstract 2003*. Washington: U.S. Government Printing Office.

Wang, Ko, Terry V. Grissom, James R. Webb, and Lewis Spellman. 1991. "The Impact of Rental Properties on the Value of Single-Family Residences." *Journal of Urban Economics* 30(2): 152–66.

Wasson, Renya Reed, and Ronald Paul Hill. 1998. "The Process of Becoming Homeless: An Investigation of Female-Headed Families Living in Poverty." *Journal of Consumer Affairs* 32(2): 320–42.

Index

183